McDonaldisation, Masala
McGospel and Om Economics

McDonaldisation, Masala McGospel and Om Economics

Televangelism in Contemporary India

JONATHAN D. JAMES

 SAGE www.sagepublications.com
Los Angeles • London • New Delhi • Singapore • Washington DC

Copyright © Jonathan D. James, 2010

First published in 2010 by

 SAGE Publications India Pvt Ltd
B1/I-1 Mohan Cooperative Industrial Area
Mathura Road, New Delhi 110 044, India
www.sagepub.in

SAGE Publications Inc
2455 Teller Road
Thousand Oaks, California 91320, USA

SAGE Publications Ltd
1 Oliver's Yard, 55 City Road
London EC1Y 1SP, United Kingdom

SAGE Publications Asia-Pacific Pte Ltd
33 Pekin Street
#02-01 Far East Square
Singapore 048763

Published by Vivek Mehra for SAGE Publications India Pvt Ltd, typeset in 10/12pt Calisto MT by Star Compugraphics Private Limited, Delhi and printed at Chaman Enterprises, New Delhi.

Library of Congress Cataloging-in-Publication Data

James, Jonathan D.
    McDonaldisation, Masala McGospel and om economics: televangelism in contemporary India/Jonathan D. James.
        p. cm
    Includes bibliographical reference and index.
    1. Television in religions—India. 2. Christianity—United States—Influence. 3. Christianity and other religions—Hinduism. 4. Hinduism—Relations—Christianity. 5. India—Religion. I. Title.
BV656.3.J365   261.2'945—dc22   2010   2010027729

ISBN: 978-81-321-0473-5 (HB)

The SAGE Team: Elina Majumdar, Anupam Choudhury

I dedicate this book, with profound gratitude, to my family—my wife, Elizabeth; children, Ben and Melissa; my siblings and their families in Singapore, Sydney and Adelaide; and colleagues and friends scattered all around the world. Without your emotional support, prayers and encouragement this book would not have been started or finished!

Contents

List of Tables and Figures

Tables

Figures

Foreword

As we move further into the twenty-first century, we are learning to un-learn many of the assumptions and lessons of the twentieth century. This process is both a temporal one—times are changing along with our senses of time and of timeliness and timelessness—and a geographic one—we have come to think very differently about spaces and boundaries and differences and commonalities. The overall theme is probably best understood to be that of cultural globalisation. Cultures today exist in less isolation than in the past and in fact understand themselves and their uniqueness in relation to their place on regional, national and global 'maps'.

This is obviously an effect of the media age to a great degree. The modern means of communication make it possible for us to know and to know about 'others' from whom we are temporally and geographically separated. And, we find, those distances both define our differences, but at the same time, define our commonalities and our means of distinctiveness. Such deeply embedded cultural dimensions naturally introduce the question of religion and those practices and places that we might once have thought of as uniquely 'religious'. Religion today functions as a primary means of identity, playing an important role in local, regional, national and global politics. And, the interaction between media and religion increasingly defines these cultural spaces and contexts.

In this globalised era, we cannot anymore assume that the modern means of communication are exclusively the property of the global 'North' and 'West'. Communication media link widely disparate spaces, cultures and histories, and the evolving religious cultures of these spaces, in globalised late modernity, increasingly define and are defined by this new reality. In this era, we can no longer think of media and communication only in terms of their technologies and channels, either. As those of us in the 'North' and 'West' experienced first, the media age has certain political-economic logics, which frame and define what once were purely 'cultural' practices and objects in new ways, chiefly experienced through processes of commercialisation and commodification. Thus, in this era of religious and media change, we must recognise that it is mediated and commodified spheres of action and cultural practices that make modern religious meanings possible.

These intersecting realities are what makes a book such as this one so valuable. The form or substance of 'televangelism' might once have been thought of as entirely a creature of the United States or of the West, or of the mission outposts of American or European evangelicalism. We might also have assumed that the meaning of televangelism was only in its purest technological forms, expressed in specific ministries and broadcasts. Careful scholarship has revealed that the phenomenon was much more than this, that to understand it, we had to understand its historical, cultural, religious, media and economic contexts. We learned that televangelism was a mediatisation and commodification of religion. We further learned that its meanings and implications stretched well beyond what might have been thought to be its delegitimation through these 'artificial' processes. No, we learned televangelism and mediatised and commodified religious expressions and movements are organically authentic in their own ways and their own contexts and we need to interrogate them in these terms. We need to understand how they 'work' in cultural and religious senses. We also need to understand the political implications of all of this. As powerful generators of cultural meanings, religious media and mediatised religion have tremendous potential for generating solidarities, movements and identities that can have powerful implications for either understanding or misunderstanding, peace or conflict.

This book in its own way, addresses these questions. It looks at the trajectory of the form and practice of televangelism as it has been expressed in an entirely new context, that of South Asia and it takes on board the realities of the form and of the broader form(s) of commodified, mediated religious experience. It looks at how these developments relate to questions of authenticity, power, politics and the future of religion and spirituality in these contexts. It looks at the histories it interrogates in their own terms and in their own contexts. As a contextualised case study outside the expected geographic and temporal contexts, it provides important insights into the general form of interactions between religion, media and markets. It tells us something about its own context, about other contexts and about the evolving situation with globalising religious and media cultures.

Jonathan James thus presents us with a unique opportunity to look carefully at the evolving global situation in the new century through the lens of a particularly complex, layered and compelling case study. We all have much to gain from this, regardless of our own cultural, religious, geographic or political contexts.

Professor Stewart M. Hoover
School of Journalism and Mass Communication
Director, Centre for Media, Religion and Culture
University of Colorado at Boulder

Acknowledgements

It takes a team to produce a book and so I wish to offer my sincere thanks to a wide range of people and institutions for their help, patience, insight and perseverance in bringing this project to completion.

I am indebted to Professor Stewart Hoover, one of the world's leading scholars in the field of Media, Culture and Religion for his encouraging and incisive foreword.

I sincerely thank all the research participants in Mumbai, Hyderabad, Indore and Chennai for their willingness to be a part of this project. Special thanks go to Raju Cherian and Dr John Eapen who both did a marvellous job as research assistants. I am grateful to the Christian Broadcasting Network (CBN) in USA and India for their generosity in giving their time, materials and helpful information in connection with my research.

I particularly want to thank: Edith Cowan University in Perth, Australia for extending support in the form of editorial services, which were ably provided by Dr John Hall; Avrille Wasserman for her understanding and painstaking efforts in the production of the manuscript and Elina Majumdar, Anupam Choudhury and the entire team at Sage Publications for their cheerful assistance and patient disposition during the entire book-writing process.

I wish to thank the following for giving me permission to use their materials: the editors of *Studies in World Christianity* and *Journal of Religion and Popular Culture*, to reproduce portions of my work which originally appeared in their journals; the editors of *Missiology: An International Review* to adapt Hiebert's (2000) diagram on Wallace's (1956) theory on revitalisation in Chapter 1; the editor of *Satellite and Cable TV Magazine* to reproduce a table on Cable TV trends in India in

Chapter 4 and Sony Music/ATV to use the lyrics of the song *Would Jesus Wear a Rolex* in Chapter 7. If any copyright holders have been inadvertently omitted, the publishers and I would be more than pleased to make proper arrangements accordingly.

Introduction

One of the largest events in the history of Indian Christianity took place in February 2004 when America-based Charismatic evangelist Benny Hinn conducted his 'Festival of Blessings' Crusade in Mumbai.[1] It was reported in the local media that 4.2 million people attended the three-day meeting (the biggest crusade held by Hinn thus far) at the 1.2 million square meter MMRDA grounds at Bandra-Kurla Complex (*Light of Life*, 2004: 97). The event was carefully orchestrated, with 20,000 volunteers, a 1,000 member choir, 32 giant TV screens, an enclosure for 17,000 sick and disabled people and parking facilities for 100,000 cars (*Light of Life*, 2004: 97).

Benny Hinn had not previously visited the Indian subcontinent. So why was his crusade so successful? The success may be attributed to a number of factors including the fact that Hinn's huge Florida-based Church entity had been broadcasting his healing and teaching programmes through satellite television to India for at least six years before he set foot on Indian soil. Benny Hinn, whose TV programme is seen in 200 countries, is an example of the growing number of Charismatic televangelists whose ministry has entered the global arena through new technology (Benny Hinn Ministries, 2006).

Background of the Book

Over the last 10 years, as I have attended and participated in mission conferences in India, I have observed the changing shape and form of Christian ministry in the church.[2] In the main, I have noticed the following changes in the church scene in India: the style of worship in the church, the emphasis and priorities for ministry, the preaching and the techniques and strategies for doing ministry. In many cases, there appears to be a subtle shift in the theological and hermeneutical framework of the church leadership, with pastoral techniques resembling the American model rather than the older models inherited under colonisation.

Two interesting points are worthy of note. First, most of the changes mentioned above seem to have taken place in churches that are not well off economically. Second, most of the leaders in question would not have had the means to travel to the United States of America or to other Western countries, which presumably, are the sources of these new influences. So what has caused the changing church scene in India?

On closer examination, I have found that the impetus for change has been television. I have learned that the Indian government's liberal attitude to satellite and cable television began in the early 1970s. This policy, which continues to be in force today, is enabling more and more Indians to access a plethora of American and international television programmes, including access to religious television or 'televangelism', to use a term coined by Jeffrey Hadden and C. E. Swann (Hadden and Swann, 1981). Thus, the question arose: What is the link between the changing shape and form of Christianity and the opening up of the airwaves in India? This book explores the hybrid phenomenon of Charismatic televangelism and its impact on the Protestant Church and Hindu community in India.

The historian Neill (1984) categorises the work of Christian missions in India in several phases: first, there was the Syrian phase (which church tradition maintains, was started with the coming of St Thomas sometime between 50–52 AD); second, the Portuguese in the early fifteenth century; third, the Roman Catholic Jesuit phase in the middle of the fifteenth century and fourth, the Dutch and English phases which began in the early seventeenth century. (I will return to a detailed account of this history up till the middle of the twentieth century in Chapter 3.) Is televangelism another missionary phase in India? If so, what new challenges will the church and the community encounter as this new missionary strategy takes root in India?

The book also reveals that, unlike the seminal missiological analysis developed by Walls (1996), that the centre of gravity of Christianity is moving from the North to the South and from the West to the East, international Christian television is still very much the domain of the Western nations and in particular of the USA. This book also differs from the findings of Goh (2004) that there is a new Asian Christian movement that is developing ministries in Asia from networks and hubs driven largely by Asian organisations and agencies (Goh, 2004). My research shows that whilst it may be true that aspects of the Asian missionary movement are becoming more indigenised, the realm of international television ministries in Asia, particularly in India, is still largely driven by the United States of America. Furthermore, these American televangelistic ministries, by and large, are not truly contextualised to the local Indian situation, thereby creating several tensions within the church and the larger community.

Aim and Definition of Main Terms

The aim of the book is to investigate the influence of Charismatic televangelism in urban India in two settings: the Protestant Church and the Hindu community.

The key research issue concerns the hybrid phenomenon of Charismatic televangelism and its influence on the Protestant Church and the Hindu community in contemporary, urban India. The advent of televangelism has raised a number of issues which will be identified and investigated along with the key issue:

1. Televangelism and how it is rooted in Christianity's history in India;
2. Critical aspects of Indian Christianity which have an impact on televangelism;
3. The standing of Charismatic televangelism in India today.

There are four main settings in the book (see Figure A): Televangelism, Charismatic theology, the Indian Protestant Church and the Hindu community.

Televangelism, will serve as the first research setting. Charismatic theology, which is a branch of Christianity with an experience-based emphasis, is the second research setting. The Christian church in India, with a 2,000-year tradition, forms the third setting, while the Hindu community serves as the fourth research setting.

Here is a brief overview of the definitions of the main terms used in the study (a fuller description is provided in Chapters 2 and 4):

Figure A: Four settings

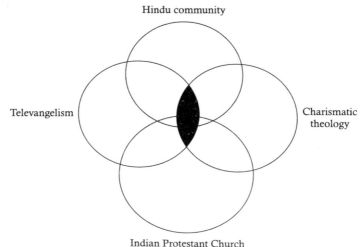

Source: Author.

1. Televangelism is a hybrid concept (from the words 'television' and 'evangelism') that refers to the use of television as a means of propagating the Christian faith.

2. Charismatic is a term that originates from the Greek language (*Charisma*, a gift of God's grace), sometimes called 'neo-Pentecostalism'. It is a reference to the movement within Christianity that focuses on the spiritual gifts of speaking in tongues, prophecy, healing, 'slaying in the Spirit' and miracles, as the norm for Christian faith and practice.

3. Church, refers in this study, to the Protestant denomination of Christian followers who adhere to the historic Christian doctrines following the Reformation movement. The term 'Protestant' is generally used in contradistinction to 'Roman Catholicism'. 'Denomination' is a reference to established Christian congregations (with similar traditions) which have been in existence for many years, with widespread geographical membership but unified in some form of administrative body (Religious Tolerance Website). The theological understanding of the term 'church' is two-fold—the universal Church which consists of Christian believers of every age and place and,

localised congregations in specific places. Together, the two-fold meaning of the term, in a theological sense, refers to 'God's new creation in an eschatological programme that was inaugurated by Christ's resurrection' (Court, 2008: 539).

Sociologically, however, the church in India is a diverse and pluralistic movement even within the Protestant denomination. Therefore, it is impossible to speak of the 'church' in a singular and 'normative' manner. For the purpose of this research, I have chosen four categories of churches within the evangelical, Protestant family in India. As these churches will form the basis of my research, references to the 'Protestant Church in India' and the 'Indian Protestant Church' or 'the church' in this book will refer to these four categories: Mainline non-Charismatic churches such as the Church of South India (CSI) and Church of North India (CNI); Mainline churches, such as Baptist and Methodist, which have appropriated Charismatic forms of worship and teaching, while retaining their denominational distinctives and traditions; Pentecostal denominational churches such as the Assembly of God and Neo-Pentecostal (Charismatic) independent churches, such as New Life.

4. Hindu, in this study, refers to both a follower of the Brahmanical religious faith of India as well as one who adheres to Hinduism as a way of life, in terms of a socio-cultural identity system. 'Hindu televangelism', in its broad context, can refer to Hindu religious content in many commercial television programmes such as soap operas and TV movies. In this study, however, 'Hindu televangelism' refers specifically to the establishment of separate Hindu channels that operate on a semi-commercial basis (like their Christian counterparts) featuring the religious and socio-cultural aspects of Hinduism.

Why This Book?

A book of this nature is important for several reasons. First, there is a tendency to think of the phenomenon of globalisation purely in economic and political terms. This study looks at globalisation from a cultural and religious standpoint. In particular, it looks at the role that religion and religious transnational organisations play in world cultures and religions. Hence, religion and globalisation are much more interconnected and implicated in each other than previously thought.

Second, whereas televangelism in America has been the subject of several academic studies, international televangelism has not attracted sufficient scholarly attention. As technology and religious fervour increase and as religion becomes a 'commodity' in the growing global market, it is likely that televangelism ministries will also continue to increase all over Asia. Hence, there is a need for the study of this phenomenon in Asia.

Third, in a country with a 2,000-year-old tradition of Christianity, televangelism is a new means of evangelising India. The American Christians are the last in a line of foreign missionaries to enter India. While the pre-colonial and colonial Christian eras were marked by oral communication and print communication respectively, the post-colonial Christian era is characterised by satellite and digital communication technology. As another missionary phase in India, after the Portuguese, Dutch and the British phases of colonial missions, what new challenges and tensions will the Church and community in India encounter from televangelism?

Fourth, the book is significant in the Indian context, where there are currently four 24-hour Charismatic TV networks. Is the church in India changing as a result of Charismatic televangelism or will the rich cultural and Christian heritage of the Indian church resist the effects of the hybrid phenomena of Charismatic televangelism? Preliminary observations and discussions with Christian leaders in India indicate that Charismatic televangelism has induced 'popular Christianity'. This is the kind of faith that appeals to the masses; arguably it is grounded in feelings and signs rather than on theological objectivity. This book aims to investigate this phenomenon.

Fifth, the rise of Hindu fundamentalism, and the *Hindutva* call for an 'India for Hindus', has seriously affected Christians and the cause of Christian evangelism and mission activity in the last few years. In light of what is perceived by Christian leaders as a disturbing trend, how will televangelism be accepted by the Hindu community and what are the implications for the ongoing activities of the Indian Church?

Sixth, an offshoot of the study is the discovery of the parallel development and growth of 'Hindu televangelism' in India, which occurred shortly after the introduction of Christian televangelism. Although a more comprehensive study on this interesting and relatively new phenomenon is warranted, my research will only address some of the issues of Hindu televangelism and its contested place in India's mediascape.

Finally, the use of the ethnographic methodology to enter into the two Indian settings: the Protestant pastoral community and the Hindu community enabled me to gain an appreciation into the deep insights, sentiments, fears and aspirations of the members of these diverse groups. Eight assertions (discussed in Chapter 9) have arisen out of the ethnographic study. As a subsidiary approach to the main methodology, I devised an historical-comparative framework from three fields of study: post-colonial studies, sociology of religion and missiology (study of Christian missions). These three fields were examined in conjunction with the three eras of Indian Christianity: pre-colonial, colonial and post-colonial. As a result, I have devised two assertions and a measurement scale: the full circle accommodation assertion, the historical roots missiological assertion and the indigenous measurement scale.

These will be discussed further in Chapters 2 and 3. It is hoped that this fresh approach and the new assertions will add significantly to the pool of knowledge and research in this particular field and potentially benefit the study of televangelism in other Asian contexts such as the Philippines or Taiwan, where there exists a liberal policy on transborder, religious television.

Scope, Approach and Presentation Style

This book seeks an understanding based mainly on the views of the Indian Church and Hindu community leaders, on the influence of Charismatic televangelism on contemporary, urban India. It does not provide a sustained critique of televangelism in India, neither does it provide a critique of Christian fundamentalism and its political agenda, although political concerns are freely expressed by various leaders and reported in the book. The focus of the book is to learn how both the Protestant Church and Hindu communities in India are being affected by global, transnational Christianity particularly through Charismatic televangelism.

I chose pastors of churches and leaders of the Hindu community, rather than lay members as my participants for research because in the Indian context, leaders are decision-makers and gate keepers as Indian society observes a hierarchical structure (Sanne, 2003).

Since the principal research interest is the combined understanding of the Protestant pastors and Hindu leaders, I chose the ethnographic approach as my primary methodology. The main methods chosen were participant observation and interviews. Qualitative interviews were conducted with 20 senior Christian leaders, 35 Hindu leaders and six key informants and specialists in Mumbai and Hyderabad. In the way of analysis, triangulation was used juxtaposing the three main qualitative methods (observation, interviews and case study) with two quantitative methods (survey and content analysis). As the principal researcher in this project, I was ably assisted by two research assistants from India.[3]

A content analysis of television programmes was undertaken with the researcher watching 12 hours of the Christian television network *Miraclenet* (6 am till 12 noon and 6 pm till midnight) and a further 12 hours watching the second network *God TV* (same time slots). Another content analysis was undertaken for the Hindu channels: *Aastha* and *Sanskar*, with the researcher watching six hours of Hindu television (6 am till 12 noon on *Aastha*) and a further four hours on *Sanskar* (6 am till 10 am). Both these telecasts were viewed in Mumbai (on Thursday) and Hyderabad (on Saturday). Therefore, the total time spent on viewing television programmes in both Mumbai and Hyderabad amounted to 48 hours (for Charismatic televangelism) and 20 hours (for Hindu televangelism).

A survey using a questionnaire for 60 middle-level pastors from both Charismatic and non-Charismatic persuasions was conducted in Mumbai and Hyderabad to gauge the views and understanding of the pastors on the topic of Charismatic televangelism. The information and views gathered from the content analysis and the survey were discussed with the senior pastors, Hindu leaders and key informants for greater understanding of the phenomenon of Charismatic televangelism.

Paley (2001) contends that ethnographic research writing should combine personal discourse with scholarship (Paley, 2001: 1–25). In keeping with this approach, I use the first person as my literary style.

Chapter Summaries

The book contains nine chapters. Chapter 1 consists of an introduction to the key metaphors used in the book: McDonaldisation, Masala McGospel and Om Economics. These are seen in relation to globalisation, 'glocalisation' and commercialisation. I also outline the subsidiary methodology I used—relational-comparative analysis, from which I devised what I term the 'historical-comparative framework'. This framework which is used to analyse televangelism in India, is drawn from three disciplines: post-colonial studies, sociology of religion and missiological studies. To conclude the chapter, I provide a summary of the key research findings. These findings are elaborated in Chapters 6 and 7 and analysed in Chapter 9.

In the second chapter, I place Charismatic televangelism in its global context by tracing its roots to black American Pentecostalism. I also explain the theological underpinnings of the Charismatic movement in comparison to the larger evangelical body of Christianity. The roots of American televangelism and its growth into a world-wide phenomenon are also explored. Finally, the full-circle accommodation assertion, which suggests a link between Hinduism and the Charismatic movement, is postulated.

Chapter 3 examines data on the history of Indian missions and relevant issues pertaining to the social and cultural aspects of Christianity in India. Televangelism is situated in India's church history as one of the missionary phases of Indian Christianity. This chapter addresses the two research issues: How televangelism is rooted in Christianity's history in India and the critical aspects of Indian Christianity today that affect televangelism. The chapter covers the following aspects: historical overview of Christian missions (from apostolic times to the present), indigenous Christianity, Pentecostalism in India, people groups and caste, urbanisation, church growth patterns and structures and Hindu–Christian tensions.

Both the historical roots missiological assertion and the indigenisation measurement scale are discussed here. The historical roots assertion concludes that the contemporary church's call for indigenisation is basically a return to the pre-colonial Christian era and the indigenisation scale is a measuring device to assist the church in assessing the level of indigeneity in the various church and parachurch ministries.

Chapter 4 establishes the place that Charismatic televangelism has in contemporary India. It traces the origins of televangelism to the time of the Gulf war in 1991 when satellite television was introduced to the nation. Three different forms of Christian televangelism are identified: global (transnational); local and 'glocal' (based on a fusion of the global and the local). The characteristics of global and local televangelism are explained in preparation for the ethnographic study on global and 'glocal' Charismatic programmes in Chapters 6 and 7.

Chapter 5 traces the origins of Hindu televangelism and analyses the two main Hindu channels in terms of programme content. A comparative study of Charismatic televangelist Benny Hinn and Hindu televangelist Shankar is undertaken. The relationship between Charismatic televangelism and Hindu televangelism is explored especially in the way the Hindu channels collude with the practices of consumerism and marketing techniques in the same fashion as Charismatic televangelists.

Chapters 6 and 7 analyse the data on the influence of both global and 'glocal' Charismatic televangelism on the leaders of the Protestant Church and the Hindu community in urban India. In the main, 'glocal' televangelism is perceived to be more culturally in tune and, therefore, more acceptable to Indians than global televangelism.

In Chapter 8, I examine the intermediary role that television plays in broadcasting the Christian faith. I do this by pointing to the areas of ownership, relationships and links to other global televangelism ministries as well as the issue of funding. I also point out the creation of the 'new' face of Christianity that is being undertaken by the Charismatic movement and televangelism together with the implications of this to the individual worshipper, the church and the larger Hindu community.

In the concluding chapter of the book, I give a summary of the study as well as an analysis of the findings. I assess the impact of televangelism in India and postulate some broad predictions on mediated faith in today's global world.

Notes

1. Apparently, Hinn's Bangalore meeting in 2005 was attended by seven million people, according to various media reports (see http//www.indiasalvationcrusade.com/newsjan05.htm).
2. The words 'church' and 'churches' are generally used interchangeably in this book to refer collectively to Protestant congregations within the evangelical tradition of Christianity, which constitute the research sample. At times the word 'Church' is used in the singular sense (capitalised) to refer to specific denominations such as the 'Protestant Church' or the 'Catholic Church'. Unless specified, when reference is made to the 'Indian Protestant Church', the 'Protestant Church in India' or 'the church'

I am referring collectively to the churches within evangelical Christianity that are the target of my research.

3. All references to 'the researcher' in the chapters refer to me as principal researcher.

References

Benny Hinn Ministries. 2006. 'Television Reaches Around the World', Retrieved from http://www.bennyhinn.org/Televison/televisiondefault.cfm on 10 March 2006.

Court, J. W. 2008. 'The Growth of the New Testament', in J. W. Rogerson and J. M. Lieu (eds), *The Oxford Handbook of Biblical Studies*. Oxford: Oxford University Press.

Goh, R. B. H. 2004. 'Asian Christian Networks: Transnational Structures and Geopolitical Mappings', *Journal of Religion and Society*, 6(2004).

Hadden, J. K. and C. E. Swann. 1981. *Prime Time Preachers: The Rising Power of Televangelism*. Reading, MA: Addison-Wesley Publishing.

Light of Life. 2004. 'News: Festival of Blessings', *Light of Life*, Mumbai, 4 April.

Neill, S. 1984. *A History of Christianity in India: The Beginnings to AD 1707*. Cambridge: Cambridge University Press.

Paley, K. S. 2001. *I Writing: The Politics and Practice of Teaching First-Person Writing*. Carbondale, Illinois: Southern Illinois University Press.

Religious Tolerance Website. (n.d.). 'Definition of Terms: Cults, Sects and Denominations' [Electronic Version]. *Denomination section*. Retrieved from http://www.religioustolerance.org/cults.htm on 9 May 2008.

Sanne, S. 2003. 'British Colonialism in India and its Influence on Indian Society' [Revised Internet Edition]. Retrieved from blog.designs-for-automotion.de/zeug/British%20Colonialism%20in%20India%20and%20its%20Influence%20on%20Indian%20Society.pdf on 11 December 2007.

Walls, A. 1996. *The Missionary Movement in Christian History: Studies in the Transmission of Faith*. New York: Orbis.

Chapter 1

McDonaldisation, Masala McGospel and Om Economics

When advocating an 'Indianised' church in India, veteran American missionary E. Stanley Jones drew a poignant analogy based on a north Indian marriage custom. The story goes like this: after the wedding ceremony, the women friends of the bride, surrounded by musicians, accompany the bride to the home of the bridegroom. Then after ushering her into the presence of the bridegroom, they quietly take their leave. That is as far as they are allowed to go. 'That', says Jones, 'is our joyous task in India—to know Jesus, to introduce him to India and then to retire,...to trust India with Christ and trust Christ with India. We can go so far. He and India must go the rest of the way' (Jones, 1925: 212–213).

To what extent has this recommendation, written in the 1920s, been followed by succeeding bands of missionaries and mission agencies in India?

A new phenomenon is taking place in India today: televangelism. Propelled primarily by the global Charismatic movement, televangelism is shaping India's airwaves producing two strands of programmes that I term metaphorically as 'McDonaldisation' and 'Masala McGospel', following studies by Ritzer (1993) and Drane (2001). I term Hindu televangelism, a consequence of satellite technology and Charismatic televangelism, 'Om Economics'. I paint these three pictures of televangelism in India with a broad brush, relying on my ethnographic research, content analysis and the relational-descriptive analysis which I call the historical-comparative framework.

'Televangelism' was coined by Hadden and Swann in their book *Prime Time Preachers* (Hadden and Swann, 1981: 4–12). It comes from the merging of the words 'television' and 'evangelism', referring to the new breed of Christian evangelists who use the medium of television to get their message across to the masses (Hadden and Swann, 1981). Hadden and Shupe (1988) argue that televangelism's roots are more than a century and a half old, going back to the revivalist movements of nineteenth century America (Hadden and Shupe, 1988). Frankl (1987) goes a step further to show that televangelism today is a direct descendent of the revival ministries of Charles Finney, Dwight Moody and Billy Sunday (Frankl, 1987). Schultze (1989) explains that televangelism is based on the following features: like its ally, commercial television, it is dependent on audience support, works best with strong and media-savvy personalities and it reflects aspects of the American culture in its materialistic and consumerist value system (Schultze, 1989). Schultze (1989) equates televangelism with the American Dream—which is a reference to the success mentality and the state-of-the-art technology used by televangelists. In other words, the medium is a product of the American value system.

A series of scandals among well-known televangelists brought discredit to televangelism in America in the 1980s but the phenomenon continues to thrive there (Schultze, 1989). Starting from the USA, televangelism has been exported to other countries, with tremendous success especially in South America and Africa (D. Martin, 1990). Televangelism has also spread to India and this study attempts to capture something of its impact in a Hindu-oriented society.

'McDonaldisation' is a term used by critics of contemporary processes and products that veer towards the anodyne, sameness and packaged happiness promoted by global franchised businesses. As a result, some Indian churches have become replicas of success-driven, American, suburban, middle-class congregations in their organisational patterns: formulaic-worship styles and upbeat preaching based on the Charismatic ideals of health, prosperity and success. McDonaldisation is a form of pre-packaged, externally imposed Christianity in today's culture of consumer worshippers. Whereas the traditional role of the Christian preacher was to exegete the text in the local context, global Charismatic preachers teach the Charismatic Gospel in a global context.

'Masala McGospel', the 'glocal' version (the fusion of the global and local Indian culture) of Charismatic televangelism was described rather cynically in the research by both pastors and Hindu leaders in India as 'two parts Indian and three parts American'.[1]

Hindu televangelism has borrowed many production and commercial aspects from Charismatic televangelism and is flourishing in India. I describe this new phenomenon as 'Om Economics' for, without its discourse orientation and the strong element of orthodox beliefs, Hindu televangelism seems even more commercialised than Charismatic televangelism. These three strands of televangelism are explored in this book to give the reader an explanation of the changing religious mediascape in India.

The approach I take in this chapter is as follows: first, I explain the key metaphors used in the title in the overall context of globalisation; secondly, I outline the methodology and situate the study alongside the main theories and concepts that I employ and, finally, I provide a summary of the key research findings.

'McDonaldisation'

Giddens (2000) defines globalisation as 'the intensification of worldwide social relations which link distant localities in such a way that local happenings are shaped by events occurring miles away and vice versa' (Giddens, 2000: 28). Birch et al. (2000) define the cultural dimension of globalisation: 'the way in which the same electronic technology is able to disseminate cultural texts—films, television shows, sporting events, cartoons, music, pornographic images and stories... across national borders' (Birch et al., 2000: 56).

In the realm of studies on globalisation and international communication, the work by Huntington (1998) gives a broad picture of the three historical phases of our world: the pre-modern world where civilizations were separated by time and space; the modern world of colonisation which effectively led to the subordination of many societies and the current post-modern world where the dominance of one civilization over all others is being replaced by 'intense, sustained, and multidirectional interactions among all civilizations' (Huntington, 1998: 66–67).

Appadurai (2000) builds on Huntington's analysis of the third phase, stating that the central issue of cultural processes in today's world is the 'schizophrenic' condition '...calling forth theories of rootlessness, alienation and psychological distance between individuals on the one hand and fantasies (or nightmares) of electronic propinquity on the other' (Appadurai, 2000: 1803).

Appadurai (2000) goes on to argue that the new global cultural economy 'has to do with certain fundamental disjunctives', which can be explained by looking at the five dimensions of global cultural flow: ethnoscapes, mediascapes, technoscapes, finanscapes and ideoscapes (Appadurai, 2000: 1806). Appadurai explains the following terms: 'ethnoscape' refers to the shifting ethnic mix of persons, 'technoscapes' refers to the 'global configuration of technology', 'finanscapes' to global capital, 'mediascapes' to the electronic and digital media capabilities and 'ideoscapes' to the prevailing political ideologies of states (Appadurai, 2000: 1806–1809).

Appadurai's (2000) analysis seems adequate for describing the process of overlaps and disjunctures with his use of the suffix 'scapes'. However, he does not address the issue of religion directly and neither does he give enough credit to the role played by organisational structures such as the church, and even the nation-states, in his discussion on global flows.

Hexam and Poewe (1997) indicate that religious movements can 'flow' in two ways: firstly as an intact global tradition that may adapt itself to local conditions or secondly as fragmented aspects of a religious tradition. These fragments are then grafted into individual experiences or prevailing folk religions (Hexam and Poewe, 1997).

The phenomenon of globalisation has also given birth to several specialised studies: Ritzer's (1993) concept of McDonaldisation and Barber's (1995) polemical study of Jihad versus McWorld. McDonaldisation refers to the ways in which the principles of the most well-known American fast-food restaurant chain operates in various social settings, such as the workplace, education and health care (Ritzer, 1993: 1). Ritzer (1994) identifies five interconnected principles of the McDonaldisation process: efficiency, calculability, predictability, increased control and the replacement of humans by non-human technology (Ritzer, 1994: 140–156). Zayani (1997) argues that Ritzer's theory, though not identical, is built on Weber's theory of bureaucracy and that both Weber and Ritzer 'describe an organizational model that strives to eliminate inefficiency, irrationality, uncertainty and unpredictability' (Zayani, 1997). The underlying motivation for these core principles is the maximisation of profit for the transnational company. Therefore, every unit of input is carefully measured so that the optimum means is always chosen for every given end.

Here are some examples of how global televangelism is built on the principles of McDonaldisation:

Efficiency

The principle of efficiency has streamlined and simplified the process of the entire food industry from the viewpoint of the consumer. In the same way the Christian faith on global televangelism has been streamlined and simplified in such a way that consumers get what they want quickly and efficiently in ways that are tested and proven by countless other people all over the world. If to what we want, is it Christianity?

The successful fast-food restaurant, McDonalds, in appealing to consumers, offers a wide array of choices at a relatively low cost with prompt service. By way of analogy, American Christianity, according to Jenkins (2000) offers Christian worshippers: a wide variety of menu choices 'designed to please our appetites and personal taste..., a variety of religious experiences, with the price of commitment in time and money kept low and spirituality without intimacy and relationships with people'. He adds '...That's why many people love the mega-church environment where they can be anonymous consumers' (D. Jenkins, 2000: paras 9–10).

The content analysis (as explained in Chapter 4) reveals that televangelists are framing their sermons to offer quick and 'efficient' fixes to deep-seated spiritual, emotional and financial problems: *Five steps to Financial Freedom*; *You can be a millionaire*; *Claim your inheritance now*; *Your deliverance begins today*; *Be a lender, not a borrower*; *You are healed*; *God is your fortune-teller* and *Be freed from the demon of jealousy*. The concept of Christian discipleship and maturity, according to a key informant, is not something that happens overnight. Unfortunately, the televangelists do not see it this way. McGrath (2002) points out that the journey of learning in the Christian life (listening, praying, heeding to counsel) is being bypassed for instant answers and quick fixes: 'Classic Christianity saw the journey of faith as significant in itself. Reaching the goal of the journey...was of course important. But the journey was itself a means of personal growth, engagement and transformation' (McGrath, 2002: 52).

Global televangelism has reduced faith to a commodity for the calculating consumer. In short it is producing 'consumer Christianity'. Jenkins (2000) defines consumer Christianity as:

...a mentality which is self-centered. One who is a consumer is concerned with the benefits to himself or herself whatever they buy or believe. Therefore, for the consumer to become interested in the product or service or belief system, it must appeal to their personal interests, concerns and opinions. (D. Jenkins, 2000: para 6)

Calculability

It seems that qualitative growth is not as important as quantitative growth in Charismatic televangelism. Spiritual success is all about numbers. In the content analysis it is shown that in the television programmes at least 20–25 shots are shown per half hour of the crowds in the churches or outdoor crusade venues where most of the sermons are preached. Television preachers like Pat Robertson, Creflo Dollar and Benny Hinn talk about the size of their operation, the crowds that come, the number of people healed and also the money needed to finance their operations on the TV programmes and their literature: 'Hundreds of verified healings and thousands of conversions have occurred including people rising from wheelchairs and leaving crutches. Several blind eyes and deaf ears have been opened and verified' (Hinn, 1992: 94–95).

Predictability

Ritzer (1993) asserts:

In a rational society, people prefer to know what to expect in all settings and at all times. They neither want nor expect surprises...In order to ensure predictability over time and place, a rational society emphasizes such things as discipline, order, systematization, formalization, routine, consistency and methodical operation. (Ritzer, 1993: 83–85)

The content analysis (as elaborated in Chapter 4) reveals that global Charismatic televangelism programmes in the main follow a formula based on the following components: 'Praise and Worship', a term which is now used in many parts of the world to refer to the segment in a church service where choruses (rather than hymns) are sung, led by a Worship leader with a full complement of musicians and, at times, back-up singers. Preaching and/or teaching is often reduced to a commercial transaction of spiritual (symbolic) goods, with statements such as 'Do you need healing? Do you need prayer? Send a donation and get this free CD or book'. 'Ritual'—healing, 'slaying in the Spirit' and special prayers and sale of products and/or fundraising also seem to be the main features of Charismatic programmes.

The underlying idea in the teaching and in the 'packaging' of the message is that Christianity is 'workable', practical and experiential. This predictable format seen on television generates a comfortable and familiar environment for the worshipper and has contributed to the portable nature and the global spread of Charismatic teaching and practices.

However, McGrath (2002) questions whether the predictability of Charismatic worship might fail to challenge and excite worshippers in the long run: 'Dulled by a sense of overwhelming liturgical over familiarity, many worshippers have been known to "switch off" and let their minds wander to other things…the dull and thoughtless food preparation routines [at McDonalds] demand little thought or attention' (McGrath, 2002: 54).

Charismatic churches all over the world are organised in terms of a 'specific transnational Christianity' that include 'the organisation of the church, preaching styles, modes of worship, and pastoral outreach that includes cell churches … these distinctions are reinforced through Christian Broadcasting' (Thomas, 2008: 26).

Increased control

Control is one of Ritzer's final categories of the McDonaldisation process. McDonalds control both their employees and the customers by encouraging fully scripted interactions complete with the employees being trained to offer friendly service with a smile and the parting words: 'Have a nice day'. Likewise global televangelists exude confidence as they preach and teach an upbeat and positive message about healing, wealth, success and deliverance with a fully orchestrated production format. McDonalds turns its customers into involuntary unpaid labour, where they must queue to give their orders, carry their food, eat most of the food with their hands and clear away their own rubbish. Customers are being socialised to become part of the routinised world of service workers. Likewise, global televangelism is turning their audiences into their 'labour force' as televangelists, such as, Benny Hinn and Pat Robertson ask for 'co-labourers' (listeners) to financially support their global ministries. Through these ways, televangelism audiences are becoming socialised to the new 'global church' built in virtual space.

Hong (2006) describes the structural control of one of the largest Charismatic mega-churches in Korea:

> In the design of the Korean mega-churches, it is stressed that the fundamental building block of the church should be a small, lay-led, home-based, homogenous group. Organized along the lines of a corporation, firm or social category, members can progress through the subgroups of the church, and this represents a step in their social journey...it remains to be seen whether the bureaucratic apparatus will stifle the life that it is supposed to assist and preserve. (Hong, 2006: 7)

The modern Charismatic ministries and churches are built as megachurches with 'a spiritual enterprise culture' that requires 'in the top echelon, a kind of international manager of the spirit' (D. Martin, 1990: 143).

Global televangelism exercises its control of viewers through a combination of spiritual Charismatic 'anointing' and television technology. Christian Research Institute (CRI) in their review of Hinn's (1990) book *Good Morning, Holy Spirit* (which became a number one best seller) discovered that Hinn's practice of 'slaying in the Spirit' is one of the key control mechanisms the televangelist uses on TV and in his crusades:

> Hinn's practice of slaying people in the Spirit by blowing on them or touching their heads bears all the marks of manipulative staged performances...Hinn announces to his congregation to get ready for the experience, he positions 'catchers' on the stage to catch those who fall; those who are 'slain' lose complete control of themselves, while Hinn remains firmly in control of himself; at times whole sections of the congregation are 'slain' at the same instant, and always at Hinn's cue. (Bowman and Carden, 1991)

The content analysis of global televangelism programmes shows that Charismatic teachers are presented as having a sense of 'aura'. Evangelists like Dollar, Hinn and Hagee are presented as 'larger than life' spiritual celebrities through the careful use of 'image management' and technology.

In short, global televangelism is offering a pre-packaged form of spirituality (wrapped in a neat wrapper served with spiritual 'fries' and 'coke' for easy consumption). This is the 'McDonaldisation of the gospel'. Historically, most foreign missionaries have tried to familiarise themselves with the Indian culture and attempted various methods of indigenising the gospel to the local context. The mainline Indian churches today, such as Church of North India (CNI) and Church of South India (CSI), which were started by the colonial missionaries, have undergone various levels of indigenisation. In contrast to this, global televangelism follows the McDonaldisation principle of 'one size fits all'. Furthermore, the rhetoric of certain global Charismatic televangelists seems to imply that their 'anointed' ministries transcend all nations and cultures without the need for any modification in their methods or message. For example, Hinn stated:

> As I've said, my ministry took quantum leaps forward in 1990 when the Lord told me to begin monthly miracle crusades around the country…There have been many extraordinary events. One that seems to happen in every crusade, usually in the teaching meetings on the morning of the second day is the directive from the Lord to have the people get quiet, with eyes closed and hands raised. The Lord will tell me 'say now' and I will touch them. That's all He tells me to do: 'say now'. It's amazing; I do it, and right away there will be gasps and even screams as the power falls. I open my eyes and invariably two-thirds of the ten thousand or more present collapse, onto the floor, healings of all kinds occur… (Hinn, 1992: 86–87)

Anderson asserts that it is characteristic of Pentecostal and neo-Pentecostal groups, that they seldom pay attention to cultural issues and matters pertaining to the indigenisation of the Charismatic gospel (Anderson, 1999).

'Masala McGospel' and 'glocal' televangelism

Is global communication creating a world of homogenised global culture? Caincross (2001) believes so, but Compaine (2002) only partially agrees with this view. Compaine points out that when *Star TV* (an Asian subsidiary of News Corp.) began broadcasting satellite TV into India, with programmes like *Dallas* and *The Bold and the Beautiful* dubbed in Hindi, audience ratings were low. Compaine adds that the: '…network only succeeded in India once it hired an executive with experience in Indian programming to create Indian soap operas and when an Indian production house took over news and current affairs programming' (Compaine, 2002: 20).

Therefore, Compaine concludes in order to succeed, global firms must produce and sell non-homogenous products or content (Compaine, 2002: 20). Regardless of whether a global homogenised culture is being created, the reality is that culture is a key player in globalisation. Hoover makes this assertion clearly:

> ...it is no longer possible to think of empire only in terms of politics or trade in raw or finished goods, but that we must now also think of culture, and second the implication that religious culture and religious cultural products may well play a role in this process. (Hoover, 2005: 127)

Barber (1995) posits that there are two major opposing forces: global capitalism (Mcworld) and factionalism or tribalism (Jihad), both of which are threatening democracy. These two forces are operating at the same time in certain countries around the world, including India: 'India is trying to live up to its reputation as the world's largest integral democracy while powerful new fundamentalist parties like the Hindu nationalist Bharitiya Janata Party, along with the nationalist assassins, are imperilling its hard-won unity' (Barber, 1992: 53–65).

Therefore, I use the term 'McGospel' in the book, following Barber's (1995) writings and attempt to relate this phenomenon also to the church and in particular to American televangelism in India. For the purpose of this study 'McGospel' refers to the Gospel originating from the USA, with all the cultural and technological additives of America including the capitalistic and corporate aspects of Christianity.

The term *masala* is a reference to the blending of Indian spices. The prolific Bollywood film industry that produces Indian movies has been referred to and known to follow a formulaic *masala* mix consisting of mainly melodramatic and romantic storylines linked with doses of song, dance and music. This mix, according to Tyrrell (2003), is rooted in Indian culture and some aspects of it are traced to Sanskrit theatre:

> Bollywood films are ... an 'Omnibus' or a 'Masala' form—combining melodrama, action, comedy, social commentary and romance violently juxtaposing intensely tragic scenes with jolly song and dance numbers, jolting the viewer from one extreme of feeling to another (an aesthetic similarly inherited from Sanskrit theatre). (Tyrrell, 2003: 314)

Hence, 'Masala McGospel' is a reference to the blending of the American gospel with Indian culture. McDonalds menus do vary from country to country. In India, Hindus do not eat beef and Islam forbids the eating of pork so McDonalds outlets in India have lamb, chicken and vegetarian burgers on their menu. In Sweden, McDonalds outlets offer a *Smulton Vanilj Paj*, a local version of McDonalds pie. Thus adapting their core culture to fit in with the local tastes, McDonalds franchises have remained successful globally (Frost, 2005).

In a similar way the American Christian media group, Christian Broadcasting Network (CBN), has adapted its core culture to fit in with certain aspects of Indian culture and customs in their televangelistic programme *Solutions*. In this way the global and what has been termed the 'glocal' are 'simultaneously apparent in interconnected ways' (Lyon, 2000: 99). The term 'glocalisation', coined by Roland Robertson, comes from the Japanese business technique of *dochakuka*, which originally was used when a company adapts a global outlook to local conditions (Robertson, 1995: 20). Therefore, it can be stated that *Solutions* is a 'glocal' version of CBN USA's global televangelism ministry.

I have used the terms 'indigenous' and 'localised' interchangeably to point towards a missiological understanding of communication. The focus is based on whether the universal aspects of the Christian gospel are expressed in culturally understandable and sensitive ways. Historically, missionaries have cautiously sought to draw the boundary between indigenisation and syncretism (Nicholls, 1995).

The Roots of Hindu Televangelism

Hinduism, unlike Christianity, does not have a single founder, a specific system of theology or morality. Nehru (1964) describes Hinduism this way: 'Hinduism, as a faith, is vague, amorphous, many-sided, all things to all men. It is hardly possible to define it, or indeed to say definitely whether it is a religion or not, in the usual sense of the word' (Nehru, 1964: 73).

Levinson (1998) contends that Hinduism consists of 'thousands of different religious groups that have evolved in India since 1500 BCE' (Levinson, 1998: 58).

Hinduism is pantheistic whereas Christianity is theistic. Pantheism sees the entire world as part of God (Kreeft, 1987) and has an animistic flavour because all objects of nature and in the heavens are worshipped. Griswold (1912) describes Hinduism's tendency to deify this way:

In the Rig Veda, the earliest literary monument of Hinduism, divine honour is paid to heaven and earth, sun, wind, fire, dawn, rivers, mountains, trees...the cow, dead ancestors etc...whatever force or object of nature was useful to man or striking in appearance or effects was a candidate for apotheosis. (Griswold, 1912: 164–165)

Griswold (1912), in presenting the syncretistic characteristic of Hinduism, argues that if Hinduism has a mission, it is a mission quite unique from Christianity:

For it too is missionary—in its own way. It [Hinduism] annexes, not individuals, but whole tribes and communities. The history of India up to the tenth Christian century is largely the history of the spread of Aryan religion...The conversion of a tribe to Hinduism meant its acknowledgement of the supremacy of the Brahmans and its enrolment as a separate caste...These were the essentials. As regards religious faith and practice, the newly Hinduized tribe would be free to make any adjustment it pleased—usually a compromise between its own gods and the gods of the Hindu pantheon. (Griswold, 1912: 167)

Griswold further explains that the syncretism in Hinduism is quite unlike other forms of religious syncretism:

The supreme tests for admission to the fold of Hinduism are not moral or intellectual, but social—the adoption of caste—organization and the acknowledgment of Brahman supremacy. The essential element in Hinduism, then, is not belief, but social organization. This fact explains why it is that the Hindu finds fault with the Christian missionary, not the preaching of Christ in India, but only for baptizing. It is the disruption of the Hindu social system rather than a change of belief, which is feared. (Griswold, 1912: 168)

Whereas the sole sacred text in Christianity is the Bible and Christianity is a text-based religion, Hinduism has many sacred texts and is, by and large, not text-based in the same way as Christianity. The main sacred texts of Hinduism (consisting of hymns, incantations and rituals) are the *Vedas*: the *Rig Veda*, *Sama Veda*, *Yajur Veda* and *Atharva Veda* (Hare, 2007). Another important text is the *Ramayana*. The *Ramayana* (dated to the first century CE) is: 'a moving love story with moral and spiritual themes that has deep appeal in India to this day' (Mana's website). It is a poem written by Valmiki, based on the exploits of Rama, an *avatar* of Vishnu, who is considered 'a principal deity in his own right' (Mana's website). Other texts include the *Mahabharata*, the *Brahmana*s, the *Sutra*s, *Purana*s and the *Aranyaka*s (Hare, 2007).

The absence of a text-based orientation in Hinduism, perceived by some as a weakness, is one of the reasons for the significant reform movement within Hinduism in 1875—the *Arya Samaj*. Founded by Swami Dayananda Saraswati, the *Arya Samaj* called for a return to the main Hindu text the *Vedas* and 'elaborated perhaps the most central and certainly the most elusive theme of Hindu discursive tradition: the authority of the *Vedas*' (van der Veer, 1998: 65). Smith (1987) disagrees with the view that Hinduism is not a text-based religion, arguing that 'all religions by definition, must have a fixed canon' and that Hindus 'do see themselves as defined, in part or whole, by their relation to the *Veda* (a relation usually negotiated by the Brahmin class)' (B. Smith, 1987: 41–42).

An important difference Hinduism has from Christianity, arising from Hinduism's non-text based orientation, is that it is an orthopractic faith (life-orientation) whereas Christianity is more concerned with orthodoxy (theological-orientation). Griswold explains this important characteristic of Hinduism:

> In Hinduism more fully perhaps than even in orthodox Judaism religion embraces the whole of life. One explanation of this is that the separation which has been made in the West between social custom and religion has never taken place in India...hence Christianity and Hinduism touch common life differently. The principle of Christianity is 'Whether ye eat or drink or whatsoever ye do, do all to the glory of God' (1 Cor. 10:31). But the principle of Hinduism is 'Whether ye eat or drink or whatsoever ye do, do all according to fixed rule and established custom'. Liberty prevails in Christianity; legalism, in Hinduism. This explains why...Hindus...seem at first sight so religious. It is because their religion consists so largely in the punctilious performance of an elaborate body of religiously consecrated custom touching every detail of life. (Griswold, 1912: 169–170)

This, in part, explains why the content, style and viewing of Hindu televangelism differs from its Christian counterpart. More aspects of these differences will be elaborated in Chapter 5.

When Hinduism's sacred text, the *Ramayana*, was serialised in 78 episodes on national television between 1987 and 1988, nearly 100 million people watched the most popular episodes (van der Veer, 1998: 175). The variability of responses by Hindus was extraordinary. Some of the difference could be attributed to: not understanding the Hindi language, caste and class of the viewers. The medium became the message when, in public places, 'the television itself was often garlanded with flowers or incense' (Mitchell, 2005: 2). Many Hindus claimed to have a *darshan*, 'a glimpse of the sacred' during the viewing (van der Veer, 1998: 175). Other viewers took part in rituals and prayers before the programme (Mitchell, 2005: 2).

In essence the lifestyle of Hinduism, based on the orthopractic nature of the faith, is what concerns Hindu television. O'Malley (1935) contends that the religion of the masses in India is not so much by way of the scriptures or the arguments of the philosophers. It is not discourse-based, as Christianity is, but more lifestyle based. In essence this is what popular Hinduism is:

> ...a mixture of Brahmanical doctrines and animistic beliefs and the position which either holds in the religion of the masses in any particular area depends on the extent to which Brahmanical influence has spread...The higher we go in the social scale, the more does Brahmanical worship prevail. (O'Malley, 1935: 129)

Another important aspect of Hinduism, besides the orthopractic nature of the faith, is the place of image in Hinduism. The Hindu tradition of idols, icons, representations of gods and goddesses is an ancient one and television and the internet have only extended this tradition. Hindu channels routinely advertise and sell Hindu idols and icons such as Ganesha images and statues and some Hindu channels specialise in marketing such cultural products.

Although Hindu televangelism is gaining prominence in India, there is no real in-depth study of this interesting phenomenon. There are brief, featured articles on Hindu televangelism that have been published in newspapers and popular magazines such as: *Hinduism Today* (January–March 2003); *The Sunday Pioneer* (2006); *The Washington Post* (2003) and *Businessworld* (2006). These articles mainly cover the growth of this new phenomenon, outlining the characteristics of Hindu televangelism, the methods, the rhetoric and the business aspects of the operation.

The research on Hindu televangelism in Chapter 5 shows that the lack of a text-based, discourse orientation, coupled with a heavily commercialised foundation, has earned Hindu televangelism the dubious title of 'Om Economics'. *Om* or *Aum* is the fundamental symbol and syllable (sound) of Hinduism, quoted in the Hindu scriptures— the *Katha Upanishad* as well as the *Mandukya Upanishad*. It represents *Brahman*, the impersonal (almost unknowable) Absolute:

Om is not a word but rather an intonation, which, like music, transcends the barriers of age, race, culture ... It is made up of three Sanskrit letters, aa, au and ma which, when combined together, make the sound of Aum ... Hindus begin their day or any work or journey by uttering Om ... a newly born child is ushered into the world with this holy sign ... during meditation, when we chant Om, we create within ourselves a vibration that attunes sympathy with the cosmic vibration ... (Das, n.d.: paras 1–4, 6)

If *Om* is synonymous with *Brahman* and if, by reciting *Om*, a Hindu attests to his or her ultimate security and sufficiency in the Absolute of Hinduism, then the disjunction of Hindu televangelism becomes all the more keenly felt, because of its contemporary collusion with the world of power flows and commercialisation.

Methodology and Theory

The main methodology I used in the field study was ethnography, a research method from the social sciences. I chose this methodology because it was important to gain an in-depth understanding of the views, perceptions, fears and aspirations of Christian pastors and Hindu leaders in the divergent cultural context of India. By using ethnography as my methodology and some of the key methods like participant observation I was able to get close to my respondents in their own contexts. During the one and a half years of fieldwork, I managed to collect sufficient data to draw a 'portrait' of two cultural contexts—Christian pastors and Hindu leaders in India (Harris and Johnson, 2000). I elaborate on these portraits in Chapters 6 and 7.

I supplemented the ethnographic methodology with survey research, conceptual analysis and the relational-comparative analysis (for which I used an historical-comparative framework).[2] I felt it was necessary to use this historical perspective because the contemporary missionary outreach of televangelism is part of a long and sustained Christian activity and, therefore, it cannot be viewed in a historical vacuum. In fact the missionary enterprise has a history dating to the apostolic times. In my historical-comparative framework, Christianity in India is divided into three eras—pre-colonial, colonial and post-colonial. Using these three eras, three fields of study pertaining to the research were introduced to provide the theoretical framework: post-colonial studies, sociology of religion and missiology (study of Christian missions).

The three fields of study mentioned above are set in relation to the different eras of Christianity and Hinduism in India. I now explain the main theories from the three fields of study, in Table 1.1a.

Table 1.1a: The historical-comparative framework

Theoretical perspectives	Pre-colonial Christianity era	Colonial Christianity era
Post-colonial studies	Syrian (Middle-Eastern) Christianity Oral communication— the primary form of communication	Portuguese, Dutch, British, American • Resistance from one Syrian group • Hybridisation from another Syrian group • Conversions from Hinduism Communities divided by British Print media—the dominant technology
Sociology of religion Wallace's theory of revitalisation	Accommodation Differentiation	• One group of Syrian Church accommodates • Hindus come to Christ (acculturation theory)
Missiological studies	Indigenisation Hindu in culture, Christian in faith, Syrian in liturgy	• Syrian Church taken over by Catholic → Fragmentation into three groups • Translation, education, Church planting of Western denominational Churches • Indigenous Groups

Source: Author.

Post-colonial studies (and globalisation)[3]

The field of post-colonial studies is the study of the relationships between the European colonial powers and the nations that were once colonised by these European nations. 'Post-colonial' refers to the time after colonial empires granted independence to colonised countries. The word post-colonial also signifies a position against imperialism and euro-centrism. Some of the questions that pertain to the discipline of post-colonisation are:

1. What were the experiences of the colonised?
2. What traces of colonialism are left behind in the education, science, technology and culture of colonised countries?
3. What types of resistance took place during colonialisation?
4. Is there a particular resistance discourse that can be identified?
5. How is colonialisation influencing the language, the arts and the knowledge systems of colonised societies?
6. What emergent forms of culture are replacing colonial culture (such as essentialism and hybridity)?

An aspect of post-colonial studies that influences this research is the globalisation of religion. Economics and politics are the two fields that concern researchers most in their discussions on globalisation (Fukuyama, 1992). However in this research I place religion and transnational religious organisations in the new space of globalisation. That is to say, I believe religion is yet another dynamic system that has left the borders of the nation-state and entered into the realm of globalisation alongside economics, politics and culture. This is the perspective of Vasquez and Marquardt (2003) who firmly place religion and globalisation within an interdisciplinary framework:

> ...the new spatio-temporal arrangements generated by globalization dovetail with religious 'morphologies of success'—forms of religious organization and practice strategically equipped to deal with the existential predicaments generated by globalization at the level of everyday life. By changing our sense of time, space, and agency, globalization clearly affects the viability of religious congregations. (Vasquez and Marquardt, 2003: 55)

In placing religion and globalisation in this setting, Vasquez and Marquardt reject the 'old paradigm' of the treatment of religion which is based on secularisation. Rather they choose a model of religion where 'ordinary believers and institutions find in religion resources to bridge the multiple identities and functions they must perform in an increasingly complex world' (Vasquez and Marquardt, 2003: 29).

Vasquez and Marquardt posit that there are five ways that religion intersects with globalisation (Vasquez and Marquardt, 2003: 51–64):

1. Deterritorialisation and reterritorialisation (religion as a map): Religion becomes a key element in the 'new spatio-temporal arrangements' and a 'cognitive map' by which people locate

themselves in the new space created by globalisation (Vasquez and Marquardt, 2003: 51–52). Deterritorialisation refers to 'breaking down' the spatial arrangement of globalisation and reterritorialisation is the 'reconstitution' of the new spatial arrangement (Soja, 2000: 200). The new spatial arrangement is a blending of 'local, regional and global dynamics' (Vasquez and Marquardt, 2003: 52). The mainline CSI and CNI churches in India are owners of huge million-dollar properties and in the last few decades, property and litigation issues have become a major snare of these post-colonial churches. In contrast to this (except for the mega churches) a growing number of Charismatic churches seem to focus more on capturing the airwaves and mediating faith to the masses, rather than being encumbered by issues of physical location and territoriality.

2. Transnational religious networks: Religious organisations take advantage of these new spatial arrangements to strategically create new religious networks and 'organizational conduits' for the flow of religious truth (Vasquez and Marquardt, 2003: 54). Levitt (2001) identifies three types of transnational religious organisational patterns—first, organisations that are connected by a single authority with local autonomy like the Catholic Church, second, organisations that are 'less centralized' and not subject to 'pre-established rules', third, franchises or chapters of the sending organisations (Levitt, 2001: 11–12). The Pentecostal and neo-Pentecostal Church follows Levitt's second model where 'flexible tie...must be constantly worked out' (Levitt, 2001: 14). According to Vasquez and Marquardt, Pentecostal churches:

> ...offer believers resources to relocalize themselves, to renew broken selves and build tight...communities...On the other [hand] Pentecostal churches, can be unabashedly globalizing, combining skilfully the use of transnational webs of missionaries and storefront congregations with sophisticated global media to highly mobile migrant populations. (Vasquez and Marquardt, 2003: 55)

3. Glocalisation: The concept enunciated by Robertson (1995) refers to the practice of adapting a global concept to a local condition. Religious organisations are involved in glocalisation because:

...on the one hand they have to reinforce their claims to universal authority...in a world...deeply skeptical of grand narratives. On the other hand, these organizations must respond to specific demands of individuals and communities who experience fragmentation and depthlessness...In dealing with this tension, religious organizations often unintentionally produce hybridity and fragmentation. (Vasquez and Marquardt, 2003: 57)

4. Hybridity: Similar words like syncretism, bricolage and creolisation have been previously used in the disciplines of religion and sociology. Bhabha (1990) uses the word hybridity to show 'fractures in the sovereign, unified and self-transparent Cartesian subject at the heart of the colonial enterprise' (cited in Vasquez and Marquardt, 2003: 60). Vasquez and Marquardt (2003) argue that: 'As globalization deterritorializes and reterritorializes culture, religion enters into recombination with multiple media, giving rise to hybrid cultural products that blur spatial, temporal and conceptual distinctions.'

   Charismatic televangelism is both local and global as it is 'a local expression of a global Charismatic culture—they are rooted in specific local contexts and at the same time, transnational...' (Asamoah-Gyadu, 2005: 21). Hexam and Poewe (1994) refer to this phenomenon as a 'multisource diffusion of parallel developments [that] encompass Europe, Africa, America and Asia' (Hexam and Poewe, 1994: 61).

5. Borders and borderlands: Religion, on the one hand, promotes hybridity 'in the same ways borderlands do' (Vasquez and Marquardt, 2003: 63). All three aspects can happen in the phenomenon of the globalisation of religion: 'border-making', 'border crossing' and 'border blurring' (Vasquez and Marquardt, 2003: 63).

Post-colonial studies, seen in relation to Christianity and Hinduism, suggest that in considering the phenomenon of televangelism, the following perspectives need to be considered:

1. Political resistance to Christianity is prevalent in the form of restrictions to missionary visas and overseas funding as well as anti-conversion laws in some Indian states.
2. Satellite and digital media have become the predominant media technology for the spread of Christianity as global, local and

'glocal' televangelism are becoming more and more prevalent. Certain states have used means to block cable operators from transmitting Christian programmes. Protestant pastors have mixed feelings about televangelism: whereas a few are in favour of the new media, others are wary of anything Western, and many are afraid that new ideas via television would undermine their authority and ministry in the post-colonial church structures.

3. The majority of Indian Christians (50–60 per cent) are Dalit (or scheduled caste) and after years of being marginalised by the nation and to some extent by the churches, a 'subaltern' Dalit Christian discourse is finally emerging.

4. Transnational Hindu televangelism has entered the scene, catering for India's population as well as the 'diaspora' Indians largely in the West.

5. Hindu televangelism, while rejecting the exclusive message of Christianity, has used the methods, techniques and marketing strategies of Charismatic televangelists to propagate the 'new spirituality' of Hinduism.

Some of these perspectives will be taken up in the research and analysis reported in succeeding chapters.

Sociology of religion and revitalisation theory

Sociological theories of religion in recent times have seen the function of religion as one of providing answers to the dilemmas and questions of life: 'religion is valuable, in that it makes for social cohesion and social continuity' (Evans-Pritchard, 1990: 48). Durkheim (1961) sees religious phenomena in two categories: beliefs (opinions and values) and rites (special actions) based on the division of the world into the sacred and the profane. For Durkheim, ordinary things, objects and words can take on a sacred meaning because certain people attribute a sense of sacredness to them (Durkheim, 1961).

Weber (1990) analyses religion in Western society in a profound way in its relationship to Western capitalism and the 'Protestant ethic' (Weber, 1990: 53). According to Weber, post-reformation thinking changed the idea of a Christian's sense of calling to include a moral jus-tification for involvement in mundane, worldly and business activities (Weber, 1990).

The secularisation theory (the loss of religion and ritual in the public domain, evidenced by the high attrition rate in churches) of Wilson (1966) has been challenged by Martin (1978) and Turner (1983). Turner states: 'Christianity in the past may have been much weaker than commonly assumed, whereas Christianity in the present may be much stronger than attritionist views normally suggest' (Turner, 1983: 145).

Evans-Pritchard (1976) suggests that the West has moved from primitive aspects of magic and witchcraft to more intellectual and cerebral forms of faith (Evans-Pritchard, 1976).

Lyon (2000) argues that religion has not gone into oblivion in the contemporary West but, rather, it has reorganised and reinvented itself. Using the 1994 'Toronto Blessing' phenomenon (sometimes called 'Holy laughter movement') as an example, Lyon explains the patterns and suggests reasons for this new packaging of religion:

> It [Toronto Blessing] became an indigenous and widely networked church, and by 1996 had attracted over 300,000 visitors from 25 countries...The 'Blessing' relies on communication and information technologies for contact and has adopted a 'showbiz' style that focuses on the [human] body as much as on words. (Lyon, 2000: 108)

Pentecostalism and 'neo-Pentecostalism' (or the Charismatic movement) are growing so rapidly around the world that Turner (2004) estimates one in 25 of the global population are Pentecostals (Turner, 2004). Pentecostalism and neo-Pentecostalism have important characteristics that partially account for its worldwide growth and the consequent repositioning of Christianity in the contemporary world:

1. It is syncretistic in that it draws from many sources including cults (Lehmann, 1998).
2. It downplays doctrine (theology) in comparison to the importance it places on ritual, symbolism and conversion experiences (Lehmann, 1998).
3. It builds on the Protestant work ethic and has made a virtue of work skills, success, self-discipline and social aspiration (Turner, 2004).
4. It gives women a public role in the life of the Church (Lehmann, 1998; B. Martin, 2001).

Hawkins asserts that the above-mentioned features make Pentecostalism:

> An eminently portable religion, ripe for export growth. There is no need for learned scholars...theological content is readily supplied by the Bible; any culture will do; rituals and symbols can be borrowed from anywhere, local or global. It is this very hybridity and fluidity that defines Pentecostalism and makes it global. (Hawkins, 2006: 176)

India's response to Christianity's influence, especially in its encounter with Hinduism, can be seen from the viewpoint of Hindu attempts to maintain meaningfulness and stability in the wake of intense modern and enlightened religious ideas. To understand this phenomena I draw on Wallace's (1956) theory of revitalisation (see Figure 1.1).

Wallace (1956) writes as an anthropologist (from a functionalist viewpoint) who conceives that the role of culture is to meet the physical and psychological needs of society. Therefore, from his perspective, revitalisation movements are 'deliberate, conscious, organised efforts by members of a society to create a more satisfying culture' (Wallace, 1956: 279). In other words, revitalisation is a social process set in force when the needs of a society are not being met. These movements occur

Figure 1.1: Wallace's revitalisation theory

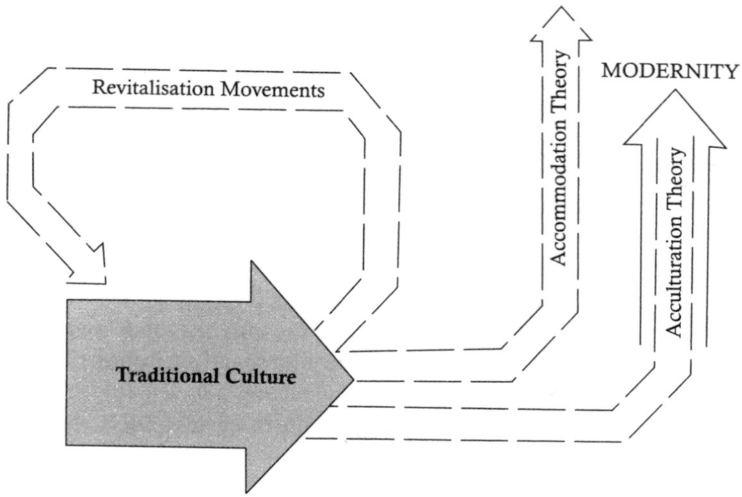

Source: Adapted from Hiebert (2000: 50) (used with permission).

under two related conditions: During times of stress for individual members of society and during times of widespread disillusionment with existing cultural beliefs (Wallace, 1956).

Wallace (1956) posits that when cultures and religions are met with powerful ideologies and movements, three kinds of responses are seen:

1. 'Acculturation' or conversion movements: where people leave their basic belief systems and practices and take on the new faith.
2. 'Accommodation movements': where people stay in their own faith but adopt some of the tenets of the new faith, such as the modifications introduced by the *Brahmo Samaj* group.
3. 'Revitalisation movements': where people go back to their roots and seek to revive their faith by synthesising the old religion with new elements so as to ensure its survival in the contemporary era.

The first response 'acculturation' refers to conversion movements and this has been an ongoing reality in India's history.

A second response is 'accommodation movements' in which the disillusionment of the present system causes people to adopt some of the elements of the new religions but interpreting these in their own terms. The *Brahmo Samaj*, which emerged in the late nineteenth century, transformed 'Brahmanical Hinduism by submitting Hindu scriptures and teachings to the test of rationality and Christian ethics. The result was a synthesis of Vedic idealism, Islamic monotheism, and Christianity morality. The caste system, untouchability... wife burning...were condemned. Reason was enthroned' (Hiebert, 2000: 50).

An example of the 'revitalisation movement' is the formation of the Arya Samaj and the Ramakrishna Mission, which gave birth to neo-Hindu fundamentalist movements (Hiebert, 2000: 51). Hiebert argues that neo-Hinduism is:

>...the result of India's encounter with Enlightenment and Christian thought...These movements also emerged out of the success of Christianity in winning untouchables. Many Hindu leaders became extremely anxious about the landslide of the lower sections of Hindu society to Christianity, a 'foreign religion'. (Hiebert, 2000: 52)

Successful revitalisation movements tend to travel in two directions and both of these are evident in the Hindu revitalisation movements (Hiebert, 2000: 51):

1. Spiritualised Hinduism—the reform movements of the Arya Samaj and the Ramakrishna Mission, which stress the spiritual nature of Hinduism.
2. Politicised Hinduism—the birth of the Hindu Mahasabha in 1909, which led to the formation of the Rashtriya Swayamsevak Sangh (RSS), a Hindu fundamental movement with a vision of a Hindu theocratic state.

There are several global Hindu organisations that promote neo-Hinduism (in both the spiritualised and politicised forms) within India and outside India, such as:

ISKCON (International Society for Krishna Consciousness), Ananda Marga, Arsha Vidya Gurukulam, Arya Samaj and RSS (Rashtriya Swayamsevak Sangh) (Hiebert, 2000: 52).

The introduction and growth of Hindu televangelism just after the introduction of Charismatic televangelism in India suggests that Hindu televangelism is yet another example of the revitalisation movement within Hinduism.

In the same way as the theory of the revitalisation movement is applied to Hinduism, it can be applied to the Charismatic movement. In many ways, the theology and style of Charismatic worship is a response to the text-based, rational approach of historic Christianity. Faith in the West, by and large, has been an intellectual exercise (Evans-Pritchard, 1976). The Charismatic movement has also adopted certain features of the materialistic, consumer culture of the West. In that sense Wallace's accommodation theory can be applied to the distinctive phenomena of Charismatic theology and worship with its focus on emotion, health, wealth and miracles.

Heelas, Woodhead, Seel, Szerszynski and Trusting (2005) state that a new 'spiritual revolution' is taking place in Christianity and other religions where the 'good life' is actually celebrated and spirituality has replaced religion: *Why is Religion so evil?*

> The 'good life' consists in living one's life in full awareness of one's states of being; in enriching one's experiences, in finding ways of handling negative emotions...the goal is not to defer to a higher authority, but to have the courage to become one's own authority. (Heelas et al., 2005: 2–4)

Sociology of religion, seen in conjunction with Christianity and Hinduism, suggests that in the overall study of televangelism in India, the following perspectives need to be examined:

1. All three aspects of Wallace's (1956) theory of acculturation, accommodation and revitalisation are evident in Hinduism. In both the colonial and post-colonial Christianity eras in India, conversions are seen, whether on a one-by-one basis or as in 'people movements'. This is 'acculturation'. High-caste Indian Hindus were attracted to enlightenment thought introduced by the British, and many low caste and tribals accepted the gospel spread by colonial missionaries. Those who did not have a significant place in the Brahmanical order are now guaranteed a place as Christians in Western-based churches.

2. In the same way, accommodation is seen in the Hindu reform movements such as *Brahmo Samaj* and revitalisation is seen in spiritualised Hinduism, politicised Hinduism, as well as in Hindu televangelism.

3. Can Wallace's (1956) theory be applied to the Charismatic movement? Are elements of accommodation and revitalisation manifest in the way experiential Charismatic televangelism has gained prominence over the more rational and orthodox Christian beliefs and practices?

4. In Chapter 4, I assert that Wallace's (1956) theory of revitalisation can be used to show an interesting interplay between Hinduism and the Charismatic movement.

These perspectives will be explored further in the book.

Missiology (study of Christian missions)

During the colonial era, the missionary leader Macdonald (1910) noted that European personnel had successfully opened up China, Asia and Africa, bringing them under the influence of the superior European economic and political powers: The 'nations which are best fitted to send missionaries abroad are the strongest and most influential in the world, and their united empires comprise the greater part of the habitable world' (Macdonald, 1910: 218–219).

Underlining this sentiment is the conviction of the superiority of Western civilisation compared to the cultures and worldviews of others. Many Christians treat evangelisation and civilisation as two necessary aspects of the mission of the church. Christianity is therefore equated with Western culture—religion, albeit under the powerful symbol of the cross (D. Smith, 2003: 119). Escobar (1994) bemoans this particular missionary approach, naming it 'imperial missiology' as it pursues mission work from a standpoint 'of superiority: political, military, financial, technological' (Escobar, 1994: 17). This trend can be traced historically, where the cross, the symbol of Christianity was linked with the following aspects:

1. The sword in the seventeenth century;
2. Commerce in the nineteenth century;
3. Information technologies in the latter part of the twentieth century (Escobar, 1994: 17).

Missiology in the post-colonial world is a highly contested arena as Christian mission is overshadowed by the processes of modernisation and secularisation. When Muslims and Hindus see the Westernised patterns of worship, the commodification of the gospel and the general lack of reverence for God in Christianity, their perception of Christianity as a 'carrier of a Western secular modernity' is reinforced (D. Smith, 2003: 112).

Christian leaders in Asia today seem to be wary of Christianity's Western influences and associations and the clarion call to the Church is for the indigenisation or localisation of Christianity:

> Apart from the evangelical doctrine...almost everything about us portrays us as a Western institution. The way we celebrate the special days in the Christian calendar, our rites of passage, our rituals and practices in the church have not much to do with the Bible but more to do with the cultural setting of the people who brought the Gospel to us. (Dhanabalan, 2003: para 6)

Missions in post-colonial India must also be understood in the context of the trenchant critiques of Shourie (1987, 2000) who, in his two books, dismisses the identity of Indian Christians who have chosen not to belong to Brahmanical Hinduism and criticises the movement of Dalits who have chosen to convert to other religions. Dharmaraj (1993) asserts that colonial mission in India was influenced by the political climate of expansionism and the concept of 'Christendom' rather than Christianity.

Missiology is the discipline that pertains to the broad approaches, theologies and motivating forces behind the spread of the Christian gospel across cultures and nations. Luzbetak (1985: 512) categorises three basic paradigms of missions that have been used historically in the Christian church: the ethnocentric model, the accommodational model and the contextual model.

The ethnocentric model of missions is based on non-engagement with the host culture. It is motivated by the missionary's sense of personal and cultural superiority and has also been referred to as a 'confrontational' method of evangelism (Copley, 1997: xiv).

The accommodational model uncritically accepts all that is in the host culture to the point that the culture overrides the Christian faith, leading ultimately to syncretism. Luzbetak (1970) defines syncretism as: '...the fusion of Christianity and what is commonly known as "paganism" resulting in a theologically untenable amalgam called "Christopaganism"' (Luzbetak, 1970: 239).

The contextual model encourages engagement with the culture and carefully synthesises the biblical text so that a culture-specific interpretation and application can be determined for a given situation. Shaw (1995: 155) explains the necessity of the two-sided concerns of the contextual model: '...the necessity of critique with a cultural context [and] the need to protect against syncretism. Both must be taken seriously.'

Hiebert (1982) explains that the concept of 'critical contextualisation', which neither rejects all traditional beliefs nor uncritically accepts all traditional beliefs, will avoid the pitfalls of syncretism and enable new believers of a culture to understand the Christian faith within their own cultural context (Hiebert, 1982: 287–294).

Gilliland (1989) explains that true theology is based on an interpretation of what the gospel means to a particular culture 'using the thoughts, values and categories of truth which are authentic to that place and time' (Gilliland, 1989: 11–12).

The pre-colonial Christians of the Malabar coast seem to have maintained a form of indigeneity through a form of contextualisation because they were 'Hindu in culture, Christian in faith and Syrian in doctrine, liturgy and polity' (Frykenberg, 2004: 116). In this case 'Hindu' is a reference to the native culture of India: 'Notwithstanding the universality of the message, where the Word has been made flesh, this flesh and clothing have been "Hindu" (native) in culture. That being granted, the gospel's expression [was seen] in indigenous motifs, style and terms' (Frykenberg, 2004: 123).

Missiological studies suggest that in terms of Indian televangelism, the following perspectives need to be examined (see Tables 1.1a and 1.1b):

Table 1.1b: The historical-comparative framework (continued)

Theoretical perspectives	*Post-colonial Christianity era*	*Colonial Hinduism era*	*Post-colonial Hinduism era*
Post-colonial studies	• Very few missionary visas, anti-conversion laws, FCRA funding guidelines, opening of airwaves, American televangelism (Charismatic) 　▪ Global or transnational televangelism 　▪ Local televangelism 　▪ 'Glocal' televangelism • Ambivalence by some pastors—nostalgic of colonial denominational churches • Resistance discourse by 'subaltern' Dalit Christians • Satellite and digital technology, the dominant technology	• Resistance • Conversions	• Resistance • Hindu televangelism (copy methods, rhetoric, global marketing strategies) • Transnational Hindu TV for '*diaspora*' Indians
Sociology of religion		• Conversions (acculturation)	• Revitalisation theory; political tensions (violence by *Hindutva*) • Socio-cultural propagation (Hindu televangelism)
Wallace's theory of revitalisation	Charismatic theology—a response to a 'rational' faith and a materialistic, consumer culture (accommodation theory)	• Hinduism is reformed (accommodation) • Birth of *Brahmo Samaj* (accommodation)	

Missiological studies	CSI, CNI, Baptists, Methodists, etc. are a 'carryover' of colonial era	• More neo-Pentecostal (Charismatic) independent churches	Indigenous Christianity • Churchless Christians • Anonymous Christians	Christianity the 'fulfilment' of Hinduism … theory of Farquhar	• A radical *Hindutva* 'India for Hindus' agenda • Propagation of Hindu spirituality
Critical contextualisation	(leaders still have colonial mindset)	• Greater openness to Charismatic teaching and less focus on denominations	• *Jesu Bakhta* • Popular Christianity • Dalit theology		• Hindu televangelists influenced by Charismatic methods

Source: Author.

1. The pre-colonial Christianity era was one marked by the indigenisation model where to be a Christian meant to be Hindu in culture, Christian in faith and Syrian in liturgy, doctrine and polity.
2. The colonial era was marked by various models of missiology where Christianity was closely related to commerce, culture and to the British empire. However, there were missionaries like Carey, who upheld indigenisation and Farquhar, who promoted the theory that Christianity is the fulfilment of Hinduism.
3. The post-colonial era is characterised by churches like Church of North India and Church of South India, which were started by the Western churches and mission agencies. These churches continue to fill the religious landscape of India today but they are not influencing the nation as much as the post-colonial, independent (and at times post-denominational) neo-Pentecostal churches. At the same time there is a clear resurgence of the indigenous movement and a growing antipathy to the Western models of Christianity, with televangelism receiving mixed responses both from the church and the community.

More discussion will take place on these perspectives in the research and analysis.

The Influence of Charismatic Televangelism

Thirty-five per cent of Indian pastors (Charismatic and non-Charismatic) attributed the Charismatic influence in India to the media, and named television as a key agent in this whole process.

Global Charismatic televangelism emanating from the West (especially America) is generally impacting the Protestant Church and the Hindu community in three ways: uneasiness and resistance, acceptance and new media formations (see Table 1.2):

Uneasiness and resistance

Both the Charismatic and non-Charismatic pastors are uneasy about the cultural disjunction caused by Charismatic global televangelism.

Table 1.2:   Global Charismatic televangelism's influence on the Church and the Hindu community

Type of influence	Protestant Church	Hindu community
1. Uneasiness and resistance	• Charismatic and non-Charismatic pastors are uneasy about cultural elements • Non-Charismatic pastors from mainline churches resist the techniques, teachings and overall packaging	• High-caste and high-class Hindus • Conservative Hindus • Hindu leaders are threatened
2. Acceptance	• Christians who watch and participate in some of the associated activities while continuing to attend their own churches • Christians who cross over into Charismatic churches/groups • Charismatic Christians whose faith and beliefs are reinforced as they watch and participate	• Adherents of 'popular Hinduism' (syncretism or 'Christo-Hinduism') • Middle and lower class Hindus (*sanskritisation*) • Hindus from various castes and classes whose needs are met
3. New media formations	• Local televangelism—the indigenous version • 'Glocal' televangelism—the hybrid version	• Hindu televangelism— imitates techniques, consumer ideas and rhetoric of global Charismatic televangelists

Source: Author.

Non-Charismatic pastors are generally more negative about Charismatic televangelism—its techniques, teachings and the overall way it is packaged.

The high-caste and high-class Hindus and conservative Hindus are generally uneasy and resistant towards global televangelism, while the Hindu leaders are threatened by its serious political and cultural overtones.

Acceptance (by Christians)

The pastors indicate that the positive responses from Christians come from Charismatic Christians who are already sold out to the teachings and practices of the movement. Global televangelism reinforces their beliefs and keeps them in touch with new teachers, methods and trends.

In addition to this, non-Charismatic Christians may cross over into Charismatic churches or groups and find more spiritual satisfaction in these groups than in their traditional churches.

Furthermore, acceptance comes for Charismatic Christians who watch global televangelism with discernment, picking and choosing the parts that they are comfortable with. These Christians have some form of participation in Charismatic activities but they continue to attend their own non-Charismatic churches.

Acceptance by Hindus
(positive response to televangelism)

The research indicates that acceptance among the Hindus comes from people of a mixture of castes and classes whose needs have been met in some way by Charismatic televangelists. These Hindus may or may not attend organised churches.

They include those from the middle to lower classes who are impressed by the wealth, health and prosperity teachings of Charismatic televangelists. To these Hindus, adherence to Charismatic teachings may aid them in their quest for a better lifestyle. Hence this is a form of *sanskritisation*, a term coined by Srinivas (1952), to refer to Hindus who try to move upwards in the social hierarchy. Most of these Hindus would continue in their Hindu traditions while espousing aspects of the Christian faith and practices.

Another category of people are those who believe in 'popular Hinduism' but who have an open mind to spirituality and therefore are impressed by some of the teachings of Charismatic teachers. These Hindus would still retain their Hindu beliefs and practices while taking on new Christian beliefs. Pastors have referred to this syncretistic faith as 'Christo-Hinduism'.

New media formations

Within the Protestant Church, two types of televangelism have emerged as a result of global televangelism: local televangelism and 'glocal' televangelism which is a hybrid version of Western (American) and Indian televangelism.

Within the Hindu community, Charismatic televangelism has influenced Hindu televangelism, in that the modes of communication utilised by the Christian broadcasters are being keenly observed and adapted by Hindu broadcasters for their own ends.

'Glocal' Charismatic televangelism, as seen in the case study I conducted on the programme *Solutions* was generally well received by pastors of both Charismatic and non-Charismatic persuasions although it was pointed out that cultural disjunctions are still prevalent.

The Hindu leaders were more open to 'glocal' televangelism than to the American varieties of global televangelism. However, some aspects of cultural inappropriateness and the presentation of the 'exclusive Christ' continued to be raised as negative issues even in 'glocal' televangelism.

The Features of Global, Glocal and Hindu Televangelism

'Global' televangelism is transnational television that is produced outside India and therefore not contextualised to the culture and conditions of Indian society. The majority of the programmes originate from the United States of America and hence they operate on a commercial basis—through aggressive fundraising and sale of products. The fundraising techniques are noticeably American in nature. Most of the programmes are produced by Charismatic churches and agencies where the themes of prosperity, health, miracles and blessing predominate. The concept of 'spirituality' in these programmes is more experience-based rather than text-based moving away from the main stream, historic, evangelical Christian hermeneutical and theological approaches. There are covert and sometimes overt political references in these 'global' programmes that are disturbing to Hindus and Muslims and even some Christians.

'Glocal' televangelism, whilst being a bold attempt to indigenise the Christian message to the Indian context, still has a long way to go because of its marked American influence. Even though it has been described as 'three parts American and two parts Indian', 'glocal' programmes mark the beginning of a new form of televangelism that has growing appeal to the middle class, English-educated urban Indian. Mediated Christianity in India may blossom more and more in this realm, catering to the televisual, Bollywood audience.

Hindu television is markedly different from global and glocal televangelism in many respects yet shares some characteristics. The launch of separate Hindu TV channels seems to be largely prompted by global Christian televangelism. Hindu televangelism propagates Hindu spirituality and the practices of Hinduism in keeping with the orthopractic nature of Hinduism. Discourse (in the way of global televangelism) is not a common feature of Hindu televangelism.

It is very interesting to note that the marketing tools, product sales and the overall commercial aspects have been borrowed from Christian global televangelism to the extent that the economics of Hindu televangelism now seem to underpin Hindu mediated faith. This trend will be studied in Chapter 5.

The changing mediascape of India brought about by the introduction of satellite television and global televangelism is one of the most interesting developments in contemporary India. No study has been undertaken that looks at the impact of Charismatic televangelism on the Protestant Church and the wider Hindu community in the gateway cities of Mumbai and Hyderabad. The findings I have produced, might challenge some widely accepted generalisations about the changing faces of both Indian and world Christianity.

In this chapter, I have introduced the key metaphors and described how these relate to the three strands of televangelism in India: global, 'glocal' and Hindu. An explanation of the methodology and the theoretical perspectives relating to televangelism have also been provided, paving the way for a summary of church and Hindu leaders' regard for televangelism. These findings are elaborated in Chapters 6 and 7.

Notes

1. Since this chapter draws on primary research, the ideas and opinions of the respondents (many of whom wish to remain anonymous) are identified in the text in the following ways: MLP—middle-level pastor/s; SCL—Senior Christian leader/s; KI—Key Informant/s; HL—Hindu leader/s and ML—Muslim leader/s.
2. The historical-comparative framework comprising aspects of three fields of study: post-colonial studies, sociology of religion and missiology (Christian missions) was used to understand televangelism in India in the global and historical context (see Tables 1.1a and 1.1b).

By combining these seemingly disparate disciplines in a synthetical way, I was able to build historical-comparative sketches of Christianity which enabled a better understanding of the present-day impact of Charismatic televangelism in India. Therefore, this methodology provided background information and fresh insights into the areas of research.

Drawing from Kurth's (1999) explication of the three historical eras to study religion and globalisation, namely: pre-modernist, modernist and postmodernist, I used as my research parameters, five successive phases or eras of the religious scene in India: Pre-colonial Christianity era, Colonial Christianity era, Post-colonial Christianity era, Colonial Hinduism era and Post-colonial Hinduism era.

3. Although I am aware of the weaknesses in the field of post-colonial studies, I still choose to use it as part of my theoretical perspective. I reject the aspect of post-colonialism that has, in some cases, been reduced to a caricature of 'third-worldism'. Neither do I hold to the polemical anti-Western heritage of post-colonial studies that fails to see that the Western values of rationalism, universalism and self-criticism are what make scholarship possible. I believe the intercultural encounter between the West and India is best seen in what Pratt (1981: 33–40) describes as 'contact zones', the social spaces between the West and the colonised. It is in this realm of post-colonial studies together with the globalisation of religion, that I frame my theoretical perspective.

For critiques of the post-colonial, post-structural and pro-Marxist approaches, I recommend the following scholars: Ibn Warraq (2007); Irwin (2006); Gellner (1992); Eaton (2000); Frykenberg (1996); Kopf (1987); Viswanathan (1998) and Dirks (2001).

Chapter 2

Charismatic Televangelism: The Global, Evolving Spirit[1]

Historians of religion inform us that the expansion of Christianity has not merely been an exercise of adding people into the kingdom but adding people of all ethnic groups and cultures into the family of God. Jenkins (2002) reveals that the map of world Christianity is changing, as a major shift is now taking place in the southern hemisphere (Africa, Asia and South America), with more Christians there than in the North—the traditional heartlands of the faith. Christians in many of the largest mega cities of the southern hemisphere—Sao Paolo, Mexico City, Kinshasa, Kampala, Manila and Seoul—boast of large numbers of Christians with the largest Protestant Church in the world being located in Seoul, Korea. Just as significant as this finding, is the fact that the explosive church growth in the South is clearly marked by the Charismatic model of Christianity.

Televangelism as a phenomenon was historically a project of the evangelical church community. However, in the last 10 to 15 years, global televangelism has become primarily an undertaking of the Pentecostal and neo-Pentecostal (Charismatic) churches. This 'made to travel' brand of Christianity, with its spirited and experiential-based worship, has freely and unashamedly espoused new technology and media strategies to literally reach the ends of the earth (Dempster et al., 1999). This openness to media technology is in part due to the Charismatic theology of communication and media (elaborated in Chapter 8), which is based on the perception that the media is firstly, a gift of God and hence all forms of electronic media can potentially be embodiments of power, 'anointing' and blessing.

In this chapter, I attempt to situate Charismatic televangelism in the context of the global Charismatic movement through the following ways: first, I trace the roots of the Charismatic movement and differentiate Charismatic doctrine from Pentecostal and evangelical Christianity; second, I give an overview of televangelism and Christian approaches to it; third, I trace the American roots of televangelism and explain its present global influence; and fourth, I postulate an interesting link between Hinduism and the Charismatic movement, in what I term the 'full circle accommodation' assertion.

Evangelical Christianity, Pentecostalism and the Charismatic Movement

The term 'evangelical' refers to the body of Protestant Christians who claim to adhere to the historic and biblical understanding of the Christian gospel. Evangelical theology, which is based on the gospel of Jesus Christ and its doctrines according to its proponents, can be summarised in the following categories: the sufficiency of the Bible, the sufficiency of the person of Christ and His work on the cross, the need for conversion through faith and the active demonstration of the gospel in evangelism and social service (Bebbington, 1989: 4–8). Based on these categories, evangelicals believe in some 'fundamental' (as opposed to 'incidental') doctrines such as the inspiration of the Bible, the deity of Jesus Christ and the resurrection of Christ.

Pentecostalism grew out of the Holiness Movement originating from the Methodist and Baptist denominations during the late nineteenth century (Synan, 1984: 836). In 1901, in Topeka, Kansas Charles Parham, a former Methodist minister, taught his students at Bethel College (USA) about baptism in the Holy Spirit characterised by speaking in tongues, as an experience distinct from Christian conversion. In 1906, William Seymour, a Black American, one of the graduates of Bethel College, taught this doctrine at his Apostolic Faith Gospel Mission on Azusa Street, Los Angeles where 'revival' broke out. From here, Pentecostalism spread to the four corners of the world (Synan, 1984: 836). Pentecostalism, therefore, had its beginnings in a Black American context where the worship had all the trappings of early Black American culture, described by Lyon (2000: 112) as 'primal religiosity'. Here we find evidences of exuberant worship, songs that portray oppression and a rhetoric of protest. Asante (1987) maintains that in protest rhetoric, the protester 'must use different symbols, myths and sounds than the established order ... The oppressed must gain attention and control by introducing another language, another sound...' (Asante 1987: 122). This is a highly interesting observation by Asante as Pentecostalism is known for its teachings on *glossolalia* or 'speaking in tongues'. The fact that Pentecostalism is rooted in Black American culture is significant to Freston (1997) who believes that this explains the movement's rapid spread to Africa, South America and Asia, where people in many of these countries experience ongoing poverty, oppression and sickness.

If Charles Parham is the father of Pentecostalism, Dennis Bennett, an American Episcopalian, is the father of the Charismatic movement (Hocken, 1988: 130). In 1960, Bennett announced to his Van Nuys congregation that he received the outpouring of the Spirit. Later, Bennett visited Vancouver, BC and conducted seminars on the Holy Spirit. Thousands of Anglicans and other Orthodox Churches in North America were influenced by this renewal movement. In the United Kingdom, organisations like the 'Fountain Trust' and men like Michael Harper and David Watson helped to popularise Charismatic teachings throughout the UK (Richardson, n.d.: paras 7–8).

The Charismatic movement (so named from the Greek, *charisma*, a gift of God's grace) is historically and theologically linked to Pentecostalism (and was originally labelled 'neo-Pentecostalism'), but unlike Pentecostalism the Charismatic movement initially stayed within historic evangelical churches (Synan, 1984). The movement today 'exists almost totally outside official Pentecostal denominations' (Synan, 1984). One of the common practices of the Charismatic movement is 'slaying in the Spirit'—hands are laid on a person during prayer and when the person is overcome by the Holy Spirit's presence he or she loses all motor control and falls to the floor (usually backwards). The context of this practice is usually at the end of a meeting during the 'altar call' when people respond to receiving greater manifestations of the Spirit in terms of power, gifts, healing and 'anointing'.

Wagner (1988) distinguishes three waves of Charismatic manifestations: the first wave was Pentecostalism in the 1960s; the second wave was in the 1970s when mainline denominations appropriated Charismatic teaching and practices into their churches and the third wave in the 1990s, was associated with John Wimber with his emphasis on signs and wonders (Wagner, 1988).

Today there are many Charismatic independent churches and several of these have become denominations in their own right, like New Life Church in Mumbai, India. Although the terms 'Charismatic' and 'Pentecostal' have been used interchangeably, there are reasons why the Charismatic movement can be seen as a separate movement in its own right.[2]

Table 2.1 shows seven points of distinction between the Charismatic movement and the Pentecostal denomination (Martinez, 2006). In the main, the differences lie in the following: the origin, Christian roots, church structure, hermeneutics, key doctrines, church worship styles and socio-economic makeup.

Figure 2.1 comprises three concentric circles that show how Charismatic Christianity relates to Pentecostalism and the broader category of evangelical Christianity. The figure also shows that while many groups associated with the Charismatic movement are within the broad category of evangelicalism, the Charismatic movement is indeed wider than evangelicalism. By this definition many Pentecostal and Charismatic churches will fall into the category of evangelicalism. However, given the dynamic nature of these movements, especially the Charismatic movement, which does not have defined denominational affiliations, some new groups with experiential theologies (see Table 2.1) may fall outside the body of historic evangelical Christianity.

According to the historian Frykenberg (2008), the impact of Pentecostalism and its close ally, the Charismatic movement, in India is quite profound with approximately 20 per cent of evangelical Protestants in India having some kind of involvement with these movements.

Figure 2.1:   Charismatic movement in the Christian context

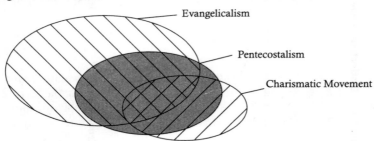

Source: Author.

Table 2.1:   Distinction between Charismatic and Pentecostal Christianity

Points of distinction	Pentecostal denomination	Charismatic movement
1. Time of origin	1900 onwards	1960 onwards
2. Christian roots	Protestant 'holiness' movements originating from Methodist and Baptist backgrounds	Protestant Pentecostal roots
3. Church structure and polity	Traditional denominations (like Assemblies of God, Foursquare) with various forms of Church Government	* Not a denomination—in the early days it transcended denominations and taught the Pentecostal beliefs to other Protestant denominations as well as to the Catholic and the Eastern Orthodox Church * Today there are many Charismatic Independent Churches and several of these have become denominations in their own right, like New Life in Mumbai, India * Some like Hillsong (Australia) are still part of the Assemblies of God Pentecostal denomination, but their growth and success are so remarkable that they can afford to have a loose relationship with the denomination
4. Hermeneutics	Historical and grammatical system (like Orthodox evangelicalism) as well as a 'pneumatic' or 'experiential' system of interpretation on certain doctrines and issues	Historical and grammatical system but moving more and more to the 'pneumatic' or 'experiential' system of interpreting the Bible—the common phrase 'the Bible says' is being replaced with 'the Lord told me'

5. Doctrines Being a Christian and speaking in tongues *glossolalia*	To be a Christian involves a two-stage experience—accepting Jesus Christ as Saviour (for forgiveness of sins) and then being filled with the Holy Spirit, resulting in the evidence of 'speaking in tongues'	To be a Christian involves a two-stage experience—accepting Jesus Christ as Saviour (for forgiveness of sins) and then being filled with the Holy Spirit. This second stage experience may result in 'speaking in tongues'. Many Charismatics believe other signs and spiritual gifts follow like 'being slain in the Spirit', 'laughter' (Toronto Blessing), prophesy, signs and wonders, miracles, health and prosperity
Holiness and Sanctification	Strong and defined positions on holiness (and almost 'perfectionism' in this life) and sanctification—growing in holiness and Christ-likeness	Very few groups emphasise holiness and sanctification—this has led some to carnality and abuse of Christian liberty
Spiritual gifts	Spiritual gifts are operated by the Holy Spirit for the building up of the Church	Spiritual gifts are generally given by the Holy Spirit for believers to use as they deem fit
6. Church worship style and emphasis	Strong emphasis on worship and singing (hymns and choruses), preaching and evangelism	Strong emphasis on worship and singing (mainly choruses), referred to as 'praise and worship', teaching especially on healing, prosperity and involvement in warfare (waging war on Satan and his hosts)

Source: Author.

Christian, Protestant Church
and Charismatic Television

In this study, 'Church' refers both to the mainline churches of the Protestant Church, as well as independent Charismatic churches in India and 'Christian' generally refers to an individual or organisational member of the Protestant denomination. Mainline churches refer to mainstream Protestant Churches ranging from evangelical orthodox to liberal, although generally theological moderation is what underpins mainline churches. In India, the mainline churches such as Methodist, Congregational, Presbyterian and Episcopalian have joined forces to form a united church under two regional groupings—the Church of North India (CNI) and the Church of South India (CSI).

Charismatic Christians or pastors are those who have experienced the 'second blessing' (see Table 2.1) of being filled with the Holy Spirit. They also believe that all the spiritual gifts described in the New Testament are available to the church today. Non-Charismatic Christians believe that accepting Christ as Savior and being filled with the Spirit is a one-stage experience that does not necessarily result in the 'speaking of tongues'. Furthermore, non-Charismatics believe that not all the spiritual gifts are available to Christians today. The term 'Charismatic' is an umbrella term referring to Christians who believe that gifts such as healing, prophecy and speaking in tongues are available to all in the Church today. Although Charismatic theology was inspired by Pentecostalism, differences prevail in certain respects (see Table 2.1). Charismatic Christians are not exclusive to any single Protestant denomination. Hence, Methodists and Episcopalians could equally be termed 'Charismatic'. In fact, the movement has also influenced the Catholic Church. In the last decade or so, independent Charismatic churches (of a non-denominational nature) have sprung up all over the world.

Charismatic television refers to Christian television programmes that demonstrate or teach the following: first, salvation is a two-stage experience involving accepting Jesus Christ as Savior and then being filled with the Holy Spirit; second, this then results in speaking in unknown tongues, and assumes that signs and wonders, prophecy, healing, prosperity and success are the will of God for all Christians. The Holy Spirit's manifestation in a person is aided through a technique called 'slaying in the Spirit'.

Christian Approaches to Television

Christian television scholars have three approaches to television's effects: to focus on television's negative effects (the iconoclasts), to glorify television's positive effects (the optimists) and to take a critical and interpretive view (the realists) seeing both the good and the bad in television (Mitchell, 2005). Here is a brief explanation of each approach.

Postman's work (1985) is based on an iconoclastic view of television's ability to turn everything into entertainment and, in the process, to trivialise all aspects of life, be it politics, education, news and even religion. In the same category of iconoclastic studies is the work of French writer Ellul (1985), who argued that whenever the visual takes precedence over the word (such as in televisual culture) it spells disaster for Christianity, which is a faith based on content. This concurs with Hendershot's (2004) research findings that many Christian television programmes, though professionally produced and equal in quality to the best commercial telecasts, are often sadly diluted in content. While Ellul focuses on the written word or the word that is heard, Muggeridge (1977), also in the first category of iconoclasts, focuses on the reality of Christ versus the fantasy of the televised Christ. He creates a fourth temptation: the offer of a televangelistic opportunity for Christ to launch a worldwide ministry (Muggeridge, 1977: 37).

In contrast to the iconoclasts, Armstrong (1979) glorifies and defends television's usefulness, especially in the context of Christian evangelism. Armstrong describes television as one of the 'major modern miracles of modern times' (Armstrong, 1979: 8). International broadcaster Robertson (cited in Hemphill, 1981: 67) refers to televangelism as 'the most formative force in America', whereas noted Evangelist Billy Graham (1976) says he 'can preach to more people in one night on TV than perhaps [the Apostle] Paul did in his whole lifetime' (Hemphill, 1981: 67; Littell, 1976: 16). This view is also shared by other Christian leaders, such as Benny Hinn, who have mega television ministries (Benny Hinn Ministries, 2006).

The third category of scholars and practitioners see television not in such black and white terms. This is the critical interpretative view, also known as the audience-centred perspective. Scholars like Fore (1987) and Hoover and Lundby (1987) identify how viewers create their own meanings and myths through their television viewing experiences. Morgan (2005) analyses the ability of audiences to come up with their own understanding of the various aspects of life through television. Clark (2003) analyses the world of teenagers and how they use television programmes like *The X Files* to understand their own lives. Audience-centred studies have increased in the second half of the twentieth century, as have studies on how viewers of different Christian traditions are involved in the activity of meaning-making (Horsfield, Hess and Medrano, 2004). Summarising both the bad and the good effects, Mitchell (2005) says: '...television need provoke neither total avoidance nor uncritical use. Another news report showing an emaciated baby in Darfur or Niger...may lead to questioning faith, but it often also provokes acts of Christian charity' (Mitchell, 2005: 7).

This book, based on the third approach which is the critical interpretative view, seeks an understanding from the perspective of Christian and Hindu leaders about televangelism and its influence in contemporary, urban India.

Televangelism in America

In this subsection, the origin of televangelism, its impact and expansion from United States of America (USA) to countries in Africa, South America and Asia are assessed.

Literature on televangelism surfaced in the late 1970s in the USA with the growth of religious television programmes. However, given the scope and prominence of religious television in the USA, the studies that deal with the various issues of religious television are surprisingly few. The studies that deal with trans-border religious television are fewer still.

One of the researchers in the field is Hadden (1981), who also co-authored with Swann (1981) and Shupe (1988). Other important studies come from Hoover (1987), Frankl (1987), Schultze (1989) and Abelman (1990) who also co-authored with Hoover (1990), Bruce (1990) and the Australian researcher Horsfield (1984).

The hybrid term 'televangelism' was coined by Hadden and Swann in their book *Prime Time Preachers* (1981) as the obvious conjunction of the words 'television' and 'evangelism'.

Hadden and Shupe (1988) argue that televangelism's roots are more than 'a century and a half old', going back to the revivalist movements of nineteenth century America. These revival movements, according to the authors, were not linked with any one church or denomination— 'they crossed sectarian boundaries... Drawing support from...a wide variety of churches' (Hadden and Shupe, 1988: 60).

While Hadden and Shupe (1988: 60) regard televangelism as a para-church movement, Frankl (1987) goes deeper into historical analysis to claim that televangelism today is a direct descendant of the revival movements of Charles Finney, Dwight Moody and Billy Sunday. Frankl's theory is that televangelism came into being with the historical roots of revivalism, coupled with the changing social climate of America, characterised by the following: 'economic growth', 'women in the workforce, flagrant sexuality, drug abuse, increase in divorce' and 'the availability of new technology' (Frankl, 1987: 23–61).

Frankl (1987: 4) sees televangelism as a 'significant organizational development' comprising 'broadcast networks and syndicated TV programmes', with a growing increase in TV and Radio Station ownership by religious groups (Frankl, 1987: 3). Bruce (1990) believes that the decentralised, market model of media adopted by America has con-tributed to the large number of religious groups who have tapped into religious broadcasting.

Hadden and Swann (1981: 60–64) have devised a typology of televangelism programmes:

1. 'The Supersavers': Billy Graham, Oral Roberts, Rex Humbard and Jerry Falwell;
2. 'The Mainliner': Robert Schuller and his *Hour of Power*;
3. 'The Talkies': Pat Robertson and *The 700 Club*; and Jim Bakker and *The PTL Club*;
4. 'The Entertainers': Jimmy Swaggart and Ross Bagley;
5. 'The Rising Stars': James Robison, Kenneth Copeland and Jack Van Impe;
6. 'The Teachers': Richard deHaan and Paul Van Gorder of *Day of Discovery*; and Frank Pollard's *At Home with the Bible*.

I add two more to these six categories, namely: 'The Dramatics' pioneered by the Lutheran Church—Missouri Synod with their production of *This is the Life* and 'The Miracle Worker' featuring Benny Hinn and other televangelists who perform miracles on air.

Hadden and Shupe (1988) theorise that even though the popular press may misunderstand and misconstrue the movement, televangelism is 'rooted in the American tradition ...it is an intrinsic part of American life' (Hadden and Shupe, 1988: 73). It must be acknowledged that televangelism is very much an American creation and that it is flourishing in its country of origin. Schultze (1989) adds that 'the American dream' is the touchstone of televangelism: just as televangelism is a product of America, it inevitably reflects aspects of American culture—materialism, hedonism, consumerism and ethnocentrism (Schultze, 1989). Besides these, two other aspects of American culture have contributed to the birth and expansion of televangelism, namely—technological optimism and expansion-mindedness (Peck, 1993; Schultze, 1989).

Australian researcher Horsfield (1990) asserts that, whereas religious television is useful in America, it is not a universal model for faith. It is his theory that religious television consists of specialised programming for a specialised audience (Horsfield, 1990: 80).

Hadden (1990: 3) lists three characteristics of televangelism ministries in USA:

1. They are dominated by Christians of the conservative evangelical traditions ... 'the large majority can be classified as either fundamentalist or Pentecostal'.
2. These ministries operate independently, that is, they operate as autonomous para-church structures with hand-selected board members even though they may be led by pastors of mega churches.
3. They operate as quasi-commercial agencies; broadcast time is purchased and contributions are solicited from viewers; also books and products are offered on air in exchange for a donation.

The number of viewers and the televangelism audience composition are hotly debated issues. Evangelist Billy Graham (1983) maintains that televangelism's breadth is tremendous:

> TV preachers touch the hearts of shut-ins, night workers, the very old, the very young, tenement dwellers—people often cut off from the comforts of a local church. Its real converts are coming not from traditional churches, but from commercial TV, whose diet of secular programming leaves viewers starved for spiritual nourishment. (Graham, 1983: 4–8)

Sociologist Bruce (1990) is actually critical of the size of the televangelism audience, stating that '...not much televangelism is consumed by not many people' (Bruce, 1990: 234). Bruce goes on to clarify, alluding to the two-step theory of communications, that although televangelism has failed in its primary purpose of converting the non-believers, it does have secondary effects, such as: 'entertaining believers...providing opportunities for young conservatives ...to have their own conversion experience as well as uniting the believing community' (Bruce, 1990:135–136).

Hoover (1987) asserts that whereas 'religious television viewing is socially desirable' in the USA, it is 'an infrequent behaviour engaged in for very short periods of time' (S. Hoover, 1987: 135–151). Furthermore, Hoover's research points to the fact that 'the aggregate audience for religious television is quite small by conventional standards' (S. Hoover, 1987: 135–151).

In light of the relatively small audiences, Bisset (1980) questions the effectiveness of televangelism, stating that 'we are not broadcasting the Good News—we are narrowcasting it to a highly defined, previously interested audience' (Bisset, 1980: 30).

Abelman (1990), basing his study on secular media researchers like Rubin (1983, 1984), Windahl (1981) and Dennis (1962), has identified three types of viewers of religious television: (1) the ritualised viewer, (2) the instrumental viewer and (3) the reactionary viewer. Abelman's research shows that 65 per cent of the religious televiewing audience consists of the ritualised viewer—those who are church members and already religious or 'born again'. About 20 per cent are instrumental viewers—those who view informational programmes like talk shows and interviews for their unique perspectives; these viewers 'are significantly less religious and more educated than ritualised viewers' (Abelman, 1990: 99–108). The remaining 15 per cent of religious televiewing audience consists of reactionary viewers:

> These are the ones who firstly turn to religious television out of dissatisfaction with the secular counterpart. Secondly they may turn to religious television out of curiosity to find out the outcomes of controversies and scandals surrounding Christian television like the sexual and fundraising problems faced by the PTL [*Praise The Lord*] Network. (Abelman, 1990: 99–108)

Hadden and Shupe (1988) have identified several problem areas relative to American televangelism. They believe that the modern media revolution, of which televangelism is a part, 'is reshaping American religion...Mass media does not expand our knowledge about particular subjects...to guard against boredom; the images must be fast paced, thus building in the inevitability of superficiality' (Hadden and Shupe, 1988: 72). Horsfield (1984) agrees with this depiction of 'over simplification' and even 'instant gratification and sensationalism', concluding dramatically that 'when religion buys into TV culture, it runs the risk of distorting not only life, but also religious faith' (Horsfield, 1984: 80).

Schultze (1989), while agreeing with this, points out the new challenges now facing the traditional Churches:

> ...televangelism's popular religiosity has seriously challenged the traditional, institutional and denominational Church...Televangelism has helped introduce to congregations such things as entertainment-oriented worship, Charismatic preaching...Instead of driving people away from the church, televangelism is changing their very conception of the church and its functions. (Schultze, 1989: 204–205)

Kintz and Lesage (1998), based on a collection of essays by various writers, assert that the 'religious right' in America, in an effort to wage war against secular humanism has given birth to several fundamentalist institutions including broadcasting and publishing. Television, radio, video/evangelism and other aspects of evangelical media usage are mentioned by the authors and critiqued from various standpoints, including that of Marxist post-colonial writer Gramsci (1978).

Hadden and Shupe (1988), taking a less critical approach than Kintz and Lesage (1998), see televangelism as a major socio-political movement led by the new Christian Right. Furthermore, they warn of the political potential of televangelism. Televangelists are a 'prophetic voice of change' as well as religious leaders. They have power, persuasive ability and financial support—all of which can be channelled for strong political purposes in the name of God (Hadden and Shupe, 1988: 71–73). However, Bruce (1990) disagrees with Hadden and Shupe's view that there is a 'stampede towards conservatism' by the American public, arguing that 'a wide-ranging review of survey studies of opinions during the first five years of the Reagan presidency could find no evidence for a general movement to the right' (Bruce, 1990: 189).

Another important problem identified by Horsfield is that the local Church and leaders view televangelists as in conflict with and damaging to their traditional functions. The perception is that televangelists build their own ministries rather than support the local churches (Horsfield, 1990). Horsfield (1985), in a study of the mailings of television broadcasters, comes to this conclusion about televangelism's empire-building propensity: 'The picture that emerges from the mailings is that broadcasters view convert-respondents to their programmes less as candidates for referral to local churches and more as candidates for membership and support of their own organizations' (Horsfield, 1985: 96).

Global televangelism

Hadden and Shupe (1988) identify another issue that paves the way for this study—the aggressive expansion of televangelistic ministries around the world. Pat Robertson's Christian Broadcasting Network (CBN) which is beamed to 43 countries five days a week was the first Christian global television enterprise in the USA. Hadden and Shupe (1988) go on to show the level of receptivity that these programmes have in these countries: 'Many of these are Third World nations...where the biblical apocalyptic and millennial themes of televangelists are going down well with audiences there' (Hadden and Shupe, 1988: 70). Apparently the emergence of satellite technology in the 1970s ensured a more efficient delivery system of international telecasts. Robertson's creation of CBN was followed by Jim Bakker, who started the PTL Inspirational Network and Paul Crouch with the launch of his Trinity Broadcasting System (TBN) (Hadden, 1990). Both CBN and TBN are multi-faceted, non-profit organisations who provide programmes by cable, broadcast and satellite to a world-wide audience. TBN's programmes are carried on 33 international satellites, including Palapa C-2 which covers India, Indonesia and Southeast Asia, (TBN, 2009) while CBN today claims to be seen in 'approximately 200 countries with a 24-hour telephone prayer line ... in approximately 71 languages' (CBN International, 2004a).

The breadth of CBN's media business empire is seen in its strategic acquisition and ownership of media-related companies:

> Pat Robertson exemplifies this strategy, both producing *The 700 Club* and owning the cable network to carry it. From the cable network, the Family Channel and a variety of other enterprises developed—CBN television productions; CBN University (now Regent University,

comprising graduate schools in business, communication, law and public policy); CBN Publishing offering a 'Superbook Audio Cassette and Colouring Book' for children ages four to eleven' 'Sing, Spell, read and Write', an instructional system for children in primary grades; and Video Tracts 'designed to be used by the individual or as a key element in a church's or organisation's overall evangelistic outreach. (Frankl, 1998: 166)

Another significant aspect to the CBN media empire is in its pursuit of a global reach CBN has had and continues to have links and connections with secular and profit-making companies such as media mogul Rupert Murdoch's *Fox Kids Worldwide* (P. Thomas, 2008).

Before looking briefly at televangelism's expansion specifically into Ghana, Brazil and India, I will attempt to understand the broad strategies used in global televangelism emanating from America, noting in particular Hadden's (1990) three main strategies for the USA: transnational strategy, syndicated programming and cooperation with indigenous leadership.

'Transnational strategy' refers to American broadcasters working to some degree with indigenous leadership to beam broadcasts into nations 'without the authorization of local officials' (Hadden, 1990: 7). 'Syndicated programming' may involve either translating individual programmes (into local languages) or adapting or creating specific programmes for specific countries. The third strategy, 'cooperation with indigenous leadership', involves identifying successful local evangelists with the aim of helping them expand their radio and television ministries. This involves financial and technical support (Hadden, 1990).

Having explored the birth and growth of televangelism in America I now proceed to understand its growth and impact in selected countries in Africa, South America and Asia.

Televangelism in Ghana

Maxwell (1988) observes that African Pentecostalism has grown enormously, in no small part due to the opening of the airwaves and electronic media and the support provided from the USA (Maxwell, 1988: 255).

In Ghana, all the four television stations give 'substantial space to mass mediated religion, particularly Christianity which commands the allegiance of 62 per cent of a population of almost twenty million people' (Asamoah-Gyadu, 2005). Pentecostal and Charismatic television, often inspired by their American counterparts, dominates the televangelism scene in Ghana (Asamoah-Gyadu, 2005). Some of the well-known TV ministries in Ghana include: Christian Action Faith Ministry International, Voice of Inspiration, Word Miracle Church International and God's Miracle Encounter and Your Miracle Encounter (Asamoah-Gyadu, 2005).

Gifford (2004) states that Christianity in Ghana has become a 'media phenomenon' as 'services are often built round the requirements of television' (Gifford, 2004: 32). Therefore, the Charismatic 'praise and worship' segment in Church services is widespread in almost all the denominational Church services in Ghana together with the practice of 'healing and deliverance' (Asamoah-Gyadu, 2005: 24). However, the ongoing impact of Charismatic televangelism is the breakdown of denominational Church loyalty as well as the decrease in the power of the local Church pastor (Asamoah-Gyadu, 2005: 13).

Televangelism in Brazil

Next to the USA, Brazil has the second largest Christian televangelism enterprise in the world (Lyon, 2000). The first North American televangelist on Brazilian TV was Rex Humbard who was on air from 1978 to 1984 (D. Smith and Campos, 2005). Even though the CBN's *700 Club* was introduced to Brazil during that time, Humbard had the biggest following—mainly from the local Assembly of God denomination (D. Smith, 1988).

In the 1980s the local preacher, Nilson do Amaral Fanini rose to fame with the programme *Reencontro*, which was aired in 88 stations. However, owing to financial problems (in spite of donations from North American media enterprises like the Billy Graham Association), he sold a large portion of his media ministry to Edir Macedo of the Universal Church of the Reign of God (D. Smith and Campos, 2005).

Macedo has built a huge media empire using all forms of media— radio, television, newspapers, magazines and internet—which routinely directed the masses to send their offerings to the 'blessing address': either one of the two mega churches in Rio de Janeiro and Sao Paulo (D. Smith and Campos, 2005: 58). His media ventures are similar to that of the Christian Broadcasting Network (CBN) in USA, in that, he has acquired the US$45 million commercial television network *Rede Record*, with 30 stations in Brazil and Sao Paolo

(D. Smith and Campos, 2005: 58). Macedo practices a Charismatic Christian theology of healing and miracles incorporating elements of 'Brazilian Catholicism, Protestantism and Kardecist Spiritism' (D. Smith and Campos, 2005: 58).

Other local groups with appreciable televangelistic ministries include: the International Church of God's Grace (a breakaway group from Macedo's Universal Church) and the Apostolic Church of Rebirth in Christ, which mainly targets the youth through music (D. Smith and Campos, 2005). The growth of Pentecostal and Charismatic Christianity in Brazil and other parts of South America, aided by televangelism, is becoming a threat to Catholic hegemony because the Catholic Church previously dominated large sections of South America (Lyon, 2000).

It is noteworthy that Brazilian Christian televangelism has several significant characteristics: first, it has entered into the commercial media market in its efforts to build a huge religious franchise; second, it has moved from using only American imports, to producing independent Brazilian programmes; third, most of the successful TV ministries are operated by Charismatic churches; fourth, shamanistic (spiritist) practices seem to be absorbed easily into the Christian message on television; fifth, religious entrepreneurs have cleverly taken religious ideas and repackaged them. Smith and Campos (2005) reveal this commercial strategy of the televangelists: 'All of human experience, including ethical values, intimate relationships and encounters with the numinous, can be commodified, packaged, and sold as consumer goods' (D. Smith and Campos, 2005: 62).

Televangelism in India

Although Christian televangelism is a growing force in India, research on this phenomenon is practically negligible. James and Shoesmith (2007) note that in spite of the fact that the Christian population of India is less than 3 per cent, there are four 24-hour Christian TV networks—*Miraclenet, God TV, DayStar* (all owned by Charismatic groups) and *EWTN* (a Catholic TV ministry). James and Shoesmith (2007) also note that only 5 per cent of programmes are of the genre of what they term 'indigenous televangelism' and that Christian Broadcasting Network (CBN) is the forerunner in the production of localised Christian television programmes (J. James and Shoesmith, 2007: 98). The nature of televangelism in India and other pertinent information on this phenomenon are elaborated in Chapters 5 to 7 (J. James and Shoesmith, 2007: 98).

Thomas and Mitchell (2005) in a study of television's impact among members of the Marthoma Christian denomination in south India, report that television has not replaced religion as such. They reveal that for the Marthomites:

> ...religion and television are considered to be different for the most part without having any influence on each other. Even religious television is not regarded as a major resource for the Christian faith or a substitute for traditional religious practices ...Televangelism may cater to the elderly...Church still remains a source of meaning and identity. (S. Thomas and Mitchell, 2005: 42–43)

Thomas (2008), in a study of Christian fundamentalism and the media in south India, posits that the Pentecostal and neo-Pentecostal churches in India with TV ministries, are exercising a political agenda with possible links to the communication-savvy 'Christian Right' group in the USA. Thomas' study is limited to the city of Chennai, using theoretical concepts from the French scholar Pierre Bourdieu (1991); Thomas uses the following constructs in his analysis: field, habitus, distinction and symbolic capital (Bourdieu, 1991).

Link between Hinduism and the Charismatic Movement

In as much as I argue that Hindu televangelism has been influenced by Charismatic televangelism (Chapters 1 and 5), I also postulate here that Charismatic televangelism has been influenced by Hinduism. This is in keeping with Lehmann's (1998) findings reported in Chapter 1, that the Charismatic movement is syncretistic and it easily draws its teachings and practices from many sources including cults.

As pointed out in Chapter 1, Wallace's (1956) theory of revitalisation in the wake of the collision of cultures and religions, is in line with my research on Charismatic televangelism. Wallace (1956) proposes that there are three responses when cultures are met with powerful counter-ideologies: acculturation (conversion movements), accommodation (cultural adaptation and modification) and revitalisation (the old faith or culture is revived by synthesising new elements into it).

There are a number of interesting parallels between Hinduism/ New Age ideology and the Christian Charismatic movement. These parallels are such that, I propose, in line with Wallace's theory (1956) a cyclical influence that I have termed a 'full-circle accommodation' assertion (see Figure 2.2).

Diem and Lewis (1992) define the New Age movement as a:

> ...unique synthesis of many pre-existing movements and religious traditions. A significant component of this synthesis is the South Asian religious tradition, particularly certain strands of Hinduism. The Hindu influence is clearly evident in the Indian yoga and meditation techniques, as well as certain key notions such as chakras and karma... (Diem and Lewis, 1992: 48)

The historical roots of Hindu influence to the West (USA) are categorised in three waves (Diem and Lewis, 1992: 48–49):

Figure 2.2: Full-circle accommodation assertion

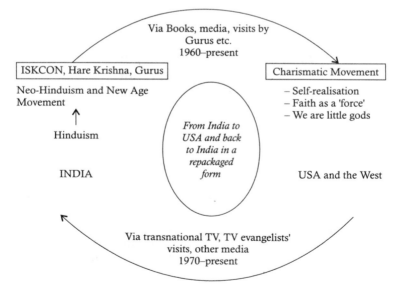

Source: Author.

1. The literary era during the latter half of the eighteenth century with the translation and distribution of Hindu literary texts. These texts influenced the Transcendentalist Movement, headed by Ralph Waldo Emerson and the New Thought Movement.
2. The visiting Hindu teachers' era during the nineteenth and early twentieth centuries, with visits from leaders such as Muzoomdar, Vivekananda and Yogananda.
3. The Immigration era after 1965, when a new wave of Indian immigrants entered the USA, coupled with ongoing visits from well-known Indian gurus who addressed audiences interested in non-traditional sources of truth and spirituality.

Alexander (1992) describes how American Transcendentalism, New Thought and Swedenborgism were influenced in some way by Hindu ideas, which in turn influenced the Unity School of Christianity, Christian Science and the Human Potential Movement. New Thought began as a late nineteenth century healing movement in New England 'within self-consciously Christian circles' (Alexander, 1992: 35). According to Alexander (1992), the Methodist minister Warren Felt Evans (a Swedenborg follower), in a book published in 1886: '...seems to return to a "Mesmeric model" by positing the existence of "mental energy" transmitted by the mind. He identified the energy with the Hindu *akasa*, the astral light of Western occults, Holy Spirit and the Platonic world-soul' (Evans, 1886, quoted in Alexander, 1992: 31).

The Human Potential Movement is built on a few key methods, one of which is 'peak performance' (feelings of bliss, ecstasy or rapture) and the other is a practice very similar to Hinduism's *prana* force called 'life force':

> ...the basic purpose of yoga is to contact and absorb prana in ever increasing quantities. Certain forms of yoga are especially directed towards channelling of energy in a very direct manner. Kundalini Yoga is described in the classical texts as 'the Yoga of Psychic Force'. (Evans, 1886, quoted in Alexander, 1992: 31)

New Thought and the Human Potential Movement ideas and practices (such as soothing music, crystals and healing) found their way into some churches. The idea that God is the source of all good, led to New Thought ideas of healing (Melton, 1992). Other ideas like 'prosperity consciousness', propounded by Cole-Whitaker, found their way into various churches:

[prosperity consciousness] is...one of the aspects of New Thought which has been able to penetrate the mainstream of American religious life through the work of ministers such as Norman Vincent Peale and Robert Schuller and Pentecostal evangelists such as Kenneth Hagin, Kenneth Copeland, Frederick Price and Rex Humbard. (Melton, 1992: 26)

I see the present Charismatic movement in Christianity as a movement that has been influenced by many disparate systems of thought and practices, including some aspects of Hinduism. The following ideas of Hinduism were propagated by the New Age movement to the West in the 1950s and 1960s:

1. The self-realisation teaching believes that people have the means within them to bring about their dreams, visions and even healing into fulfilment. Gawain (1985), a popular New Age author influenced by the concepts of Hinduism, says: 'Our bodies are simply a physical expression of our consciousness. The concepts we hold of ourselves determine our health and beauty or the lack thereof. When we deeply change our concepts, our physical self follows suit' (Gawain, 1985: 59).

    Korean Charismatic teacher Cho (1979), who teaches the concept of visualisation—a technique for prayer, faith and church growth—has borrowed New Age/Hindu concepts when he says:

    > We've got to visualize and dream the answer as being completed...we should always try to visualize the end result as we pray. In that way, with the power of the Holy Spirit, we can incubate that which we want God to do for us. (Cho, 1979: 26–27)

2. Faith as 'force': Swami Vivekenanda, a stalwart of neo-Hindu philosophy, says:

    > Any word, any action, any thought that produces an effect is called *karma*. Thus the law of *karma* means the law of causation, of inevitable cause and effect...The child is ushered into the world...to workout his own past deeds...Each one of us is the maker of his own fate. (Vivekenanda, quoted in Soper, n.d.: 100–101)

Many Charismatic teachers have borrowed the aforementioned concept in their teachings. Here is a sample of these statements by Charismatic teachers that show a reliance on Hindu/New Age thinking: '...our faith is measured by our confessions...our confessions rule us...It's not God who heals you, it's your faith' (Barron, 1987: 61; McConnell, 1988: 96–97).

3. 'We are little gods', a concept taught by many Charismatic leaders, stems from the pantheistic nature of Hinduism. Hinduism believes that each individual has the spark of divinity because we are part of the universal consciousness of Brahman—the life force. The Ramakrishna Mission in its official leaflet *Vedanta in America* states: 'Man's real nature is divine. If in this universe there is an underlying reality...it must be within each one of us...therefore man in his true nature is God' (Ramakrishna Mission, quoted in Soper, n.d.: 94).

   Charismatic teacher Copeland states, 'You imparted into your child the nature of humanity...That child wasn't born a whale...You don't have a god in you. You are one' (Copeland, quoted in Martin, 1989: 76). Paulk, another Charismatic teacher says, 'Until we comprehend we are little gods...we cannot manifest the Kingdom of God' (Paulk, quoted in Martin, 1989: 76).

So, Hinduism (from India) influenced the USA over a period of years. As stated above, the influence was felt in the Transcendentalist Movement, New Thought and the Human Potential Movement which, in turn, influenced the Charismatic movement (neo-Pentecostalism). Now the Charismatic movement is impacting India through transnational television and a full-circle has been reached in respect to Wallace's (1956) theory of accommodation. Hence I call this the full-circle accommodation assertion (see Figure 2.2). This assertion highlights several significant implications in the realm of religious and cultural globalisation: first, media and religion interact to reshape and modify existing religious ideas and practices; second, this cultural flow is multi-directional and not just one-way as it is often assumed; and third, in this instance the centre–periphery assumption (that the West is at the centre and the rest of the world is the periphery) has been disproved.

In this chapter, I have argued that televangelism, rooted in the American context, is now a global reality mainly due to various aspects of American culture (such as expansionism) and the global Charismatic movement whose adherents believe that the media is

God's gift for the propagation of the faith. Charismatic Christianity (also known as neo-Pentecostalism) an experience-based faith that celebrates God's direct intervention in human life through 'tongues' healings, signs and wonders was born in the context of early black American Pentecostalism. Although Charismatic practices and doctrines taught on television have American roots, the full-circle accommodation assertion shows that it has also been influenced by some Hindu and New Age ideas, pointing to the dynamic nature of this global movement.

Notes

1. Some of the findings in this book were originally published in *Studies in World Christianity*, 13 (2) under the title *Masala McGospel: A Case Study of CBN's Solutions Programme in India.*
2. Although I show the subtle differences between the Charismatic movement and Pentecostalism, in reality it is difficult to separate the two Christian groups and hence in this book, I treat the Charismatic movement and Pentecostalism as one.

Chapter 3

Televangelism in India's Context: Historical and Cultural Issues

Christianity has a long history in India; in fact, it has a longer history than most nations of the world as Christianity came to India before the first Western missionaries arrived. One of India's early Presidents, Dr Rajendra Prasad observed:

> Remember St Thomas came to India when many countries of Europe had not yet become Christian, and so those Indians who trace their Christianity to him have a longer history and a higher ancestry than that of Christianity of many of the European Countries. (Prasad, quoted in Moffett, 1992: 24)

This chapter contains a historical background to Indian televangelism by presenting an overview of issues in the history of missions and the Church, as well as relevant social and cultural aspects of Indian Christianity. These are documented as background material so that the reader can see how televangelism is rooted in Christianity's history in India. A two-fold perspective is adopted: First, I present a record of the history of changes in Indian Christianity of which televangelism is yet another. Second, I seek through the historical overview, an understanding of the reasons why Hindus converted to Christianity. The chapter is divided into the following parts: historical overview of Christian missions, indigenous Christianity, Pentecostalism in India, people groups, caste and class, urbanisation, church growth patterns and structures and Hindu–Christian tensions.

Historical Overview of Christian Missions

Kane (1971: 103), divides India's political history into six distinct periods of time:

1.	Indus civilisation	3000 to 1500 BC
2.	Aryan civilisation	1500 to 500 BC
3.	Indian kingdoms	500 BC to AD 1000
4.	Muslim rule	AD 1000 to 1700
5.	British rule	1700 to 1947
6.	Modern independent India	1947 to the present

The 250-year period of British rule made a huge impact on India paving the way for India to establish itself in the modern world. Kane (1971: 103) asserts that India today has:

1. A reputation as one of the few genuine democracies in Asia;
2. A parliamentary government;
3. A well-trained civil service;
4. A free press;
5. Universal education;
6. English as *lingua franca*.

The well-known scholar of Tamil literature, Pope (1886), commenting on the ethical quality of the *Tirukurral*, the greatest of all Tamil poetry classics, which was composed in the second century AD, states: 'I cannot feel any hesitation in saying that the Christian Scriptures were among the sources from which the poet derived his inspiration' (Pope, 1886: xviii).

An important aspect of the existence of early Christianity in India is the evidence of Christianity's influence in early Tamil literature. Tamil scholar Gnanasigamani states: 'From the first century AD many Tamil Christian literary works were made. The Christian thought found entry in secular literature also. Scholars point to this in *Tirukurral*' (Gnanasigamani, 1981: 24).

Arulappa (1974) and Theyvanayagam (n.d.), India's foremost scholars on the *Tirukurral*, argue that the following ideas of Valluvar (the writer) are irrefutably from a Christian base: The attributes of God and the doctrines of repentance, reconciliation and unmerited grace, heaven, hell, sin and the devil.

Even though this belief is not held by all historians, these assertions cannot be easily dismissed when faced with the fact that the *Tirukurral* is unmatched by other writings in its time, in its closeness to the values and ethics of Christianity. If Pope and the other historians are right, then the fledgling early Christian church exercised a far more significant influence in the life and culture of early India than has been documented.

Early apostolic years

In the absence of early written records of the coming of the Apostle St Thomas to India, strong traditions and rich legends abound pointing to the historicity of his life and ministry in India.

Farquhar (1913), a well-known Indologist, asserts that Thomas first arrived in Punjab about AD 48–49:

> Then he left Taxila when the Punjab and its capital were seized by the Indo Scythian Kushans from China about AD 50 and went from there to Muziri on the Malabar coast via Socotra reaching Muziri in AD 51–52. (Farquhar, 1913: 20)

The historicity of the Apostle's life and ministry in India being based on strong traditions is also confirmed by Keay (1931) and Mundadan (1984). Moffett (1992) reveals that:

> [O]ne of the oldest and strongest traditions in Church history dates as far back as the year 200 AD when a Christian in Edessa, on the great bend of the Euphrates River between Roman Asia and Persia, wrote a lively account of how the apostle [Thomas] had been sent out from Jerusalem to India…he…preached fearlessly before kings and founded the Indian church. (Moffett, 1992: 25)

According to Moffett, tradition and historical records date Thomas' arrival to somewhere between AD 50–52, most likely to the southern part of India where he preached the gospel and established churches (Moffett, 1992: 34).

Christian Topography by Cosmas Indicopleustes, a Greek writer (c. 500) is another historical record stating that there were communities of Christians and priests in India before AD 550 (Cross, 2005; Neill, 1970).

The belief held by the Syrian Christians of Kerala is that Thomas landed in Cranganore in AD 52, he 'founded churches in seven places in Kerala, later proceeded to the east coast and indeed beyond India, and finally was martyred at Mylapore [within Madras] in 72' (McMahon, 1974: 503).

The early Christians were called *Syrian Christians* and some-times *St Thomas Christians* (or *Nasranis*), because of the Syrian liturgy (from Syria, Middle East) that was adopted in the church services (John, n.d.). Syriac is an ancient Semitic language, an early form of Aramaic, a language spoken in Palestine during the time of Jesus. The Syrian churches in India were led by bishops appointed 'by the patriarch of Antioch from the beginning of the third century till they were invaded by the Portuguese' (Newcomb, 1855: 732). Besides clergy from Syria, there are also records of visits by merchants; one of the most well-known merchants was Thomas Cana or Mar Thoma Cana (*The Catholic Encyclopedia*, 1912). Thomas Cana sought permission from the Rajah of Malabar, Perumal to build houses and a church and many of the early Christian followers who joined him obtained a higher class status equivalent to the Nayars, who were the middle-class of the day (*The Catholic Encyclopedia*, 1912).

Hambye (1952) calls attention to the unique way in which Syrian Christianity has survived the test of time: 'Being a minority in a closed milieu and not always well-trained and instructed, it is remarkable that [the Syrian Christians] kept the faith together with their social status' (Hambye, 1952: 386).

The historical and literary evidence together with strong trad-itions point to the fact that non-Western Christianity was present and flourishing in pre-colonial India, even before the first Western mis-sionaries came there in the latter part of the thirteenth century.

Thirteenth and fourteenth century

Historical records reveal that Marco Polo visited India in 1288 and Catholic priests like Monte Corvino stopped over in India around 1308 en route to China. Corvino baptised 100 converts in Madras and recommended mission work to be launched in India (Hedlund, 1982; McMahon, 1974). The first known claim to papal authority of the Syrian Christians in India was when a French Dominican (Catholic) priest, Jourdain de Severe, brought a letter from the Pope in 1330 urging the Syrian believers to submit to Rome (McMahon, 1974).

Fifteenth century to the seventeenth century

In 1503, there were upwards of 100 Christian churches (Syrian) on the Malabar coast (Newcomb, 1855). Around AD 1503, Patriarch Elija ordained and sent a Metropolitan to India. Therefore, this suggests there must have been 6 to 12 Indian bishops with large communities of Indian believers (Stewart, 1961).

The coming of the Portuguese after the discovery of the Cape Sea route to India in 1498 affected the Church in several ways. First, the early Indian Church, originally under the Church of the East, was fragmented when one of its sections eventually came under Rome's jurisdiction (McMahon, 1974). Second, the Pope gave the Portuguese King the 'right of church patronage' and a bishop was appointed in Goa (McMahon, 1974: 504). However, the Church in Goa was not known for its high view of morals and ethics and when the Jesuit missionary Francis Xavier arrived in 1542, his approach and character was a 'breath of fresh air' in the community that earned him the respect of the local people (McMahon, 1974). Xavier's ideals of humility and resignation to the world's material possessions struck a responsive chord with the early Christians and many people from the lower castes and the outcastes were converted as Christianity became known as 'the religion of the poor' (Kooliman, 1983: 102).

The Portuguese came to India in the ships of Vasco da Gama with mixed motives: commercial interests and missionary intentions sanctioned by the Pope. The Church exercised 'strong pressure though not actual coercion on the inhabitants to become Christians' (Cross, 2005: 832). However, their efforts to 'Christianise' were localised and not much was done to convert people outside the immediate region.

The Portuguese compelled the churches nearest to the coast to come under papal authority and in 1599 all Syriac and Chaldaic books and records of the Syrian Christians were burnt (Newcomb, 1855). The Christians who came under Rome were called Syro-Roman Christians but the Christians in the interior, after a false show of union, fled to the mountains around 1633 to escape Roman rule, continuing to call themselves Syrian Christians (Newcomb, 1855).

The entry of the Portuguese to India and their missionary efforts signalled a significant change in Indian Christianity. Indian Christianity was challenged decisively by this new and foreign version of the Christian gospel. The new challenge was to be followed by successive flows of various foreign missionaries, '...As time went on Dutch, English and French settlers moved into India bringing their own versions of Christianity with them' (McGrath, 2001: 124).

An Italian Jesuit, Robert de Nobili, worked in the south of India and was the first-known missionary to adopt an 'indigenous' approach to reaching the Hindus. Nobili, in an effort to nullify the foreign aspect of the gospel, disassociated himself from the church and dressed and lived like a Brahmin guru. He encouraged several high-caste Christian converts to stay within the parameters of Hindu culture (Cross, 2005). De Nobili 'probably baptised 600 high caste converts and made a powerful contribution to Dravidian (Tamil) Literature' (Hedlund, 1982: 77).

Nobili's controversial methods (by the Portuguese ecclesiastical standards) have been described as 'radical cultural adaptations' where he 'appropriated "harmless" customs and ceremonies' of Hinduism into the Christian faith (Hedlund, 2004: 2). In short Nobili 'Tamilized the gospel' (Hedlund, 2004: 2). Nobili's success in mission work points to the effectiveness of the indigenisation of Christian ministry and the importance of incorporating aspects of Hindu culture into the Christian faith.

From 1600, both the English and the Dutch came to India and had a Christian presence there although their work was mainly in the area of pastoral care through Chaplains who were appointed to take care of their own people. Nevertheless some of the locals benefited as 'there are records of missionary work and a few conversions' (Cross, 2005: 832).

Protestant missions in the eighteenth century

Protestant missionary work began in a significant way in 1706 when the King of Denmark sent a German Lutheran missionary, Bartholomew Ziegenbalg, together with Henry Plutschau to Tranquebar (now Trangambadi). Although the Lutheran missionaries had very few precedents to emulate, their mission was marked by lasting significance: 'Tranquebar was a tiny territory but the mission had reverberations to the ends of the earth. A new missionary conscience was stirred as news was spread in the annual letters distributed' (McMahon, 1974: 505).

Ziegenbalg's missionary strategy, of which many principles have been followed by succeeding missionaries even till today, may be summed up in the following ways:

1. Placing the Bible (translated in various languages) in the hands of people as soon as possible;
2. Establishing schools as an 'adjunct of the Church' to teach literacy skills so that people can read the Word;
3. Training missionaries to understand the culture, beliefs and social structure of the Indian people (Neill, 1970: 56).

Muthiah (2006), of *The Hindu*, in a special tribute commemorating Ziegenbalg's work, attributed India's current thriving printing industry to Ziegenbalg's painstaking and longsighted vision:

> Ziegenbalg...was convinced that the Mission's work could prove successful only if the press produced books and other literature in Tamil. He therefore sent back drawings of the Tamil alphabet to Halle with the request to create Tamil typefaces there. The Tamil type arrived in Madras on June 29 1713. (Muthiah, 2006: para 16)

In 1714, Ziegenbalg translated and printed the Tamil New Testament, the first in an Indian language (McMahon, 1974). The publication was an exercise in international, ecumenical cooperation: 'The Tamil New Testament, translated by a German [Lutheran], in the service of the Danish crown, was printed on an English printing press...[owned by the Anglican Society for Promoting Christian Knowledge—SPCK]' (Neill, 1970: 56).

Ziegenbalg also wrote a book, *The Genealogy of the Malabarian Gods*, which perhaps could be the first record of the ethnography and cultural anthropological analysis of the Indian people. Unfortunately, his mission did not recognise or encourage this work saying that Ziegenbalg 'was to proclaim the eternal gospel in India' and 'not to propagate heathen superstition' (Neill, 1970: 57).

After 13 years of extraordinary service, Ziegenbalg died in 1719 leaving some 350 Indian Christians. These were the first fruits of the Lutheran church in India and future Lutheran missionaries such as Frederic Schwartz (1726–1798) and John Zachary Kier Ander (1714–1798) continued to build on this work (Cross, 2005; Hedlund, 1982). The example of Ziegenbalg shows again the significance of the indigenous principle—how the Christian tradition of Halle was adapted to the formation of the Indian church in Tamil Nadu. Ziegenbalg's understanding of the culture of the Tamils, through his painstaking scholarship in language learning and ethnography, resulted in much success.

When William Carey and Dr John Thomas of the English Baptist Missionary Society arrived in Calcutta in 1793, the East India Company was committed to the separation of trade and faith, a decade-long policy of non-missionary involvement. Carey, therefore, secured links with the Danish crown to establish mission work in Serempore, which later became known as the 'birthplace of the modern missionary movement' (Cross, 2005: 832).

Carey left his mark not only in the Indian Church but also in the nation: '…he compiled and published grammars in Sanskrit, Bengali, Marathi, Telegu…and dictionaries in Bengali and Marathi…Carey and his colleagues founded twenty-six churches and one hundred [and] twenty-six schools' (Kane, 1971: 111).

As professor of Indian languages, Carey helped to train young men for the Indian Civil Service, worked towards the abolition of *suttee*—the Hindu practice of burning widows alive on the funeral pyres of their husbands and even translated Hindu texts (such as *Ramayana* and the *Mahabharata*) into English (Kane, 1971). The translation of Hindu texts was considered controversial and drew criticism from the mission-sending churches but it reflected Carey's conviction that converts to Christianity need not discard that which was good in their cultural and religious traditions.

Nobili, Zeigenbalg and Carey shared two common characteristics in their mission approach. First, they recognised the importance of indigenising the Christian gospel, embarking on a strategy of adaptation. Second, their early efforts in translation, printing and literary work, can be considered as the precursors of televangelism today.

It is also important to observe that just as the early missionary efforts in education and literacy brought Hindu converts into the church, these efforts also brought Westernisation to a wider group and opened the door for Hindus to be 'Westernised' without becoming converts. Berreman (1979) states that lower castes emulate the behaviour of higher castes by adopting the behaviour and attributes of the ones they admire. Dumont (1980) refers to Hindus adopting Western ways as a form of *sanskritisation*—a term used by sociologist Srinivas (1952) to refer to the upward pull of low caste Hindus towards the social status of the higher castes.

English, under British rule, became the official language and Hindus learned English to get into the administrative positions in the civil service. Does this phenomenon have a bearing on televangelism today? Are Hindus watching and responding to Charismatic televangelism for social benefits as well? This issue will be explored in the research in the forthcoming chapters.

Missions in the nineteenth century to the present

Until the 1750s the British East India Company (EIC) was a typical trading company with interests in the major trading outposts of Calcutta, Bombay and Madras. However, shortly after 1750, political events changed the EIC's purely trading concerns. England's political relations with France were at an all time low at that time over the issue of 'hegemony on the Indian subcontinent' with both France and England employing Indian soldiers (known as *sepoys*) to fight for each other (Kitchen, 1996: 6–9; Sanne, 2003: 4). Hence, the supremacy of British interests in India became increasingly dependent on the British army.

The eighteenth century saw changes in the British concept of empire. The theory of Social Darwinism was prevalent and ideas such as the 'survival of the fittest' were transferred to human beings (L. James, 1994). But how could England with its long tradition of liberalism and personal liberty take an authoritarian stance in India? England decided to resolve the dilemma by introducing the concept of 'benevolent despotism' arguing that law and order was the pressing need in India (L. James, 1994: 219). As a result, one of the new goals of the administration was the introduction of Western enlightened ideas and ideals to India. It was at this time that the Indians feared most that Christianity might be imposed as a foreign religion (L. James, 1994).

In 1813, the East India Company revised and relaxed its charter on missionary involvement which later resulted in the establishment of the bishopric of Calcutta. Other notable developments as a result of the policy change included the launch of Bishop's College in Calcutta to train Anglican ordinands in India (Cross, 2005). Also at this time the mission arm of the Anglican Church, Church Missionary Society (CMS) began to send missionaries and clergy from England 'in increasing numbers' (Cross, 2005).

In 1833, restrictions on non-British missions were lifted (McMahon, 1974: 505). This accelerated mission work from all quarters and by the end of the century, American clergy and missionaries outnumbered the British and were joined by groups of missionaries from Switzerland, Germany, Sweden and Norway (Cross, 2005). With the influx of

Protestant missions from various lands, the rules of 'comity' were observed. These were rules for regulating boundaries for various denominational groups which helped to prevent friction over territorial and ministry matters (McMahon, 1974).

Christian missions placed a great emphasis on education as a bridge to evangelism and this was seen especially in the efforts of Scottish missionary Alexander Duff. Also at this time, the focus of missions seemed to move from reaching the high caste intellectuals to reaching the marginalised and tribal peoples, including the 'untouchables'. The Lutherans met with success in reaching the Oraon tribes in Nagpur, the Welsh Calvinists worked among the Kharsis and the Baptists reached many of the tribes in the north east.

Although missions by and large were foreign-based, a few notable nationals (converts of the foreign missions) took up the challenge of evangelising their own people. Some of these leaders included Pandita Ramabai, Narayan Tilak and Sadhu Sundar Singh (McMahon, 1974: 505). A native village ministry formed through the ordination process was in place with the first priestly ordination of Indians in 1850 and from then on the number of ordained Indians very soon outnumbered the missionaries (Cross, 2005). The training of Indian candidates for ministry in the Anglican Church began in 1833 and the United Theological College was founded in Bangalore in 1910, in line with this purpose. The proliferation of Christian missions and the increasing dialogue between Christianity and Hinduism 'undoubtedly influenced the nineteenth century reform movements within Hinduism' (McMahon, 1974: 505). Some of these movements that came into being included the Brahmo Samaj (1829), the Arya Samaj (1875) and the Ramakrishna Mission (1938).

One of the most remarkable reformers of Hinduism, Raja Rammohun Roy (born in 1774) was greatly influenced by Christianity. Roy was impressed by the ethics of Christianity but not necessarily with the overall doctrinal teaching of the gospel: He gradually became convinced that Hinduism must remain Hinduism, but that an injection of Christian principles could bring that renewal and purification of the ancestral faith which was his dearest object (Neill, 1970: 117).

Singh (1992), a journalist writing from a secular perspective assesses Christian missions as follows:

> More far-reaching than the number of converts it made was the influence of Protestantism on Hinduism. Protestants took active part in suppression of suttee, ending female infanticide, and suppressing the thugs;

alleviating the condition of Hindu widows and temple prostitutes...It was the Christian missionaries...[who] roused the admiration of Hindu reformers like Ram Mohun Roy, whose Brahmo Samaj...drew a great deal of inspiration from Christianity. (Singh, 1992: 76)

Significant inter-denominational missionary efforts within the Protestant movement were seen during this time. The community-operative efforts between the Madras Christian College and the 1910 World Missionary Conference (Edinburgh) gave birth to the ecumenical movement which 'led directly in India to the formation of the National Missionary Council (1914), which evolved into the National Christian Council' (McMahon, 1974: 505).

A long series of ecumenical conferences led to the formation of the South India United Church in 1908, a union of churches from the Presbyterian and Congregational denominations. This union ultimately gave birth, in 1947, to the present Church of South India (CSI); with a similar regional union which occurred in 1970, resulting in the Church of North India (CNI) (Cross, 2005; McMahon, 1974).

The London Missionary Society (LMS), a British inter-denominational mission started work in 1795 and had as its objective the spread of the gospel rather than the starting of denominational churches (Kane, 1971). The Church Missionary Society (CMS) another British mission affiliated with the Anglican denomination started its mission in India in the early 1800s.

American missions came *en masse* after the inauguration of the American Board of Commissioners for Foreign Missions in 1810 with the arrival of Dr John Scudder. Later on, the American Presbyterians established their presence in 1834, while the American Baptists came in 1836, followed by the American Lutherans in 1840s and the American Methodists in 1856 (Kane, 1971).

In 1887, the Christian and Missionary Alliance (CMA) established work and in 1899 the Mennonite Brethren entered India (Kane, 1971).

Besides church-based missions, specialised missionary organisations also established work in India with the following ministries: Bible translation—The Bible Society in 1811 and Wycliffe Bible Translators in 1966 and Radio—The Far East Broadcasting Company (FEBC) in 1969.

Even though it was impossible to buy time on commercial radio stations for Christian broadcast, FEBC produced Indian programmes in Manila, Philippines and beamed its programmes to India via powerful transmitters (Kane, 1971).

FEBC's work in India was followed by other radio ministries, such as, Trans World Radio (TWR) foreshadowing the present state of Christian televangelism through satellite and cable television. Christian Broadcasting Network Inc (CBN), headquartered in Virginia USA, is the televangelistic ministry started by Pat Robertson in 1970. According to their website (accessed 2008) the strategy of CBN is:

> ...the development of daily or weekly television programmes on terrestrial TV stations in selected countries. These programmes are often produced in country by local production staff. The objective is that each programme will be culturally sensitive and relevant to the ethnic audience as it is viewed in their own language. These broadcasts are complemented by effective follow-up via mail and telephone counseling. To further sustain regular programming, CBN WorldReach has developed production facilities in Cambodia, Costa Rica, England, Hong Kong, India, Indonesia, Nigeria, Middle East, Philippines, South Africa, Thailand, and Ukraine. CBN WorldReach also produces TV specials that are placed on national TV in strategic countries. These programmes are broadcast in 'prime time' and are designed to generate a mass response from the audience. Follow up is handled by a CBN WorldReach office or a partner church or organization. (CBN, 2008: paras 3–4)

> On November 1997 the *700 Club* a magazine-type TV programme produced by CBN premiered in India. Today CBN has its own local office and broadcast facility in India (CBN International, India) and its programmes are telecast on several Indian cable channels—Zee Music, Zee English, Zee Cinema, God TV, Jaya TV and Maa TV. (CBN India, n.d.: para 5)

CBN International, India, telecasts programmes in the following languages to cater for India's multi-linguistic population—English, Hindi, Tamil and Telegu.

Other transnational Christian agencies started telecasting their regular programmes through the 24-hour networks such as *Trinity Broadcasting Network* (*TBN*) (1973), *God TV* (2002) and *DayStar* (2005).

A local association of groups and individuals under the name of the Evangelical Fellowship of India (EFI) was formed in 1951 'owing to the inspiration of the National Association of Evangelicals in the USA' but leadership is now completely Indian (McMahon, 1974: 506). The EFI operates as an overarching body of evangelical missions and churches and has given birth to subsidiary groups such as the Indian Missions Association (IMA) (Rajendran, 2000).

Televangelism versus Foreign Mission

The main characteristics of missionary work seen in the survey of missions in India, compared with global televangelism ministries (which will be discussed in Chapter 5), indicate key differences (see Table 3.1):

1. Televangelism has a global focus while foreign mission historically established itself in specific locations (mostly in south India).
2. Televangelism is generally not as church-based or indigenous as is foreign mission.
3. Televangelism crosses all church denominational barriers while foreign mission established its own denominational structure.

These characteristics will be referred to in this chapter and discussed further in the book.

Table 3.1: **Comparison between televangelism (global) and foreign mission**

Foreign mission	Televangelism (global)
1. Localised ministries	Globalised ministries
2. Church-based	Generally not church-based
3. Aimed for contextual, indigenous approach while retaining foreign character	Generally not contextual or indigenous
4. Used literature and print media primarily	Uses digital media and satellite technology primarily
5. Denominational-centred	Not bound by denomination—crosses all segments of the church

Source: Author.

Indigenous Christianity

Historically, one of the greatest challenges facing Christianity in India is the issue of indigenisation (localisation) or adapting the faith to the Indian culture:

Despite Hindu willingness to adopt Christianity into their religious system, Christians have encountered difficulties in the absolutism of Christian theology. The doctrine of Christianity that was most problematic was the proclamation of Christianity as the only true religion, viewing it as a manifestation of the hated colonialism. The assimilation of Christianity into the Indian populous required an incorporation of Christianity within the regimes of Indian culture. (Park, 2000: para 6)

That is why Indian Christian leaders and Indian churches have embarked on a policy of indigenisation with less and less dependence on foreign missions (Borgard, 1997).

One of the most successful Indian Christian leaders (a convert from Hinduism) was V. S. Azariah, the first Indian bishop of the Anglican Church from 1912 onwards (until his death in 1945). Azariah had great skills in:

> ...dealing with language, culture and different denominations, [to embody] the conflicts and challenges of both Christian evangelism and British rule. He also bridged the differences between ordinary Indians and British elite...Azariah is known to be someone [who] would not compromise the doctrines of Christianity and Indian culture. (Park, 2000: para 10)

Stanley Jones, an American missionary serving in India with the Wesleyan movement, was a champion of indigenous Christianity: 'His style was Indianising and de-westerning in the cultural, social, economic and political spheres—all treated evangelically. This style was based on deep and extensive immersion in many aspects of contemporary Indian culture' (Taylor, 1992: 195).

Farquhar (1913) is another missionary who promoted indigenisation. Farquhar's approach to indigenisation was based on 'the fulfilment view' (the dominant Protestant view up till the twentieth century), suggesting that Christ is foreshadowed in the Hindu scriptures and is therefore the fulfilment of Hinduism's quest for spiritual reality (Richard, 2001).

India has given birth to a number of notable Indian Christian leaders who have propagated and practiced an indigenous faith. Some of these leaders, according to Daniel (1984: 40) and Hedlund (1982: 80) are:

1. Sadhu Sundar Singh (Sadhu, a Sikh convert) is reputed to have championed the cause of the indigenisation of the Christian

faith with the famous comment that India needs the 'water of life in an Indian cup' not a European cup (Sadhu, quoted in Mathew, n.d.: paras 1, 7);

2. Nehemiah Goreh;
3. Brahmobandhav Upadhyaya;
4. P. Chenchiah;
5. Bahkt Singh;
6. M. M. Thomas.

Indigenous churches, although few in number, are growing rapidly. Some of these include:

1. The Bakht Singh movement (Jehovah Shammah), a non-Pentecostal, evangelical group with a Plymouth Brethren style of church government and worship, has a constituency of 80,000 members.
2. The Ceylon Pentecostal Mission, an Indian body, has a membership of more than 30,000 people.
3. The Indian Pentecostal Church of God (IPC) has approximately 350,000 members.
4. The Indian *ashrams*—these are worship centres that keep Christian worship along indigenous patterns, thus encouraging Hindus not to give up their culture when becoming Christians; some of the well-known *ashrams* include: *Sat Tal Ashram*, *Christian Ashram* and Andhra Evangelical Lutheran Church at Guntur (Hedlund, 1982; Johnstone and Mandryk, 2001).

Hedlund (1999: 13–27), a scholar in Indian indigenous movements, categorises Indian Christians of indigenous origins as follows: members of tribal communities, converted Dalits and converts from earlier indigenous churches such as St Thomas Christians.

Hedlund (2001) also lists several indigenous Christian groups (not in the mainstream of Christianity) within India, such as:

1. Fellowship of the Followers of Jesus (whose founder Chetti confessed faith in Christ but declined baptism);
2. Group of secret Christians in Sivakasi, south India (mainly women) who have been known to profess Christ deeply and continue to privately partake of the sacraments for as long as two to three generations;

3. 'Churchless Christians' in Madras (a description of scores of unchurched Christians in India by Herbert E. Hoefer): A survey conducted through the Research Department of the Garukul Lutheran Theological College concluded that Madras has a large number of secret believers, persons not yet baptized, at least equal to the size of the Christian community in the city (Hedlund, 2001);

4. Hindu-Christian movement started by K. Suhba Rao in Andhra Pradesh in 1924.

The aforementioned groups are successful because the Hindu converts remain in their communities upon conversion to Christianity. Evangelical scholar Richard (2001) asserts that indigenous Christianity in India will only thrive when the primary issue of community identity is adequately dealt with. That is, the situations when Hindu converts (to Christianity) are not transferred from their community to a new, alien and Western-type community: The disciple of Christ needs to own his own people's community designation and adamantly affirm that he remains with them sociologically and will follow Christ among them and will not join the 'Christian community' (Richard, 2001: 5–9).

New assertions based on Indigenisation

An indigenous church is one that has grown out of the local context or rooted sufficiently in the culture of its origin (Hedlund, 2004). Sanneh (1991) refers to the principle of 'translatability' in relation to indigenisation, pointing out that 'translatability is the source of the success of Christianity across cultures' (Sanneh, 1991: 51). Walls (1996) refers to the biblical account of the incarnation as the basis of all translation:

> Christian faith rests on a divine act of translation—the Word became flesh...Any confidence we have in translatability of the Bible rests on that prior act of translation ...

> But language is specific to a people or an area. No one speaks generalized 'language'; it is necessary to speak a particular language. Similarly, when Divinity was translated into humanity, he did not become generalized humanity. He became a person in a particular locality and in a particular ethnic group. The translation of God into humanity...was effected under culture-specific conditions. (Walls, 1996: 26–27)

Early missionaries like Nobili, Carey and Ziegenbalg understood the social customs and culture of the Indians and adapted aspects of these into Indian Christianity. In spite of this:

...the churches arising from the missionary presence was inevitably European in form—German Lutheran in Tranquebar, English Baptist in Bengal, Church of England in Tirunelvelli and Calcutta, American Presbyterian in Punjab, Welsh Presbyterian in Shillong, American Methodist in Bareilly, American Baptist in North East India and Andhra, Salvation Army, Quaker, Alliance—each according to the image of its missionary creator. (Hedlund, 2004: 2)

The earliest example of indigenous Christianity is found in the St Thomas Christians of Malabar, south India. The coming of the Portuguese seems to have been the time when the Indian (Malayalam) traditions of the Church were severely threatened leaving only the Syriac ecclesiastical traditions (Aythal and Thatamanil, 2002).

Since indigenisation is one of the common denominators of the success of the Christian church in India in terms of results (Hindu conversions) and community acceptance, I have devised 'the historical roots missiology assertion'.

The 'historical roots missiology assertion' is based upon the fact that the form of Christianity that was prevalent in India before colonisation was 'Hindu in culture, Christian in faith and Syrian in doctrine' (Frykenberg, 2004: 116).

Walls (1996) speaks of indigenisation as something that is part and parcel of Christian theology and missions:

The impossibility of separating an individual from his social relationships and thus from his society leads to one unvarying feature in Christian history: the desire to 'indigenize', to live as a Christian and yet as a member of one's society, to make the Church...a place to feel at home. (Walls, 1996: 7)

Early indigenous Christianity was at peace with society and 'at home' with Hindu culture. However, foreign missionary encounters have introduced multiple versions of Christianity in India. This coupled with the *Hindutva* allegations of an international conspiracy to Christianise India has led many Christian leaders and churches to promote a return to the indigenous model (Borgard, 1997).

Current missiological scholarship is proposing a Dharmic Christian faith, one that does not cancel out the Hindu elements and does not extract converts out of their Hindu culture into Christian enclaves (Bharati, 2004). This is highly reminiscent of Christianity in the pre-colonial era; therefore I name this the historical roots missiology assertion referring to the fact that this is a return to the first era of Christianity as diagrammatically explained in Figure 3.1.

Even today, the militant Hindu RSS group considers the historic Mar Thoma Church (Syrian) 'one of the few real Indian churches' (Ananthakrishnan, 2008: 14). This *Hindutva* attitude reveals something of the complex nature of the politics of identity in contemporary India. It also points to what may be the heart of the *Hindutva* concern namely cultural identification. The fact that the Mar Thoma Church has been identified as an indigenous church by the *Hindutva* is significant and it suggests that Christian churches in India need to seriously revisit the whole issue of indigenisation.

I have also devised a scale to measure various levels of indigenisation which I term 'indigenous ministry scale'. This is necessary, as some ministries are more indigenous than others and therefore an accurate tool is needed for measuring indigenisation (see Figure 3.2). These levels are explained below:

1. Level One—The base of this scale pertains to local staff.
2. Level Two moves on to the area of local directors and administration.
3. Level Three is achieved if the ministry has adopted local leadership, philosophy and style of governance.
4. Levels Four to Seven pertain to the practice of ministry and consist of four subdivisions: culture-specific evangelism,

Figure 3.1: Historical roots assertion

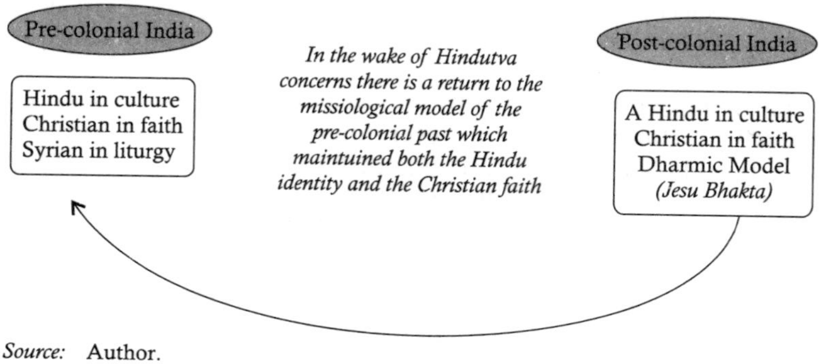

Pre-colonial India

Hindu in culture
Christian in faith
Syrian in liturgy

In the wake of Hindutva concerns there is a return to the missiological model of the pre-colonial past which maintuined both the Hindu identity and the Christian faith

Post-colonial India

A Hindu in culture
Christian in faith
Dharmic Model
(Jesu Bhakta)

Source: Author.

Figure 3.2:   Indigenous scale

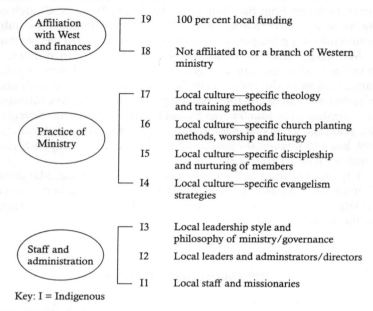

Key: I = Indigenous

Source: Author.

culture-specific discipleship of members, culture-specific church planting and worship and culture-specific theology, training and church structure models.

5. Level Eight is achieved if the ministry is independent of any links with Western agencies.

6. Level Nine is achieved if the ministry raises 100 per cent of its funding locally.

As many Christian agencies working in India (including CBN India) claim to be 'indigenous', this index helps these agencies to gauge more adequately the extent of their indigeneity and enable them to aspire for deeper levels of success in their ministries.

Prior to independence in 1947 there were only three to four indigenous mission organisations. Since independence there are now more than 125 indigenous Indian mission groups (Rajendran, 2000). Some of the more prominent Indian missions agencies are the Indian Evangelical Mission (IEM) and the Friends Missionary Prayer Band (FMPB). The IEM, founded in 1965, is an interdenominational mission fully staffed and financed by Indians with a local board of directors drawn from the Methodist, Anglicans, Baptists, Church of Nazarene and CNI (Kane, 1971: 125). The IEM upholds the indigenous ministry principle in missions especially in light of the fact that '...Missionary visas for Western missionaries were turned down... [therefore] Indigenous mission agencies sprung up' (IEM website, n.d.: para 2). Most of the Indian churches have their own outreach and mission committees and the church with the most extensive missions programmes is the Mar Thoma Syrian Church of Malabar: 'Seventy-five years ago it had one mission station. As a result of ...a revival...it now has 145 mission stations in all parts of India ...it supports 250 workers' (Kane, 1971: 125).

The mission wing of the Church organises the annual Maramon Convention in Maramon (Kerala, south India), which is known to be the largest Christian meeting in Asia with 200,000 Christians gathering for the week-long convention.

Pentecostalism in India

The first known Pentecostal-like revival meetings in India took place in Madras (now Chennai) and Travancore (south India) between 1860–1861 (Burgess, 2001: 87). The practice of the gifts of the Spirit such as prophecy, speaking in tongues and teachings on restoration of the offices of apostle and prophet were undertaken by the leader John Aroolappen, a local Anglican catechist who was trained by pietistic missionaries (Burgess, 2001).

However, it was only when American Pentecostal missionary Alfred Garr arrived in India in 1907, fresh from the experiences of the Azuza Street revival in USA, that Indian Pentecostalism embraced the direct connection between 'baptism of the Spirit' and tongue-speaking as a consequence (McGee, 1999).

Alfred Garr and his wife Lilian travelled all over India teaching the Pentecostal gospel, with a revival breaking out in Calcutta (now Kolkota) in 1907. However south India was more responsive to the Garrs' teachings on Pentecostalism than north India (Burgess, 2001).

Between 1900–1910, Charismatic manifestations, such as *glossolalia* (speaking in tongues) took place in the state of Maharashtra at the Mukti Mission run by Brahmin convert Pandita Ramabai (McGee and Burgess, 2003; Wacker, 2001).

Other Pentecostal missionaries like George Berg and Robert Cook preached the Azusa-type gospel in 1908 whereas the first Assemblies of God (AOG) missionary, Mary Chapman, came to Madras in 1915 and laid the foundation for the Pentecostal movement there (Burgess, 2001: 90). Robert Cook went on to found Mt Zion Bible Institute in 1929 in Chengannur.

In 1930, Indian pastor K. E. Abraham broke away from Robert Cook and later started the Indian Pentecostal Church of God (IPC). The breakaway seemed to be a positive step (from IPC's perspective) as IPC became more indigenous in structure and style and today is one of the largest Pentecostal church denominations in India (Burgess, 2001). The IPC, governed by a general council, has established churches extensively in most of the Indian states as well as churches for 'diaspora' Indians in USA, Canada and the Middle East (IPC website, n.d.).

The IPC denomination split in 1953 leading to the creation of the Sharon Fellowship Church (McGee and Burgess, 2003).

In 1936, Cook joined the Church of God denomination in Cleveland, Tennessee (USA) and brought all '63 churches, 2,537 members and 43 pastors', under the umbrella of the Church of God (*History of Church of God Missions*, 1943: 135–141).

The Assemblies of God and the Pentecostal Holiness Churches (both American denominations) have exercised considerable influence in India. However, classical Pentecostalism on the whole is diminishing in its impact, giving way to neo-Pentecostal or Charismatic churches, organised as independent churches:

> While classical Pentecostalism has significantly impacted specific regions throughout the subcontinent...it is the slowest growing wave in the Indian Renewal Movement...India has responded less favourably to Christian culture imposed from abroad than to those forms that have a more indigenous base. (Burgess, 2001: 94)

In 1972, a Parsi by the name of Minoo, introduced the Charismatic teaching to the Catholic Church and was responsible for launching the Charismatic movement among the Catholic churches. Starting from Mumbai the movement spread all over India's Catholic community (Burgess, 2001: 94).

Hedlund (2004) agrees that much of the renewal movement in India today is taking place largely (although not exclusively) among the Pentecostal and Charismatic sections of Indian Christianity

(Hedlund, 2004). Some of these groups of Pentecostal and non-Pentecostal traditions are: *The Inheritors, Maharashra Village Ministries, Emmanuel Ministries* (Calcutta), *the Pentecostal Mission, GEMS House of Prayer,* Chennai and the *Pentecostal Mission.* The exclusivist Pentecostal Mission (originally the *Ceylon Pentecostal Mission*) is an indigenous movement that originated in south India (P. Martin, 1998).

One of the largest mega-churches in India is *New Life Assembly of God* (Pentecostal) in Chennai which has 25,000 worshippers. Patterned after the Korean Church model of Rev. Paul Yonggi Cho, where participatory lay leadership is the feature of the church administration, New Life has 2,000 care cells that meet in homes (Hedlund, 2004). The Charismatic (or neo-Pentecostal) churches are leading the renewal movement in India today: 'There are Christian bodies with Pentecostal-like experiences and a common emphasis on the Holy Spirit that have no traditional Pentecostal...denominational connections' (Burgess, 2001: 95).

Many of the newer churches are independent in structure and seem to move away from denominational links or affiliations. Some of these Charismatic churches, according to Burgess (2001: 95), include:

1. *New Apostolic Church* (founded in 1969 with 1.5 million adherents);
2. *Manna Full Gospel* (founded in 1968 with 30, 000 adherents);
3. *New Life Fellowship* (NLF) (founded in Mumbai by Pastor S. Joseph, a former member of the *Plymouth Brethren Assemblies,* informally with 60 people meeting in 1968 in Byculla then officially in July 1980). The NLF was one of the main sponsoring churches for American televangelist Benny Hinn when he had a large crusade in Mumbai in February 2004 (Eapen, 2006).

Another noteworthy Charismatic group is *Gospel For Asia* (GFA), a mission organisation started by a high-profile south Indian, K. P. Yohannan in Texas, USA, with churches established all over India under the name of 'Believers Church'. The church has an estimated following of 100,000 members (Johnstone and Mandryk, 2001: 311). GFA also uses radio and television extensively and their daily TV programme is available on several secular and Christian networks. The parent organisation in the USA, GFA (USA), is the third largest financial donor to India (see Table 3.6).

People Groups, Caste and Class

With a population of more than one billion people, second only to China, India's 15 major languages and 700 dialects make it one of the most culturally diverse countries (Kane, 1971). Kane (1971: 104) identifies seven main physical types of people:

1. Dravidians—considered the oldest inhabitants are found in the south with such groups as the Tamils, Telegus and Kanarese;
2. Indo-Aryans—the ones who entered the nation around 1,500 BC through the Khyber Pass and drove the Dravidians south and are today located in Kashmir, Punjab and Rajasthan;
3. Aryo-Dravidians—the mixed group that is also known as the Hindustani people who make their home in the Ganges valley;
4. Scytho-Dravidians—a mixed group of Scythian invaders and the Dravidians found in Gujarat and western Mumbai area known as the Marathis;
5. Mongol—considered to originate from China and Tibet and located in the north eastern part of the nation near Assam;
6. Mongol-Dravidian—a mixture of the Mongol and Dravidian groups resulted in the birth of the Bengali people;
7. Aboriginal hill tribes—the peoples who predated the Dravidians, found in the north east with groups such as the Santals, Khonds, Bhils and Karens.

A survey of people groups reveals the existence of at least 4,635 distinct peoples, but adding to the complexity of India's population is the division of people into the various castes (Johnstone and Mandryk, 2001). The Indo-Aryan invasion led to the 'marginalisation of the original inhabitants and the subjugation of much of the Dravidian population and the emergence of multiple mixed race groups' (Johnstone and Mandryk, 2001: 309).

When the Aryans invaded India more than 3,500 years ago they introduced a new social order that divided the community on the basis of four castes (D'souza, 2004: 33–34). The *Manusmriti* book of Hindu legal code suggests that each caste descended from a specific part of the body of the Hindu god, Brahma. The four castes are: Brahmin,Kshayriya,Vaishya and Sudra.

It is believed that the three upper castes were taken from the head, arms/shoulder and belly/thigh of Brahma respectively. The Sudra caste were taken from Brahma's feet (D'souza, 2004).

Today the Indian government has recognised the following caste groupings:

1. Forward castes (around 15.4 per cent of the population) the Brahmin priestly caste constitutes nearly 34 million people, with other groups like the *Rajput Nayar* and *Kayastha* also in this category;
2. Backward castes—(around 56.6 per cent of the population) with groups like *Yadava*, *Kurmi* and *Ahir* in this category;
3. Scheduled castes—or Dalit (around 18.1 per cent of the population) are generally exploited and landless and were formerly known as outcastes, untouchables or *Harijan*. Dalits have very low literacy levels Dalit women for example have a literacy rate of only 11 per cent compared to other communities that enjoy a 20 per cent literacy level (Rajendran, 2000: 328). It is important to note that Dalit and tribal Christians form the majority of the total Christian population (see Table 3.2). As a result, of the years of oppression, a 'Dalit theology' is emerging in the Indian church. Ayrookuzhiel (n.d.) states that Dalit Christians are coming to terms with their past and expressing their awareness as 'members of an ancient primeval society disinherited and uprooted by the...*Brahmanical* civilization' (cited in Oommen, 2000: 22);
4. Tribal or *Adivasi* (around 9.5 per cent of the population) have the following groups in this category: Gond, Bhil, Santal and Koli (Johnstone and Mandryk, 2001: 309–310).

Although caste discrimination is outlawed by the constitution, it is still a part of the social fabric of Indian life 'serenely colouring

Table 3.2: Christians in India (Dalit and non-Dalit)

Dalit/Non-Dalit	*Number of people in millions*[*]
Dalit Christians	15
Non-Dalit Christians	10
Total Christians	25

Source: Material adapted from Johnstone and Mandryk (2001: 312).
Note: *Based on approximate figures.

and influencing everything and determining almost everything' (Samuel, 1977).

The fact that 70 per cent of Indian Christians are of Dalit and tribal origins and the remaining 30 per cent of Christians from middle to upper castes, is significant in the study of Indian Christianity for two reasons (see Table 3.2). First, the forms of present-day Indian Christianity and theology are the outcomes of the experiences of the minority middle and upper caste Christian converts who interpret their new faith in the light of Brahamanical and Sanskritic traditions. Dalit and tribal Christians are by and large strangers to Brahamanical and Sanskritic forms of Hinduism (Massey, n.d.). Second, as a consequence of this situation, there is a need for a more inclusive study of Indian Christianity, which takes into consideration Dalit Christianity and its particular problems and struggles of identity within India.

Whereas caste is based on one's birth into a social system with established rules and boundaries, class is defined in economic terms. Economist Ram-Prasad (2007) explains the concept of the 'middle class' in India and points out the basis for the use of this term:

...the term 'middle class' applies to those earning between $4,000 and $21,000 a year...in purchasing power parity terms. But this definition suits only 30 million...of the population...A recent study by CNN-IBN and the *Hindustan Times* suggested a 'simple consumer-based criterion' for membership of the middle class: ownership of a telephone, a two or four-wheel (motorised) vehicle, and a colour television. Under this definition, the middle class makes up nearly 20 per cent of the population— 200 million people. (Ram-Prasad, 2007: 5)

Gokran (2006) states that India's middle class primarily originates from the secured work positions of its citizens in the public sector although with market liberalisation, entrepreneurs and citizens from the private sector are also entering the middle class bracket. Economist Das (2004) argues that India's growing middle class reflects a shift in community thinking: 'Traditionally, the merchant was placed third in the four-caste hierarchy. But since the economic reforms, making money has become increasingly respectable...' (G. Das, 2004: 1, 5). Therefore India's middle class is currently somewhere between 10 to 20 per cent of the population and with the present economic policies, it is expected to grow.

Urbanisation

Although 70 per cent of the Indian population lives in rural areas, urban centres have grown rapidly in the last 50 years (Rajendran, 2000). There are six mega cities with more than eight million people in each and more than 300 cities with populations of 100,000 people each (Samuel, 1977).

Various factors have caused the rapid urbanisation of India. Samuel (1977) states some of these reasons: 'Poverty in depressed areas, slight opportunities for securing land for cultivation, reduced opportunities for employment, migrational tendencies of certain castes, and observing the prospects of friends and relatives already moved to the cities' (Samuel, 1977: 35).

Abraham (1992) discovered that, even though living conditions in cities for new migrants are generally deplorable, many villagers from rural centres move to cities in search of better work prospects and improved education (Abraham, 1992: 9).

Rajendran (2000), lists five factors that shape the urban worldview of city dwellers: the environment and associations education and enlightened minds industrialisation and technology materialism and consumerism primarily through the influence of the mass-media—radio, television, cinema, newspaper and internationalism and globalisation—'opening people's minds to new worlds' (Rajendran, 2000: 325–326).

Barnett (1953) suggests that urban dwellers are more open and responsive to new ideas: 'Migrants and dispossessed populations are characteristically receptive to new ideas, whether these ideas are developed by their own members or suggested by outsiders' (Barnett, 1953: 87).

McGavran (1970) suggests that rapid urbanisation means more people will be open to the message of Christianity and also the mass media:

> Uprooted and transplanted immigrants, starting life anew…flood into cities. These newcomers are away from the close control of family and intimates. Their priests and religious leaders do not know where they are…they should be receptive to the Gospel…They are also open to the mass media. (McGavran, 1970: 282)

Rajendran (2000) agrees with the view that urbanites are more open to the mass media but adds that people in urban centres can be swayed by the media 'for both good and bad' (Rajendran, 2000: 326).

Since my research for this book is conducted primarily in Mumbai (Maharashtra) and Hyderabad (Andhra Pradesh), a brief overview of these two urban centres is provided.

Mumbai

Mumbai (old name Bombay, meaning *Good Bay* in Portuguese), the capital of the state of Maharashtra, is India's commercial, economic, industrial and film entertainment hub. The city generates one-third of the nation's Gross Domestic Product (GDP). In the 1860s, it was described as 'the first city in India' and today: 'It's the home of India's stock exchange and the film-making industry (Bollywood)' (Johnstone and Mandryk, 2001: 328).

With a population of close to 18 million people, it also claims to be the most cosmopolitan city of India. 'Almost all Bombayites are either migrants or descendants of those moved into the city during the last 150 years' (Samuel, 1977: 27). Mumbai has the second highest Christian population (5 per cent) of the mega cities of India and is the hub for various Christian activities and agency offices (Johnstone and Mandryk, 2001). Although the city has transformed itself into a global centre for communications and trade, it is also home for many slum dwellers. Asia's largest slum, Dharavi with one million people on 170 hectares is located in Mumbai (Johnstone and Mandryk, 2001).

Hyderabad

Hyderabad, the capital of the state of Andhra Pradesh (AP), has a population of close to eight million people. Hyderabad is the nerve centre for Islam in south India, with nearly 40 per cent of its population being Muslims (Johnstone and Mandryk, 2001). However, the state of AP has also seen much growth in the Christian Church. There are more than 66,000 churches in the state and 150 Christian organisations based in Hyderabad (Johnstone and Mandryk, 2001).

Middleton (1977) asserts that AP is one of the states which has seen great and sustained 'people movements' to Christ: 'Two outcast communities, the Malas and the Madigas have been responding in ever increasing numbers over the past four decades' (Middleton, 1977: 357).

The Christian Broadcasting Network (CBN), an American Christian television network with ministries in 160 countries, has an Indian office and broadcast facility in Hyderabad where Christian televangelistic programmes are produced and broadcast to all of India.

Hyderabad is also home to 'Tollywood' the Telegu film industry and is competing with Bangalore to become the major hub for the information technology industry.

Church Growth Patterns and Structures

Patterns of Church growth

McGavran (1979), whose church growth strategies have greatly influenced the Indian church, observes: 'Sociological/anthropological considerations are exceedingly important if we are to comprehend the ability of congregations ...to flourish on new ground, reproduce themselves,...influence the nation' (McGavran, 1979: 2).

Two major patterns have been identified in church growth in India: one, in many parts of north India evangelisation, mainly through 'a one-by-one conversion pattern', has resulted in church growth; two, while in the south and north east India the main pattern of Church growth is through 'multi-individual' (group) conversion, that is, people movements from caste and tribe (Hedlund, 1982).

In many states of north India such as Maharashtra, Madhya Pradesh and Uttar Pradesh, early missionaries established mission compounds (with a school and a church) and undertook itinerant work. The itinerant missionary travelled from village to village near the mission compound with few conversions. Those who accepted the new faith were often expelled from their communities or persecuted, so they fled for refuge to the mission compound. In this way, the fledgling church grew through a one-by-one pattern of mainly displaced individuals (Hedlund, 1982: 65).

Stock and Stock (1975) explain how this pattern affected the Church in Punjab: 'Converts, cut off from their friends and relatives...soon lost their interest in trying to win others. The resulting Church became increasingly ingrown and self-centered' (Stock and Stock, 1975: 24).

As stated above, in the south of India the main pattern of Church growth has been through the 'people movement', that is 'multi-individual conversion' (Hedlund, 1982: 68). This is also true in the Punjab area in the north of India where, according to McGavran (1979), there were mass conversions among the Chuhras when 'a third of the caste became Christians, about a third Muslims and about a third Sikhs' (McGavran, 1979: 109). The motivation for these conversions was a dissatisfaction with the present status in society and an understanding that conversion would improve their status in society (Stock and Stock, 1975).

Church structures

As denominational groups entered India, churches were established according to the respective distinctiveness of churches and mission agencies. However, it would be helpful to analyse churches according to cultural and sociological factors as well. Samuel (1977) groups Indian churches according to four ways:

Syrian Churches

These churches are made up of 'Syrian Christians'—followers of the ministry of the Apostle Thomas who were later assisted and influenced by the arrival of Christians from Syria. The church has three ecclesiastical divisions: Roman Catholic (Syrian rite), Orthodox (Malankara) Syrian, and the Mar Thoma Syrian (Protestant). Syrian Christians of all three divisions are endogamous, that is they only marry within their group and are found in Kerala, all over India and even outside India (Samuel, 1977: 35).

Single ethnic Churches (one-caste Church)

Most of the large churches are the result of 'people movements' where groups of people from one caste convert to Christianity: According to Donald McGavran, 'when enough persons of one caste or tribe...in a short enough time and in a small enough area become...Christians a people movement is born...' (Samuel, 1977: 37). Some examples of people movements resulting in the establishment of single ethnic churches are found among the Nadars, Pulayas, Madigas (in Andhra), the Chamars (in northern India) and the Chuhras (in Punjab) (Samuel, 1977: 37).

'People movement' Churches (tribal converts)

Tribal people are strictly speaking not bound by caste and 'tribal structure is different from caste structure' (Samuel, 1977: 38). The tribals are aboriginals who were driven by the Hindus back into the forests. Most of the tribal people are animists, that is, they worship the spirits and the forces of nature. In Christian missions, people coming to Christianity in large numbers, is a phenomenon referred to as 'people movements'. These people movements took place primarily in Andhra Pradesh, Assam and Nagaland (Samuel, 1977).

Conglomerate Churches

McGavran (1955) refers to these churches as 'mission station approach' churches or 'gathered colony' churches. These churches are the result of the mission efforts of mission organisations with a 'mission station' approach where the mission, church and hospital or school are usually housed in the same compound. Converts are from diverse backgrounds (hence the name 'conglomerate') from the surrounding areas where the mission is located. Depending on the area and the ethnic mix, some conglomerate churches are fully conglomerate (with many ethnic groups) and some are partially conglomerate. The partially conglomerate churches would have the majority of converts from one ethnic group and a trickle of converts from another ethnic group (McGavran, 1955). In large cities, most of the churches are somewhere between partially conglomerate churches and fully conglomerate churches, therefore, the churches are composed of different ethnic groups (ranging from churches with two ethnic groups to churches with more than two ethnic groups).

However with urbanisation and migration in the last few decades, the four categories of churches previously mentioned, may not fit urban churches as neatly as it used to. Samuel (1977: 38–42) suggests three factors that influence church attendance, composition and structures in urban centres:

1. Denominational alignment—When migrants arrive in the cities they naturally look for churches that they attended back in the home villages or towns.
2. Linguistic alignment—Migrants coming to cities like Mumbai are sometimes forced to learn Marathi for work purposes. However, they continue to speak their own language among friends and family. Therefore these migrants would also look for churches that have services in their own languages.
3. Community alignment—The word 'caste' is avoided in Christian circles and in polite conversation. Nevertheless, caste still exists and the word has been replaced by 'community':

> As Christians from the 'single ethnic group' churches [of people movement] origin moved to Bombay...most of them were employed in factories, cotton mills...[as] labourers and unskilled workers...
>
> Now they were grouped in working class settlements with other people of similar employment and income...the results of such regroupings affected the churches structurally and sociologically. (Samuel, 1977: 42)

Certain missions and church groups would do outreach work among these communities on the basis of the language of the workers: Tamil, Telegu or Kannada and yet other missions or churches would simply continue with their own services in languages foreign to the workers (Cherian, 2006: interview). The fate of some of these groups, according to Samuel (1977), is changing and regrouping:

> Due to intense intermingling of Christians from different ethnic backgrounds, a new group of those who have 'forgotten' their ethnic background was also born among the second and later generations. Those who were elevated to the level of upper middle class...due to the educational processes...were also regrouping themselves along communal lines. (Samuel, 1977: 42)

In the main, there are three denominational groupings of churches—Catholic with nearly seven million followers: Orthodox (Malankara Syrian) with approximately 1.2 million followers and Protestant with approximately 16.8 million adherents (see Table 3.3) (Johnstone and Mandryk, 2001).

The Church of South India (CSI), with nearly four million members, is the result of the merger of various Protestant denominations: Anglican, Methodist, Congregational, Presbyterian and Reformed Churches in south India (Andhra Pradesh, Karanataka, Tamil Nadu

Table 3.3:   Christians in India (Catholic, Orthodox and Protestant)

Denomination	Number of people in millions*
Catholic	7
Orthodox	1.2
Protestant	16.8
TOTAL CHRISTIANS	25

Source: Adapted from Johnstone and Mandryk (2001: 310–311).
Note: *Based on approximate figures.

and Kerala states). The church is organised into dioceses under a bishop. The church explicitly recognises that: 'Episcopal, Presbyterian, and Congregational elements are all necessary for the Church's life. The Scriptures are the ultimate standard of faith and practice. The historic creeds...and the sacraments of baptism and the Lord's Supper are...binding' (Church of South India website, n.d.: para. 1).

The Church of North India (CNI) established in 1970 has a membership of approximately 1.5 million members. The Church is an amalgamation of the Anglican, Congregational, Presbyterian, Baptist, Methodist and Disciples of Christ denominations of the Protestant church and shares a similar church governance style as the CSI (Church of North India website, n.d.).

Hindu–Christian Tensions

Chowgule (n.d.) a leader of the *Hindutva* suggests that there are two fundamental differences between Hinduism and Christianity which have historically given rise to misunderstanding and a measure of tension:

1. For Hindus, religion is not a mere ritual, but a philosophy of life encompassing the entire gamut of culture. Christianity, unlike Hinduism, is based on a doctrinal book and a centralised hierarchy.
2. Hinduism is a pluralistic faith which believes 'that there are multiple paths to salvation and one chooses the path that one thinks is valid...' (Chowgule, n.d.).
3. Christianity believes in exclusivism 'that there is only one true religion and "Christ" is the only Son of God' (Chowgule, n.d.).

The pre-colonial era of Christianity was a period marked by the absence of tensions and animosities between Hindus and Christians as the early Syrian Christians were rather inward looking and there was very little evangelism as we know it today: 'The Syrian Christians, like the Jews of Cochin and Bene Israel of Bombay, survived and indeed flourished because they accepted the social system within which they found themselves and observed its norms' (Forrester, 1979: 100).

The *Sepoy* mutiny of 1857 was a clear indication of how the British army's lack of knowledge of the Hindu religion led to a period of insurgency and a worsening of Hindu–Christian relations. The mutiny was caused by false rumours that beef fat (Hindus do not eat beef as the cow is sacred) was used as grease for army rifles. When the *sepoys* refused to handle the rifles, they were punished which led to rebellion, insurrection and the murder of many Westerners before peace was restored (Vohra, 2001).

Webster (1992) and Mallampalli (2004) posit that between 1909 and 1935, British reforms divided India's people into a general electorate and a separate electorate for Christian, Muslim and Sikh minorities. Christian leaders like Bishop Azariah criticised this policy of alienating Christians from the national mainstream (Mallampalli, 2004; Webster, 1992).

Speaking at an Indian conference, sociologist, Gopal (1993), suggests that the whole issue of communalism was introduced during the period of colonialism: '[The British asserted that] India is not and can never be a nation...India is a collection of religious communities...so British interpretation plus the shortsightedness of our own leaders, not excluding the Mahatma [Gandhi], together resulted in this dreadful phenomenon of communalism' (Gopal, 1993, quoted in M. M. Thomas, 1996).

Mundadan (1984) emphasises the fact that the early Syrian Churches had interactions with the Hindus at many cultural and social levels. It was the Portuguese (Catholic) missionaries who taught communal exclusiveness and furthermore they identified 'conversion to Christianity as an extension, not only of western culture but also of western Christendom...the pattern of integration of church, community and politics of mediaeval Europe' (M. M. Thomas, 1996).

Tharamangalam (2004) contends that the current rhetoric of Hindu fundamentalism in India is a:

> ...search for a pan-Indian Hindu identity, and in the assertion of a pan-Indian 'Hindutva' (Hinduness) that is claimed to be the true heritage of Indians. This discourse inevitably involves the demarcation of the 'Hindu' from the 'other'—minorities defined as less Indian, if not foreign. (Tharamangalam, 2004: 232)

Frykenberg (2004), asserts that the militant Hindu nationalistic movement known as *Hindutva* is a reaction to the large-scale conversions of tribal and village Hindus to Christianity in the early 1790s

(Frykenberg, 2004). The *Hindutva* and its agencies such as the VHP (Vishva Hindu Parishad) and the Bajrang Dal, as branches of the RSS (Rashtriya Swayamsevak Sangh): '...have always reacted violently when whole families and villagers of low-caste people have forsaken "proper place" (of thraldom) and when, by becoming literate and educated, they have set in motion a social revolution' (Frykenberg, 2004: 113).

Michael (2003), disagrees that any significant mass movement of Christian conversion has taken place:

> ...the accusation against Christians as involved in mass conversion does not stand the scrutiny of the population trends ...The Christian population in India has been decreasing rather than increasing...The real reason for the violence...is not conversion but the Hindu fundamentalists' non-recognition of the pluralistic nature of Indian society. (Michael, 2003: 2)

Michael points out that 60 per cent of the Christians in India are Dalits (or untouchables) and this coupled with the alleged inducements to conversion given by Christian missionaries has led to five Indian states passing anti-conversion legislation: Orissa, Madhya Pradesh, Arunachal Pradesh, Tamil Nadu and Gujarat (Michael, 2003).

Sundar (2005) agrees with Frykenberg's assessment viewing conversion unlike the generally held 'adherent-centred view', rather he views conversion as a:

> ... political phenomenon, aimed at expanding numbers and keeping alternative religions out.... [Sundar, 2005: 1] [T]o place the RSS activities [re-conversions] in the context of conversion may itself be misdirected, given that its objective is not simply to convert adivasis, but to consolidate *Hindutva* as a political phenomenon. (Sundar, 2005: 3)

Chowgule, admits that the *Hindutva*-inspired re-conversion ceremonies convened to bring back the Hindus converted to other faiths was a reaction to the aggressive activities of Muslim and Christian missionaries:

> Until recently, Hinduism did not have a ceremony which would initiate a non-Hindu into Hinduism. It was invented in the 19th century by Swami Dayanand, as a reaction to the threat of the aggressive proselytising programmes of Islam and Christianity. (Chowgule, n.d.)

Besides re-conversion ceremonies, the *Hindutva* members also worked towards rewriting history textbooks excising 'inconvenient' and 'objectionable aspects' of Brahmanical history from many textbooks, including those authored by a well-known historian, Romila Thapar (*Frontline*, 2001: paras 1, 3).

The Niyogi Commission was established in 1954 in the state of Madhya Pradesh to enquire into complaints of the Christian use of force or monetary incentives to convert people to Christianity. The commission, in response to what they pictured as a world-wide conspiracy to 're-establish Western supremacy', recommended:...to ban all missions activity in labour recruitment, place controls on the entry of foreign missionaries and conversions and increase government involvement in the running of orphanages, schools, hospitals etc. (Sundar, 2005: 14).

Hindutva agencies, in a study by Raj (2001), have criticised the fact that Indian Christian organisations and churches are being assisted by foreign funds in the conspiracy to 'Christianise' India:

> Every Christian activity in India is dollar directed; every soul that embraces Christian faith is snared in by foreign money. The foreign-funded Christian institutions are conversion shops in camouflage. But for the overseas monetary crutches, Christianity in India will crumble down. (Raj, 2001: 37)

In 1976, the Indian government passed an act in Parliament known as the Foreign Contribution Regulation Act (FCRA). The main purpose behind the act was to regulate the acceptance and use of foreign funds:

> The need for...such regulatory law was felt in the late sixties when foreign agencies including CIA were suspected of having links with various...organisations....It was agreed that the Government would not allow foreigners or foreign money to dictate or influence with functioning of the Government, Political parties and other institutions of India. (FCRA website, n.d.)

All Christian organisations regarded as Non-Government Organisations (NGOs) are able to receive funds from overseas but they have to report all foreign receipts to the central government and use the funds received for social and education purposes only, and not for direct evangelism (Cherian, 2006: interview) (FCRA website).

The FCRA website (FCRA website) reveals some significant statistics as seen in Tables 3.3 to 3.7:

Table 3.4:   Increase in foreign donations

Year	1968/1969	2004/2005
Amount	INR 24 Crores*	INR 6,256 Crores*

Source: FCRA website.
Note: *1 Crore is equivalent approximately to US$250,000.

Table 3.5:   Top 3 donor countries (2004–2005)

1. USA	(INR 1,927 Crores)*
2. Germany	(INR 930 Crores)*
3. UK	(INR 765 Crores)*

Source: FCRA website.
Note: * 1 Crore is equivalent approximately to US$250,000.

Table 3.6:   Top overseas donor agencies (2004–2005)

1. Foundation Vincent E Ferrer (Spain)	(INR 184 Crores)*
2. World Vision International (USA)	(INR 124 Crores)*
3. Gospel for Asia (USA)	(INR 110 Crores)*

Source: FCRA website.
Note: * 1 Crore is equivalent approximately to US$250,000.

Table 3.7:   Cities and districts which receive highest foreign funds (2004–2005)

1. Chennai (Tamil Nadu)	(INR 560 Crores)*
2. Bangalore (Karnataka)	(INR 377 Crores)*
3. Mumbai (Maharashtra)	(INR 322 Crores)*

Source: FCRA website.
Note: * 1 Crore is equivalent approximately to US$250,000

1. Foreign donations are increasing year by year.
2. The top donor country is the USA.
3. Two of the three top donor agencies are Christian organisations from the USA.
4. Chennai, Bangalore (south India) and Mumbai (north-west) are the three city districts which receive the highest amount of funds.

The Indian government has restrictions on foreigners being involved in Christian missionary activity: 'Foreigners who wish to be involved in any form of Christian work must obtain missionary visas although these are not easily granted' (Cherian, 2006: interview).

Christians have come under increasing attacks in India and Mangalwadi, Martis, Desai, Verghese and Samuel (2000) have documented at least 63 such attacks from the middle of 1997 to the end of 1999 (Mangalwadi et al., 2000). The attack which drew widespread media attention occurred in 1999 when Australian missionary Staines and his two young sons were burnt alive in the state of Orissa (Mangalwadi et al., 2000). In December 2007, hundreds of Hindu radicals destroyed more than 700 Christian homes in India's eastern state of Orissa. The incident was reported by both the Christian and secular media and CBN described the violence as 'perhaps one of the worst attacks on Christians ever in India's history' (CBN, 2008: para 3; Human Rights Watch, 2007).

As outlined earlier in the chapter, the heart of contemporary Hindu–Christian tensions lies not merely in the rapid expansion of Christian mission, but the fact that this expansion is perceived to be aided and funded by Western sources with processes, projects, personnel and strategies that are alien to the Indian cultural context.

Factors that Help Hindus to Respond to the Church

The survey of missions and the critical issues facing the Indian church have a bearing on televangelism today. From the record of history and the understanding of the socio-cultural aspects of Indian Christianity there seem to be three common factors for success in winning Hindu converts and establishing the Christian community with relative peace (see Figure 3.3).

Figure 3.3: Why Hindus respond to the Church?

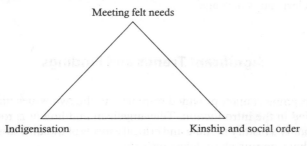

Source: Author.

The first factor, indigenisation, has already been touched upon in the earlier section. The church grows when it is rooted in the Hindu (Indian) culture. The second factor, which is related to indigenisation, concerns the social order and the kinship issues related to Indian culture. Stock and Stock (1975) have shown that the practice of extracting Hindu converts from their kinship ties and cultural networks, to be placed in Western-type churches, eventually led to weakened churches. In addition to this, the churches were seen to be destabilising the Indian community. Organised Christianity may win sporadic converts but in the process it has been accused of disintegrating the fabric of Hindu society. Hoefer (1991) challenges Indian Christians to maintain their Hindu cultural identity and take the gospel into their respective kinship circles. The indigenous models associated with the *Jesu Bhakta* (devotee of Jesus) movement and the *ashram*-type structures allow the new Christian converts to remain as part of the larger Hindu culture and the familial system. They do not encourage converts to break away. The third factor that stems from the study of Indian Christianity, as to why Hindus responded to the church, is the issue of the meeting of needs. Conversions took place generally, when Hindus, who were dissatisfied with their present status—socially, educationally or materially—saw conversion as a means to redress their situation.

How do these three factors affect televangelism today? What lessons can televangelism learn from Indian church history? The forthcoming chapters will address these questions:

1. Does televangelism practice the indigenous principle?
2. Does televangelism in any way threaten the kinship and social order of Hindu viewers and potential converts?
3. Are the felt-needs of Hindus being targeted as Charismatic televangelists promise prosperity and wealth as part of the Christian's heritage?

Significant Trends and Findings

The foregoing chapter provided responses to the two issues that were identified in the introduction: Televangelism and how it is rooted in Christianity's history in India and critical aspects of Indian Christianity which have an impact on televangelism.

With respect to the first issue, I gave an historical overview of Christian missions from the apostolic times to the present and also provided material pertaining to present-day church structures. With respect to the second issue, the following factors that affect televangelism were dealt with: indigenous Christianity, Pentecostalism, urbanisation, India's people groups, caste and class and Hindu–Christian tensions.

By dividing the church into three epochs—pre-colonial, colonial and post-colonial—and drawing out the salient features of each epoch, I was able to identify several significant trends. Pre-colonial Christianity, the time before the Western missionary influence, was a period marked by the influence of Syrian (Middle-Eastern) Christianity which appeared to be at ease with Indian culture. In pre-colonial times, Christianity seemed to be relatively thriving (although it was by and large an insular religion) and tensions between Hindus and Christians were not heard of.

Colonial Christianity opened the doors to the Portuguese (Catholic), Dutch, British and American Christian influences. The colonial era was marked by the military power of the British and the technological superiority of the different Western missionaries who used their skills in printing, translation and the establishment of schools in a far-reaching way which touched and transformed the lives of the rich and poor, high caste and low caste alike. The forms and structures of Christianity, unlike the pre-colonial era, were now clearly Western. As a result of this, tensions ensued both within the indigenous Indian Church and outside the church, especially amongst the Hindus, many of whom had real fears that Christianity would be established as a national religion. The British administration and the missionary force as a whole did not really understand the social context of Hinduism and the important role the caste system played in the life of the faith. Missionaries like Nobili, Zeigenbalg, Carey and Farquhar were discerning, even in the early days about the benefits and indeed the critical need of indigenising the church. The greater influence of Christianity in the colonial era seemed to be in its ability to reform Hinduism rather than to bring Hindu converts to Christianity, although this did take place in two distinct patterns: individual conversions in the north and mass 'people movements' in the south and north east of India. The result of colonial missions was the establishment of churches which today come under the banner of CSI, CNI, Baptist, Lutheran and other Western denominational Church structures. The Indian experience of Pentecostalism clearly points to the fact that

Pentecostalism was inspired and guided by the Azusa Street revival in California (USA).

In today's post-colonial Christian era the churches established during the colonial period (although completely Indian in leadership) are not growing and impacting on the community as the newer post-colonial and 'post-denominational' Churches and movements are doing. Some of these new movements include the independent Churches (evangelical and neo-Pentecostal) the Indian Pentecostal Church (IPC) and the so-called 'Churchless movement'. Christians from the Dalit (scheduled caste) and tribal communities outnumber Christians from the rest of the castes.

The underlying factor in the three epochs of Indian Christianity seems to be that churches grow in an indigenous context rather than in a Western mould. The three factors that encouraged conversions of Hindus to the Christian faith are: Christianity being rooted in indigenous Hindu culture, respect for the Hindu social system and meeting the felt-needs of converts.

The patterns of church growth differ in the north, the south and the north east of India pointing to the importance of ethnic background, language and caste in the overall aspect of Christian missions and conversion. Hindu–Christian tensions, which have been present since colonial days, seem to increase when Christianity is not adequately indigenised into the Indian context. With the rise of the *Hindutva* sentiments in contemporary India, tensions between Hindus and Christians are likely to be on the increase. Western forms of evangelism, Western funds and structures seem to exacerbate the growing tensions between Hindu nationalistic groups and the Christian church.

The colonial era was marked by the first wave of communications technology, namely the Church's production and use of literature through the print media, foreshadowing the current wave of technology in the post-colonial era—electronic and digital communications, namely the Church's use of satellite and cable television.

The use of satellite and cable television and the spread of Charismatic televangelism in the post-colonial era of the Indian church will be explored in the next chapter.

Chapter 4

The Construction of Charismatic Televangelism in India[1]

T he West's military victory during the Gulf war in 1990 also brought about another major victory in the global world of satellite technology in India. This was the period when CNN, Star, ATN, BBC and other media giants were busy establishing a beachhead in the Indian airwaves. It was the reporting of the news of the war that first opened the doors of satellite television to India. CNN delivered hourly updates and insights of the US-led allied war against Iraq's Saddam Hussein. Prior to this, Indian viewers were only exposed to *Doordarshan*, the national government-owned television station, whose daily fare consisted of largely educational and non-commercial programmes with a heavy focus on socio-economic and cultural development.

So great was the impact of the satellite TV invasion after 1990, that even *Doordarshan* responded by launching a new entertainment-oriented and commercially-driven channel in its network.

In this chapter, I explore the place that Charismatic television has in India. I do this by firstly, taking a snapshot of the birth of satellite television and its growth. Secondly, I give the reader an overview of televangelism and the various formats with which it operates. I identify and differentiate the three types of televangelism: local, global and glocal. Since the overview of televangelism in India is largely drawn from my content analysis of programmes, I also explain the use of content analysis in this chapter, prior to the discussion on televangelism.

Satellite Technology: Origin and Growth

The Indian government's open policy on satellite and cable TV since the mid-1990s has created a miniature media explosion. The Gulf war in 1991 and broadcasting giant CNN's inaugural telecasts of the war to South Asia was the seed planted in the Indian satellite and cable market that has now blossomed to a full-fledged industry. From only 410,000 cable and satellite households in 1992, in 2007 there were 72 million cable TV houses and 100 million TV homes (Government of India White Paper, 2003; Satellite and Cable TV Industry, 2007). In 2008, the number of cable and satellite households increased to 82 million (Contractor, 2009: interview).

According to the Government of India white paper on the cable and satellite industry (1 March 2008) there are eight major satellites surrounding India. From these eight satellites more than 250 channels are available in India:

> Major broadcasters are Doordashan, Zee (12 channels), Star (7 channels), Sony (4 channels), Sun TV, ESPN–Star Sports (2 channels). Other prominent broadcasters are ETC, ETV, Turner and Discovery. The broadcasters' present business model has a mix of revenues from advertisements and incremental revenues from subscription. (Government of India, 2003)

Ongoing liberalisation of India's uplinking policies (as of July 2000) now means that Indian private companies and news agencies (their foreign equity holding should not exceed 49 per cent) can set up uplinking teleports for other broadcasters and uplink any television channel from India.[2]

Business Line, a financial daily from the Hindu group of publications. states that, based on a Television Audience Measurement (TAM) report,

> [R]eligious channels had a viewership share of 0.63 per cent of the total television pie in 2004, and it rose to 0.72 per cent in 2005, which, when rounded off, is almost equal to the viewership from the music channels (1 per cent). (Shashidar, 2006: paras 2–3)

The article also mentioned that 'religious channels like *Aastha* [Hindu] and *God TV* [Christian] had an all-India viewership share of 28 per cent in 2005' (Shashidar, 2006: paras 2–3). Given India's ▪

population of more than 1.2 billion people, this may not seem significant. However, the number of cable homes is rising every year and the costs are getting more and more affordable at approximately Rs 300 (US$5) per month for nearly 150 channels. Therefore, community leaders are predicting more and more Indians will be able to access cable TV in the ensuing years (SCL; HL, 2006). Figure 4.1 shows the future growth trends of the Indian Cable and Satellite industry.

Satellites and televangelism

The Indian cable industry is highly fragmented, with 20,000 cable headends (master facilities for receiving television signals for processing and distribution over cable systems) and with 40, 000 cable operators. Some major Multi-Satellite Operators (MSOs) include *Siti Cable*, *Hathway*, *SCU* and *RPG*, all of which operate in the major metropolitan cities. These operators work 'on a similar model of franchising cable TV feed to cable operators who in turn provide last mile connectivity to the subscribers' (Government of India, 2003). Among the cities, Mumbai has the largest cable market and New Delhi is second.

Figure 4.1:   Future cable and satellite trends

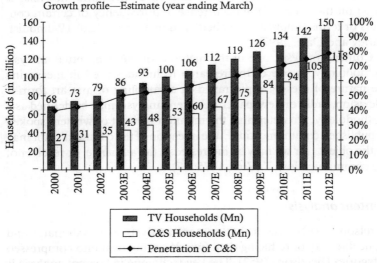

Growth profile—Estimate (year ending March)

Source: White paper on Indian Cable and Satellite Industry from an article in *Satellite and Cable TV Magazine*, 2007 (used with permission).

The following states have the highest penetration of cable TV: Maharashtra, Andhra Pradesh, Punjab and Gujarat (Government of India, 2003).

The Multi-Satellite Operators (MSOs) have been the subject of criticism due to several complaints of corruption and underhand dealings (KI, 2006). The Indian government is the gatekeeper of the airwaves only in so far as their national channel, *Doordarshan* is transmitted according to government specifications. Cable operators have the freedom to decide on the rest of the programmes and these decisions vary from operator to operator in the different regions (KI, 2006). A key informant in Madhya Pradesh (which currently has a Hindu state government) said that because of strong Hindu leanings in the state, cable operators have stopped the availability of the God TV Channel (KI, 2005).

Overview of Methodology

To understand the nature of televangelism in India, I used conceptual analysis as my main methodology. Conceptual analysis (a quantitative methodology), also known as thematic analysis, is based on the study of the occurrence and frequency of certain concepts or terms (implicit or explicit) within a text or texts (Palmquist, Carley and Dale, 1997).

Content analysis, one of the methods of the conceptual analysis methodology, is one of the research techniques used in measuring the nature of messages portrayed in a sampling of any art form—television, radio or newspaper: 'Content analysis may be defined as a methodology...to determine the manifest content of written, spoken or published communication...the intention of the communicator may be the object...or we may be interested in the audience, or receiver of the communication...' (Zito, 1975: 27).

Content analysis

Berelson (1952) asserts that content analysis is a systematic and replicable way of reducing data (words or theories) into compressed categories (Berelson, 1952). The key technique in content analysis is breaking down the many words and/or images in a certain text into fewer and representative categories based on acceptable coding systems (Lewis-Beck, 1990).

Three types of religious television programmes were singled out for content analysis—Charismatic television on the *Miraclenet* and *God TV* channels; Hindu television on the *Aastha* and *Sanskar* channels and Episode Three of Christian Broadcasting Network's (CBN) *Solutions* programme. I watched 12 hours of the Charismatic network *Miraclenet* (6 am till 12 noon and 6 pm till midnight) and spent a further 12 hours watching the second Charismatic network *God TV* (same time slots). Another content analysis was undertaken for the Hindu channels: *Aastha* and *Sanskar*, with the researcher watching six hours of Hindu television (6 am till 12 noon on *Aastha*) and a further four hours on *Sanskar* (6 am till 10 am). Both these telecasts were viewed in Mumbai (on Thursday) and Hyderabad (on Saturday). Therefore the total time spent on viewing television programmes in both Mumbai and Hyderabad amounted to 48 hours (for Charismatic televangelism) and 20 hours (for Hindu televangelism).

I avoided some of the common problems encountered in conducting content analysis, by following a series of systematic steps which I adapted from Krippendorff (1980):

1. **Selection of categories**

   I chose to analyse certain words and phrases for existence as well as frequency. In Charismatic televangelism, words such as 'prosperity', 'health', 'anointing' were selected as categories. Synonyms for these words were also coded into the respective categories. Likewise, phrases such as 'slaying in the Spirit' and those associated with rituals and prayers, were used as categories for analysis.

   Categories were also used to distinguish three types of televangelism: local, global and 'glocal'. Whereas, there were many programmes that came under the first two categories, only one programme matched the third category 'glocal'—*Solutions* produced by CBN India.

2. **Viewing of programmes/texts**

   Initially the programmes were viewed without any categories or codes so that I could get an overview of the nature and character of the various types of programmes. Once the categories were confirmed, viewing took place individually and each researcher manually recorded the concept and word occurrences. On an average, a research assistant and I viewed each programme.

3. **Irrelevant material**
   Materials that did not fit the categories were kept until the
   end of the ethnographic research. Occasionally, I referred to
   these materials and re-examined my coding system. Once the
   participant observation sessions were over, these materials were
   eliminated (Weber, 1990).
4. **Problems encountered**
   The main problem I encountered was in viewing Hindu televangelism as most of the programmes were in the Hindi language (which I do not understand). Therefore I had to rely on
   my research assistants to select the categories in the coding
   system. To overcome the problem, I also enlisted the help of
   one of the key informants who had vast knowledge of Hindu
   televangelism, to cross-check the coding system.

The Nature of Televangelism in India

There are currently four 24-hour Christian networks—*Miraclenet,
God TV* (both of which are owned by Charismatic Christians) and
a Catholic network *EWTN*. Another Charismatic 24-hour network,
DayStar, was launched in early 2006 after the initial field research
was completed. The religious fervour and flavour in India is further
evidenced by the existence of a 24-hour Islamic TV channel (*Q Channel*)
originating from Pakistan and a 24-hour Hindu TV channel, *Aastha.*
There are five other Hindu TV channels; however, they did not operate
on a 24-hour basis at the time of the research. This openness to religious television is remarkable in the light of the latest census figures
depicting the population by religion: Hindus 80.5 per cent, Muslims
13.4 per cent, Christians 2.3 per cent, Sikhs 1.9 per cent, Buddhists 0.8
per cent, Jains 0.4 per cent and others 0.6 per cent (Roy and Katoti,
2004: 34). Based on the number of 24-hour religious channels,
Christians do seem to be a growing force in the religious television
scene in India. In the balance, it must be pointed out that in keeping
with my definition of Hinduism as a way of life, many elements of
Hindu myths, folklore and practices are routinely featured in many
commercial programmes on television such as TV movies, talk shows
and advertisements.

There are four outlets for Christian televangelism in India (Thomas,
2007: 23–31):

1. *Doordarshan* (the national public broadcaster). The series on the *Life of Christ* was featured in *Doordarshan*. However, the space in this broadcaster is highly contested for programmes that adhere to government policies and, ostensibly, benefit the larger community. Hindu cultural and religious programmes are mainly featured in *Doordarshan*;
2. Transnational satellite channels like *God TV*, *Miraclenet* and *DayStar*, which are available on cable TV;
3. Indigenous Christian cable channels like *Blessing TV*, *Angel TV* and *Jeevan TV*;
4. Secular cable channels like *Zee*, *Star* and *Maa*.

The following results are based on a content analysis of the two 24-hour Christian channels *Miraclenet* and *God TV* in Mumbai, India (see Table 4.1).

About 85 per cent of Christian television originates from Western countries such as USA, Great Britain and Australia.

Locally-produced Indian televangelistic programmes amount to 10 per cent of the total programmes (see Table 4.1).

Ninety per cent of Indian programmes are also of the Charismatic Christian persuasion. Some well-known Indian Charismatic televangelists include: Brother Dinakaran, K. P. Yohanan and Sam Chelladurai. Brother Dinakaran follows the methods and style of the American Televangelist Oral Roberts from Oklahoma. Both TV programmes by Dinakaran and Roberts are hosted by a father and son team and have a strong emphasis on encouraging listeners to send in personal prayer requests. Both ministries have built huge 'prayer towers' at their respective headquarters where prayer requests from viewers are prayed for on a 24-hour basis (SCL, 2006).

An interesting phenomenon noted in the content analysis, is the availability of televangelistic programmes originating from Asia, namely Singapore and Indonesia. While Western countries are currently dominating the Christian media flows into India, a few Asian countries

Table 4.1:   Televangelism—origins

Origin	Percentage
1. Western countries	85
2. Indian (local productions)	10
3. Asian and other countries	5

Source: Author.

are also moving into global media evangelism ministries. Charismatic televangelist, Kong Hee, of City Harvest Church (Singapore), represents the new pattern of Christian media flows from Asia. Hee's broadcasts are taped for telecast to Asia from his Sunday services and the worship segment resembles the American and Australian (Hillsong) model of entertainment-oriented, rock-style singing. Hee is decidedly charismatic in his preaching content and approach. *You Can be a Millionaire* was one of the titles of his sermons which was telecast on India's *God TV* (God TV, 2006).

The content analysis also revealed that 90 per cent of all Charismatic programmes are based on the genre of 'straight preaching' (see Table 4.2). In other words, the programmes are basically the weekly church services broadcast to the masses with some editing. The remaining 10 per cent of programmes have the following formats: teaching, drama and magazine, that is, two to three segments such as interviews, short reports and news. Christian Broadcasting Network (CBN), an American-based Charismatic media agency, is the forerunner in the development of what I term 'indigenous or localised televangelism' in India. This new approach to Christian television will be addressed in Chapters 6 and 7.

Approximately 90 per cent of all Christian television is based on or contains strong elements of the Charismatic Christian persuasion. Messages on financial prosperity, 'wealth transfer', healing, success and miracles seem to predominate (see Table 4.3).

Hundred per cent of Charismatic programmes touch on prosperity theology, healing, miracles and 'slaying in the Spirit', which are teachings generally associated with the Charismatic doctrine.

Table 4.2:   Televangelism—programme typology overview

Type of programme	Percentage
1. Straight preaching (church services)	90
2. Teaching, drama, magazine	10

Source: Author.

Table 4.3:   Locally-produced televangelism

Theological background	Percentage
Charismatic	90
Non-Charismatic	10

Source: Author.

A common word used in Charismatic programmes (see Table 4.4) is 'anointed' or 'anointing' (which usually refers to a person or object set apart for a divine task and imbued with God's special power). Both American televangelist, Oral Roberts and his Indian counterpart, Brother Dinakaran, give the impression that because of the 'anointing' on them, prayer requests sent in by viewers would be answered favourably by God. Other words commonly used by televangelists include: 'miracle', 'prosperity', 'riches', 'healing' 'success', 'faith', 'blessing', 'favour' and 'sacrificial giving'.

Seventy-five per cent of all programmes are produced in the English language (see Table 4.5).

Almost all programmes have a 'multi modal' flavour, because products (CD's, DVD's, books, anointed handkerchiefs and religious jewellery) are promoted for sale and viewers are encouraged to download messages and other information, or to purchase products from the respective websites like *God TV*'s Godshop (www.godshop. com). Benny Hinn's worldwide crusades are accessible on the internet as webcasts. Eight out of 10 televangelistic programmes have a local telephone number for prayer and product purchase and some have a 24-hour prayer line.

About five to 15 minutes of air time per half-hour programme are spent raising funds and asking for donations for specific projects. These

Table 4.4:   Televangelism (Indian and Western): Key words

Words	Number of counts #
1. 'Anointing', 'anointed' or 'anoint'	95
2. 'Miracle' or 'miracles'	80
3. 'Prosperity' and 'riches'	65
4. 'Health', 'healing' and 'heal'	60
5. 'Success'	20

Source: Author.
Note   # The number refers to a combined counting of words based on viewing six hours of *Miraclenet* on one day and six hours of *God TV* another day in the city of Mumbai.

Table 4.5:   Televangelism—languages

What language	Percentage
English	75
Indian languages	25

Source: Author.

programmes operate on a semi-commercial basis, they are dependent on viewer funding and product sales to keep them on air. Most of the funding appeals are direct and some are embarrassing to local Indian Christians who are generally conservative on such issues (SCL, 2006).

Global, local and 'glocal'

As outlined above, three types of Charismatic televangelism programmes are identified: global, local and 'glocal'. Global Charismatic programmes refer to programmes that originate from overseas from transnational Christian broadcasters like *God TV*, *Miraclenet* and *DayStar* and are shown primarily on transnational, but also on local Christian and secular channels. Local Charismatic programmes are produced by local preachers for local (national or regional) consumption and can be shown on transnational channels (like *God TV*); on local Christian channels (such as *Jeevan TV* or *Angel TV*) or on secular channels like *Zee* and *Star*.

'Glocal' refers to hybrid productions of Charismatic programmes using Western and Indian resources such as CBN's *Solutions* programme which will be studied later in Chapters 6 and 7. These programmes are shown on secular channels or local Christian channels.

Table 4.6 shows the differences between global and local televangelism programmes according to six different aspects of comparison:

1. Language

Most global televangelism programmes are produced in English, while some are translated or dubbed into local Indian languages; whereas most local televangelism programmes are produced in the Indian languages.

2. Goal

The goal of the global programmes is to establish a worldwide ministry and donor base; whereas the local televangelism programmes have as their goal, the incorporation of people into their local churches.

Table 4.6:   Differences between global and local televangelism programmes

Aspects of comparison	Global	Local
1. Language	English (some translated or dubbed into local languages)	Hindi and Indian languages, some in English
2. Focus	The regions beyond with the goal of establishing a worldwide donor and ministry base	Immediate context—the goal to get people to attend local church
3. Discourse style	Literacy based	Orality based
4. Delivery/preaching style	Preacher's space is not fixed	Preacher's space is generally fixed
	Preacher is performer	Preacher is generally faithful and subservient to text
5. Media style	Preacher uses media skillfully (with a wide range of shots and close-ups)	Preacher's use of media is very basic
6. Politics	Preacher uses the politics of representation	Generally no political issues
7. Fundraising	At least 15 minutes per half hour	5–10 minutes per half hour

Source: Author.

3. Discourse style

Reddy (2006) refers to the discourse style of global televangelists as 'literacy based'. This refers to the 'unilinear time concept, a structured system that is characteristic of Western thought…' (Reddy, 2006: interview). In contrast to this, the local televangelists use a discourse style that is cyclical—where there is an ongoing shifting of time frames from past, present and future (Reddy, 2006). The cyclical style is more in keeping with Indian culture. The ethos of Hindu folk narrative lies in 'voracy' or orality (Reddy, 2006)—a term that depicts the sound produced through utterance. As sound travels in cycles, Hindu folk narrative functions in a cyclical nature. Reddy explains: 'Voracy depends on two organising principles: *scruti* (recitation) and *smriti* (memory). Therefore Hindu oral culture oscillates between the past and present in a cyclical fashion' (Reddy, 2006).

Hindu televangelism and local Christian televangelism by and large follow the orality approach whereas global Christian televangelism which follows the 'literacy' (based on writing and words as linguistic signs) functions in a linear nature (as opposed to the cyclical nature).

4. Delivery/preaching style

In local televangelism the preacher's space is fixed and so the tendency is for the preacher to stay in one place; whereas in global televangelism, space is not fixed and the preacher moves across the platform freely. In local televangelism, the preacher by and large remains faithful and is subservient to the text (Bible); whereas, in global televangelism the preacher uses his own experiences and anecdotes ('mental text'), his performance skills, as well as the written text. The portrayal of the preacher as a performer and an entertainer is a radical concept in Indian Christianity according to a senior Christian leader (SCL, 2006).

5. Media style

In global televangelism the preacher uses the media skilfully as a wide range of camera shots and close-ups are used to communicate to the audience the total message of the preacher, especially the miracles and signs being performed.

In analysing the Pentecostal televangelist, Asa Alonzo Allen, Pullum (1999) states:

> Like many other faith healers…to Allen seeing is believing. When he told his audience about the skepticism of the hotel clerk in Los Angeles, he turned to the camera and reminded his viewers that what they saw was actually what happened: 'the camera picks them [miracles] up just as they happen. Actually it's a part of the service'. Then turning his back to the audience and addressing the guest ministers…on stage, he reminded them, 'You preachers…know what we televise here in these healing lines…it has not happened before'. (Pullum, 1999: 79–80)

6. Politics

In global televangelism, political issues like the war in Iraq and references to political leaders are routinely raised as part of the programme. In local televangelism (except in a few local Charismatic televangelism programmes), political issues are not raised.

7. Fundraising

In global televangelism, at least 15 minutes is taken up per half hour in fundraising and the sale of products; whereas in local televangelism, only five to 10 minutes per half hour is allocated for fundraising. Benny Hinn's half-hour programme, *This is Your Day*, is a good example of a global programme aired on *God TV* in Mumbai. It was analysed in terms of the time allocated for various segments of the programme (see Table 4.7). This programme, like most of the other televangelistic programmes, is recorded during Hinn's crusades around the world and edited for television broadcast. The table shows that greater importance was given to the miracles of healing and fundraising than the preaching. During the eight-minute healing segment, at least 15 people were 'slain in the spirit' while a few others testified how they were healed at previous crusades. References were made by Hinn, during the preaching, to political dignitaries like the Prime Minister of Fiji. Hinn has local politicians seated on stage in almost every crusade, which was not well received in the Indian context by the press and other media agencies. *The Star of Mysore* went so far as to quote a well-known Indian dignitary who saw a link between Sonia Gandhi and the Hinn movement, when told that six Chief Ministers of the Congress-ruled states were in attendance at Hinn's various crusades. Sonia Gandhi, the current leader of the ruling Congress Party, is the Italian-born wife of the late Prime Minister, Rajiv Gandhi (Star of Mysore, 2005).

During the eight-minute fundraising segment Hinn seeks funds for two aspects of the ministry: funding to keep the programme on air as well as for special projects such as upcoming crusades, new TV equipment, a private jet for his 'mercy ministries' and humanitarian needs. Hence, television is used not only for outreach in the fields but also to keep the home base in USA informed. However, the 'home' communication and the 'field' communication are fused as one through global television. The Indian audience views both the 'home' and 'field' aspects of the communication. Therefore, confusion and misunderstandings can easily take place as Indians (Christians and Hindus) may not be able to appreciate the cultural issues at play in the fusion of 'home' and 'field' communications. For example, a senior

Table 4.7:   Programme analysis of Benny Hinn on _God TV_

Time	Segments	Features	Key statements
40 seconds	Introduction		'...featuring Benny Hinn's Miracle Crusade'
4 minutes	Choir	All Fijians from Fiji Crusade singing traditional hymns	
7 minutes	Hinn's preaching	Excerpts of his preaching on Jesus the Healer. Makes reference to the Fijian Prime Minister who is seated on stage.	'Jesus came to heal'
8 minutes	Miracles on stage (interviews and 'slaying in the Spirit')	A woman deaf for 30 years can now hear and a man from New Zealand testified how he was healed from a previous Crusade	
8 minutes	Appeal for funds	It costs on an average US$1.5 million per crusade	'If you send US$1,500 your name will be on the Tree of Remembrance at our Florida headquarters'
40 seconds	Closing		'Send us your email address so you can receive our monthly E-newsletter'

TOTAL: 28 mins 20 secs.

Source: Benny Hinn's *This is Your Day* on *God TV* (Mumbai) on 9 March 2006 at 7.30 pm.

Christian leader described Benny Hinn's pleas on television for funding to purchase a Learjet for his ministry as 'simply outrageous and even obscene in the Indian context ...' (SCL, 2006).

The *700 Club* hosted by Pat Robertson of Christian Broadcasting Network (CBN) is another example of global Charismatic televangelism. Based on a talk-show format, this programme is taped before a live audience in Virginia Beach (USA) and is seen in India on *God TV*. It is interesting that the *700 Club* is hosted on Indian television by the United Kingdom branch of CBN rather than CBN India. CBN India seems to have moved away from its association with its parent company, CBN International in USA because of adverse reactions from many Hindus and Muslims over comments made over the years by Pat Robertson, the founder and director of CBN International (KI, 2006).

In one of the programmes, aired on India's *God TV*, Robertson closes his eyes and says, 'The Lord told me someone in our audience is suffering from terrible pains on the right side of the hip...' (*God TV*, 2006). Viewers then call the toll-free number for prayers and counselling. Reddy (2006) refers to this as an example of Robertson establishing himself as one who has a 'special standing with God...it reveals that the preacher's basis of authority in communication is not only the written text but also his anointed standing before God...or a kind of "spiritual text"' (Reddy, 2006: interview). This explains why words like 'anointing' and 'anointed' appear so often in global televangelism programmes.

Edwards (2003: 1–5) in a content analysis of the *700 Club* found the following results about the frames presented in the programme:

1. Miracles are happening for people in developing countries because of the televangelistic and missionary intervention.
2. Giving to the needy will bring material prosperity to the giver.
3. Christianity is good, Islam is evil and Christians are being persecuted by Muslims.
4. America needs to pray for the victory of Israel over the Palestinians.
5. It is the responsibility of Christians (Americans) to help people in developing countries.

John Hagee's television programme on *God TV* reveals his often quoted biblical-political stand on Israel, interspersed with his preaching on prophecy '...that Israel may be giving too much land to the

Palestinians' (Berkowitz, 2006: para 2). The content analysis of one of the programmes showed Hagee's involvement in calling 400 Christian American leaders for a 'summit on Israel' resulting in the launch of a new pro-Israeli lobbying group called *Christians United for Israel* (CUFI) (Berkowitz, 2006: para 3; *God TV*, 2006). This is a good example of the fact that global televangelists do not only preach the gospel, but also articulate strong political views. While these views are acceptable in the USA, they may be confusing, inappropriate and out of place in India according to senior Christian leaders (SCL, 2006).

Televangelism was introduced into India when satellite television made its entry into India during the 1990 Gulf war. Content analysis, employed to analyse televangelism, revealed that the majority of the programmes are from the West, in the English language and of the Charismatic persuasion. These are mainly 'global' programmes as distinguished from local and 'glocal' programmes. Global programmes have a different discourse style and many seem to accentuate a strong political message.

Therefore, global Charismatic televangelism, with programmes produced by Americans like Benny Hinn, Pat Robertson and John Hagee are finding their place on Indian television. The influences these programmes have in India on both the Christian and Hindu communities will be discussed in the forthcoming chapters.

Notes

1. Since this chapter draws on primary research, the ideas and opinions of the respondents (many of whom wish to remain anonymous) are identified in the text in the following ways: MLP—middle-level pastor/s; SCL—Senior Christian leader/s; KI—Key Informant/s; HL—Hindu leader/s and ML—Muslim leader/s.
2. The term 'uplink', used in satellite communications, refers to the establishment of a communications link from a ground station to an orbiting satellite. The term is contrasted with another term 'downlink', which is the establishment of a link from an orbiting satellite to one or more ground stations.

Chapter 5

Hindu Televangelism: The Economics of Orthopraxy

In 1912, the film *The Life of Christ* premiered in Bombay. Dhundiraj Govind Phalke watched this movie and was seized by an urge to produce movies that depicted Hindu mythologies. He left for England to study cinematography and upon his return, on 3 May 1913, he released the Hindu mythological film *Raja Harishchandra*, India's first full-length, indigenous, silent film. This was to be followed by many Hindu mythologicals on film produced by Phalke, which later earned him the title: The father of Indian cinematography (George, 1989).

This is yet another instance of the interesting interplay between Christianity and Hinduism. In Chapter 1, I made the assertion that Hinduism influenced the Charismatic movement. In this chapter, I explore this ongoing interplay and point the reader to the influence of Charismatic televangelism on Hindu televangelism.

While using the broad description 'Hindu televangelism', it must be pointed out that the concepts of Christian evangelism and Hindu evangelism are not identical as they represent different epistemologies. As already discussed in Chapter 1, because of the orthopractic nature of Hinduism, the promotion of the Hindu faith is usually done in the context of the 'practice' of Hinduism rather than the 'theology' of the faith. Therefore, the term 'televangelism' is used in the Hindu context for comparative study purposes (alongside Christian televangelism) and it refers to the evolution of Hindu channels with TV programmes that promote the practice and lifestyle of the Hindu faith.

An interesting development in my research is the discovery of the growth of Hindu televangelism in India during the last decade.

The fact that Hindu televangelism emerged shortly after the introduction of satellite technology and Charismatic televangelism, suggests that Charismatic televangelism may have some influence on
the evangelistic activities of Hinduism. This is not to suggest that
televangelism is having an influence on Hinduism *per se* but that the
modes of communication utilised by the Christian broadcasters are
being observed and adapted by Hindu broadcasters for their own
ends.

As indicated in Chapter 1, when one of Hinduism's sacred texts,
the *Ramayana*, was serialised in 78 episodes on public television
between 1987 and 1989, it was estimated that up to 100 million people
watched the most popular episodes—bringing Indian life almost to a
standstill (van der Veer, 1998: 175). *Doordarshan*, India's public TV
station, has been the main carrier of Hindu programmes much to the
despair of certain Christian and Muslim families who virtually felt
marginalised and at times even boycotted the public station (Thomas
and Mitchell, 2005: 42). On the other hand, Hindu nationalism
'received a cultural boost... and an all-India Hindu self-consciousness'
was fostered when the *Ramayana* and *Mahabharata* appeared on state
television (Haynes, 2003: 14). The serialised religious programme reveals
several aspects of the politics of religion, television and nationalism.
Strangely enough, the *Ramayana* on public TV was sponsored not by
the pro-Hindu BJP but by the Congress-led government: 'in the hope
that its flagging electoral fortunes might be revived with an infusion
of [the] "Hindu vote", votes inspired by Hindu solidarity' (Rajagopal,
2001: 72).

During the two years of the *Ramayana* broadcast (1987–1989) the
Ram Janma Bhumi (birthplace of the Ram movement), which planned
to demolish a Muslim mosque in Ayodhya and build in its place a Ram
temple increased in importance (Rajagopal, 2001: 30). The publicity
grew to such an extent side by side with the televised serial that the
pro-Hindu BJP party seized the political and cultural opportunity to
declare, by the middle of 1989:

[T]hat the Ayodhya movement 'had reached a state and status in Indian
public life when it was no more possible to ignore its effect in politics
including electoral politics'. The issue was... political, with...BJP
making it their number one priority that 'a temple to Lord Ram' would
be built at the site of the mosque. (Rajagopal, 2001: 30)

Media critics and secularists condemned the religious broadcasts
as a 'communal' text suggesting that the TV serial 'might have

participated in a reconfiguration of discourses of nation, culture and community that overlapped with and reinforces Hindu nationalism' (Mankekar, 1999: 165).

As already mentioned in Chapter 1, side by side with the political impact of this TV phenomenon, was the equally extraordinary impact on various Hindus, including: those who did not understand the Hindi language, the untouchables and middle class Hindus—all of whom had their own share of spiritual responses. Many Hindus claimed to have a *darshan*, 'a glimpse of the sacred' during the viewing (van der Veer, 1998: 175). Other viewers took part in elaborate rituals and purification prayers before the start of each programme. The medium became the message when, in public places, 'the television itself was often garlanded with flowers or incense' (Mitchell, 2005: 2–3). Belief in Hinduism is grounded in practice rather than in a set body of truths. Therefore, the diversities of practice in Hinduism, when captured on television elicit different types of responses from various Hindus.

This television phenomenon illustrates, in part, why the style, content and viewing of Hindu religious television differs from Christian television. Hinduism is an orthopractic religion—it has a lifestyle orientation as opposed to a theological orientation. Belief is not always grounded on historical facts, as seen in the recent Hindu demonstrations when the Archaeological Survey of India (ASI) revealed in a 400-page affidavit that there was no historical evidence to back up the existence of Lord Ram and other characters in Hinduism's ancient text the *Ramayana* (O'Connor, 2007: 16). Professor Venkatasubramaniam, history professor at Delhi University, explained that 'Ram Setu has gotten into the culture and psyche. Even in the 21st century it is very difficult to come out of that belief' (O'Connor, 2007: 16). However, the Hindu nationalist BJP party accused the Congress-led government of 'assaulting' Hindu sentiments in bringing out this report (O'Connor, 2007: 16).

This lifestyle orientation explains why, among other things, Hindu folklore and practices find their way into public and commercial television programmes as they do into many other aspects of life. This also explains why theological discourse does not play such an important role in Hindu televangelism as worship and prayers, lifestyle teaching and *bhajan*s (Hindu repetitious worship songs with simple melodic lines). All these components of televised Hinduism are present in other commercial channels as well as on *Doordarshan* (Indian public television). Almost all the television channels, even the secular ones, 'have at least one 60-minute, early morning time slot dedicated to *bhajans*, discourses and yoga teaching sessions' (Malik, January–March 2003: para 23). It is important to note that what is different in the last decade in Hindu televangelism is the establishment of separate Hindu TV channels that operate on a semi-commercial basis like their Christian counterparts.

In this chapter, I trace the beginnings of Hindu televangelism; give a brief overview of the main Hindu channels; analyse the construction of Hindu television and explore the influence that Charismatic televangelism has on Hindu televangelism.

The Beginnings

As discussed in Chapter 4, it was during the Gulf war in 1990, when satellite television was introduced to India. It was the reporting of the news of the war that first opened the doors of satellite television to India. CNN delivered hourly updates and insights of the US-led allied war against Iraq's Saddam Hussein.

This then led to a plethora of programmes being offered via private media companies, bringing about increasing criticisms from social and cultural groups including the Hindu magazine *Hinduism Today*:

> Along with CNN, viewers rushed to embrace the new STAR TV channels like STAR Plus and MTV, England's BBC followed with its new Asian programme. Recently, a Hindi version of STAR Plus has been launched and also MTV begun by ATN...
>
> Asia Today Network (ATN) is owned by a non-resident Indians (NRI's) headed by a Suresh Shah. It is out to exploit the market in India by competing with the Star TV by presenting Zee TV programmes sexier than the Star TV presentations. ATN uses a satellite called Asianet... (Sinha, 1993: paras 6–7)

Sinha writing in *Hinduism Today* (1993) also included a discussion of the impact of satellite TV on India pointing out that it was more of a cultural bane than a social boon:

> The satellite television programmes have become so overpowering in their influence that they dominate every aspect of the life of an Indian. Whether at the dinner table, bus, train, or government office, the talk

centers around Mason's witticisms or Sinhead O'Connor's blasphemies or Ridge Forrester's lady admirers. Housewives discuss every episode of the popular soap operas, aired nightly.

It is not that there is no concern about the impact the satellite television has begun to make on India's rich cultural heritage, values and beliefs. The concern is being voiced in different quarters prominent citizens, educators and even the newspaper media. India's premier newspaper, Times of India recently carried a feature 'Sex Among Teenagers' which maintained that the overexposure of sex on MTV was responsible for powerfully inciting the new sex craze among the school kids in India. (Sinha, 1993: paras 8–9)

Aastha, Sanskar and other Hindu Channels

By the time CNN made its entry into the Indian airwaves, criticisms were mounting towards *Doordarshan*, the national broadcaster for 'aping what the foreign television offered as popular fare…for years *Doodarshan* had gradually lowered its standards…' (Sinha, 1993: para. 5).

Hence, the perception of *Doordarshan*'s loss of standards and the introduction of Western satellite channels created the need for specialised Hindu religious channels to counter them. The founders of *Aastha*, India's first Hindu TV Channel, explain the aims and aspirations of this 24-hour channel:

Aastha means faith…the aim is to increase faith in our people, faith in our country, faith in our religion…we are definitely propagating… Hinduism. We have no shame in admitting…As Bill Gates had a dream of putting a computer in every house…we have a dream that every house around the globe should be watching Aastha… (Sinha, 1993)

Kirit Mehta, one of the founders of *Aastha*, suggests that the harmful influence of the West is the fault of fellow-Hindus for not doing anything positively for the faith and, therefore, *Aastha* has been created to rectify the West's harmful influences:

The negative influence of the West on our youth is partly our fault… Aastha tries to show both the East and the West from a positive point of view…We are making a great effort to produce yoga and meditation programmes for the youth. (Sinha, 1993)

Aastha gives TV coverage of the main religious festivals like *Kumbha Mela*, as well as the festivals where thousands 'reconverted' to Hinduism from Christianity. According to *Hinduism Today* (2003), the channel is proving to become a rallying point for Hinduism: '... hundreds of people told us they had come to the Kumbha Mela only after watching it on our channel. During the next Mela, we plan to provide live broadcast of the whole thing right through' (Sinha, 1993).

Aastha TV in 2006 faced programming challenges and many 'fillers' and 'reruns' were telecast. In contrast to this, their 2008 programme schedule (see Tables 5.1a and 5.1b) reveals that the station now produces its own specials—*Aastha Special*, apportioning at least five hours per day to live telecasts of Hindu festivals (these cost between Rs 150,000–250,000 per hour) and has increased its array of new programmes.

Rajshekhar (2003: para 5) reported on a five-day festival *pravachan* (Hindu discourse) conducted by Hindu televangelist Guru Ma in Delhi. It was revealed that the talks given by Guru Ma were recorded and edited into 20-minute segments and telecast on various Hindu channels (Rajshekhar, 2003). The organiser and producer of this event was Kumar, a leading member of the Rashtriya Swayamsevak Sangh (RSS) as well as the Vishwa Hindu Parishad (VHP) (Rajshekhar, 2003). Both the RSS and VHP have been known to have links with Hindu nationalism and the *Hindutva* agenda.

Hindutva has two arms—the one associated with a violent agenda of Hinduisation and the other 'with cultural affirmation and cultural heritage—within a Hindu vision of Indian nation-building' (Hawkins, 2006). Hindu televangelism seems to fit in with this second aspect of the *Hindutva*'s cultural affirmation agenda.

Gupta (2006), writing in the *Sunday Pioneer*, says that in recent years Hindu gurus are filling the vacuum after a long period of silence when there was no united Hindu voice in India. Today television channels like *Aastha, Sanskar, Maharishi, Sadhna, Jagran* and *Om Shanti* all feature Hindu televangelists (Gupta, 2006). Gupta cites an instance, when Hindu televangelism was used to mobilise Hindus for a cause with Hindu televangelist Bapu:

> The fact that Hindu televangelism has succeeded in great measure to mobilise Hindus, irrespective of their caste or their personal preference for a god or goddess was evident in ample measure when Asaram Bapu joined the BJP's *dharna* to protest against the arrest of the

Table 5.1a: *Aastha* **programme schedule (indicative)**

IST	Sunday, 14 December 2008
0:00	Shiv Krupa
	Avdhoot Baba Shivananad ji
0:20	Discourses
	Swami Hari Caitanya Puriji
0:40	Sujok Therapy
1:00	Rajendra Jain Bhajans
1:30	Mata Ka Jagrata—Ramesh Oberoi
2:00	
2:30	Lokgeet
3:00	Rajsthan Day Celebration
3:30	Sant Geet
	Indians Saints Devotional Songs
4:00	Mangal Maitri/Manglik
	Darshanam
4:20	Sai Baba Kakad Aarti—Shirdi
4:40	Shiksha Aur Adhyatma
	City Montessory [sic] School—Lucknow
5:00	Yog Shivir Live Telecast from Auragabad
	Yogrishi Swami Ramdevji
7:30	Ayurved Evam Jivan Darshan
	Shradhey Acharya Balkrishnaji
8:00	Temples of India
8:20	
8:40	Seva Ganga
9:00	Sadhu Kailash Manav
9:20	Kal Chakra
	Pt. JayPrakash Sharma (Laldhagewale)
9:40	Vipassana
	Pujya Satyanarayan Goenkaji
10:10	Live Telecast of Shrimad Bhagwat Katha by
12:40	Pujya Swami Avdheshanand Giriji Maharaj from
	Fogla Ashram, Vrindavan
13:00	Jyotish Shikhiye
	Dr H. S. Rawat

Source: Aastha TV website http://www.aasthatv.com/Aastha_Schedule.pdf,
Programme Guide section (2008).

Shankaracharya of Kanchi...Thousands of men and women who
regularly watch Asaram Bapu's telepravachan joined the *dharna*...a
demonstration of emerging Hindu unity... (Gupta, 2006: paras 7–8)

Sanskar TV (*Sanskar* means rich values), according to its website,
is dedicated to 'Indian philosophy, religion and spiritual solidarity,
culture and dissemination of the vast and timeless knowledge of our

Table 5.1b: *Aastha* **programme schedule (indicative) (continued)**

IST	Aastha special
13:30	Sai Amrut Varsha
	Shri Subhram Bahl
13:50	Navgrah Aur Jyotishgyan
	Pandit K. P. Tripathi
14:00	Live Telecast of Bhagwat Katha by
17:00	Pujya Didi Maa Ritambhraji from Vatsalya Gram
17:40	Aastha Special
18:10	Shri Gagangiri Maharaj Laksh Laksh Deep Mahayagna
18:30	Discourses
	Swami Kriyanandji
18:50	Oshodhara
19:10	Awakening with Brahma Kumaris
19:40	Seva Ganga
	Sadhu Kailash Manav
20:00	Yog Shivir
	Yogrishi Swami Ramdevji
21:00	Ayurved Evam Jivan Darshan
	Shradhey Acharya Balkrishnaji
21:30	Talks on Oneness
	By Amma Bhagwan (English)
22:00	Talks on Oneness
	By Amma Bhagwan (Hindi)
22:20	Gyan Sagar
	Acharya Anil Vtasji
22:30	Awakening with Brahma Kumaris
23:00	Baba Gangaram Bhajans
23:20	Aastha Special
23:40	

Source: *Aastha* TV website http://www.aasthatv.com/Aastha_Schedule.pdf, Programme Guide section (2008).

great "*Sanatana Dharma*" [Hinduism] to the people of the world.' The TV channel broadcasts the following types of programmes: Hindu *bhajans*, good healthy living (such as yoga); documentaries (of worship sites and festivals); educational (such as *Ayurveda*) and special projects (such as animated movies and religious discourses) (*Sanskar* TV, n.d.).

Zee Jagran, another Hindu channel, was launched in January 2004 with the expressed purpose of 'awakening people to realise the spiritual aspects in their life and hence enriching their lives' (*Zee Jagran* website, n.d.). The channel has regular segments featuring gurus such as Sri Sri Ravi Shankar, Guru Osho, Aasaram Bapu and Prajapita Bhramakumaris.

The Construction of Hindu Television

The following results are based on a content analysis of the two Hindu 24-hour TV Channels, *Aastha* and *Sanskar.*

1. Eight out of 10 programmes are in Hindi or one of the Indian vernacular languages.
2. Nine out of 10 programmes are based on 'life skills', for example meditation, yoga demonstrations, breathing or stress reduction.
3. Eight out of 10 programmes show the priest or teacher seated in the yoga position and keeping at all times to that space, this is in contrast to Charismatic televangelists who move all over the platform.

It is interesting to note that two out of the 10 Hindu programmes involve teachers or priests who move around the stage, like the Charismatic televangelists; and two out of 10 teach in English, both using a 'three point sermon' outline, a popular technique used by Christian preachers. Swami Sukubutananda, who is known for his 'relax your mind, transform your mind' rhetoric, communicates with passion like the American Charismatic televangelists. Sukubutananda is one of the few Hindu televangelists who speaks in English as his audience extends to Indians in the diaspora, in Switzerland, USA and England as well.

Sukubutananda's preaching is a mix of slogan-filled messages on mind, body and soul transformation: 'If you are frustrated you have created that frustration…there is divinity in you…relax your mind transform your mind' (*Aastha* TV, 4 October 2006).

Guru Yashpal Sudhanshu chants a prayer and then begins his 'feel-good' lecture on coping with stress: 'Begin each day with a pure thought…when you do breathing exercises, when you control your anger, when you laugh, you're actually prolonging your life' (*Aastha* TV, 5 October 2006).

In another programme, a Hindu priest dressed in orange robes, is seated in a yoga position and gives demonstrations on the correct way of breathing. The camera moves into a close-up of the priest's stomach and chest to show his ability to hold his breath and exhale at the appropriate time.

In a different programme, Sai Baba, a well-known guru from a Hindu sect, is shown in extreme close up shots doing meditation. There is very little discourse or preaching in this programme. The opening and closing shots of Baba's 15-minute programme build him up as a 'celebrity guru'—he walks on the middle of a red carpet flanked by devotees—women on one side and men on the other. The women hand him their handkerchiefs as he walks, he touches them and returns it to the women. On his way out, he blesses a baby and then the camera pans to his bare feet walking on the carpet. The women devotees bow down and almost kiss the ground on which Baba just walked.

Sociologist Haribabu (2006) reports that female Hindu televangelists have increased in the last five years or so in India: 'This is a significant development. The women [evangelists] pick up issues not handled by male counterparts…also the female interpretation of the texts is quite different' (Haribabu, 2006: interview).

Divya Maharaas Leela from the *Golokdham Ashram* in Delhi is one of the more popular female televangelists. Speaking primarily in Hindi, with a sprinkling of words from the English language, Leela, dressed in maroon robes speaks in an almost trance-like manner. She repeats the mantra '*Om Namah Shiva*' several times for five to six minutes. At the conclusion of her talk, her audience applauds.

Sonalia Guswari, another female teacher, demonstrates the various yoga positions. In her programme, an 'enchanted' chain with a pendant, is heavily advertised for Rs 2,990. Testimonies are shared by various people as to how they have been helped by this chain, with a greater degree of concentration and better overall health. Guswari's programme and a few others seem to be entirely devoted to the sale of religious products. They are a religious version of the 'shopping channel' and the first of their kind in Indian religious televangelism.

Books and CDs, amulets, special oils and chains with pendants, are all heavily advertised during and after each programme. There are two daily time slots (6.30 am–8 am and 5.30 pm–7.30 pm), which Hindu televangelists consider as holy times for prayer, worship and the singing of *bhajan*s (Hindu worship songs). During these times an average of 20 channels would feature Hindu televangelists.

A content analysis of the two main Hindu channels in the years 2005 to 2006 revealed that 55 per cent of the programmes are dedicated to the practical aspects of Hindu living—yoga, meditation and dealing with

Table 5.2:   Programme content on Hindu channels

Demonstrations and teaching on yoga, meditation, life skills	55%
Bhajans (songs) and prayers	35%
Teaching from sacred texts	5%
Events, festivals, news	5%

Source: Author.

stress and coping with the pressures of living in a modern, urban society (see Table 5.2). *Bhajans* (worship songs), *poojas* (prayers) and the worship and ritual elements of Hinduism take up 35 per cent. Preaching and teaching from the sacred texts only occupy 5 per cent of the total programme content. There is teaching but it is directed more towards practical Hinduism, in terms of living a life free of stress and exercising control over the forces of life. As Pavarala observes:

> More and more, we are seeing the 'new age' spirituality of Hinduism (which involves life skills rather than the moral and ethical teaching of Hinduism). Ravi Shankar is the Hindu version of Christianity's Benny Hinn. Ravi's 'art of living' seminars are attracting many people to a new form of Hinduism packaged in attractive ways. (Pavarala, 2006: interview)

Sudhanshu, a well-known TV guru, said in an interview that his goal is to enhance people's aura (a halo of coloured light that surrounds each person):

> That aura protects you from negative forces…when the aura weakens, other people's words and actions have a negative impact. My message is to strengthen the aura around you by meditation, introspection and worship, so you can create heaven around you. (Lancaster, 2003)

Shankar (Hindu) versus Hinn (Christian)

A comparative study between Hindu televangelist Ravi Shankar and Christian televangelist Benny Hinn revealed several interesting similarities and differences based on themes, techniques, change agent, text, political economy, products and funding (see Table 5.3).

Table 5.3: Comparison between televangelists Shankar (Hindu) and Hinn (Christian)

Evangelists	Major themes	Technique	Text	Change agent	Political economy	Products	Funding
Sri Sri Ravi Shankar (Hindu-New Age)	Success in Life	The use of elementary principles	Hindu texts blended with success principles	The individual	Satelllite TV, Website, Seminars, Books, DVDs, World-wide offices	Books, DVDs and paraphern-alia	Sales and Seminar Fees
Benny Hinn (Christian-Charismatic)	Healing of Body	Slaying in the Spirit	Biblical Text	Jesus through Benny Hinn	Satelllite TV, Website Crusades, Books, DVDs, World-wide offices	Books, DVDs and paraphern-alia	Sales, TV Donations, Home Church Donations

Source: Author.

Major themes

Success in everyday life is the theme of Shankar's Art of Living seminars and TV programmes while the healing of the body preoccupies Hinn in his televised crusades.

Techniques

Shankar uses the elementary principles of breathing, meditation and serenity. *Sudarshan Kriya* is a breathing technique invented by Shankar '...it has the power to relieve stress so people feel joyous' (Morente, 2006). For Hinn, the main techniques used for healing are prayer, laying on of hands and slaying in the spirit.

Text

Shankar vaguely alludes to Hindu texts but seems to blend the principles of the faith with success, management and psychological principles. Hinn uses the Biblical text, especially the New Testament, but keeps referring to the same portions which support his teachings on healing.

Change agent

The individual is the change agent in Shankar's teachings. By practising deep breathing, meditation and other techniques, healing, success, joy and serenity are guaranteed for the individual. For Hinn, Jesus Christ is the healer who chooses to heal people through Benny Hinn, the powerful and 'anointed' miracle worker.

Political economy, products and funding

While Charismatic televangelism (especially the global programmes) is characterised by aggressive fundraising, Hindu televangelism does not seem to solicit donations, relying solely on sales of products. Hindu culture seems averse to asking for donations which explains why Indian Christian and Hindu leaders in Chapters 6 and 7 criticised the aggressive fundraising strategies of Charismatic televangelists.

By 'political economy', I infer that both the Shankar and Hinn organisations are part of a larger global project where various media are interlocked wielding both political and economic influence. Both televangelists use satellite TV, books, CDs and DVDs in the market of religious consumerism and have large world-wide audiences. Shankar's Art of Living Seminars are based on fees which consist of 'differently priced packages for each city and more expensive advance courses in big cities' (Bhuskute, 2005). Hinn's world-wide and televised crusades are basically financed by TV donors, Christian businessmen and his own home church and TV ministry. Both Shankar and Hinn attract influential people from the media, business and political realms of society.

Deepak Chopra, a well-known Hindu/New Age teacher, has a huge following, both from India and overseas. Chopra, also seen on Hindu channels, is like Shankar, an advocate of mind and body healing therapies based on *Aryuveda*—the traditional system of Indian medicine.

High-profile Hindu televangelist, Ramdev who teaches and demonstrates his *pranayam* (breath control) techniques, has cashed in on television to build a huge religious enterprise. Ramdev owns an *ayurvedic* pharmacy which is:

> Now part of Ramdev's burgeoning empire estimated to be worth Rs 100 crore. It includes a sprawling ashram ... and a 150-acre nursery and farm... money is churned out by the media wing which sells VCD's, books, magazines and TV rights. (Mishra, 2006: paras 4–5)

When Ramdev was recently embroiled in controversy about his *ayurvedic* preparations with the government authorities, he received massive support from political parties and leaders including the BJP, the controversial Shiv Sena, the NCP and other groups (Mishra, 2006). This is an example of the links and interconnectedness that are shaping the political economy of Hindu televangelism, not unlike Charismatic televangelism.

Charismatic TV's Influence on Hindu Televangelism

Whereas there are differences between Hindu televangelism and Christian televangelism, the similarities between the two are quite striking. A leading business paper discovered that many of these daily programmes, like their Christian counterparts, are recorded during 5 to

10-day festivals and the messages by gurus are edited into 20-minute segments and telecast on religious television (Rajshekhar, 2003). The gurus are aware that they are being recorded for broadcast at these live preaching sessions so they start 'summing up their message every 19 minutes or so. That simplifies the editing process' (Rajshekhar, 2003: para 24). Bapu, as well as a few other Hindu TV preachers, like the Christian Charismatic televangelists, offer Hindu products on air and there is a prayer line that viewers can call. *Businessworld* quotes a study by Samit Mehrotra who says the gurus are master communicators 'their dialectic is a mix of religion and entertainment...they make deft use of metaphors' (Rajshekhar, 2003: para 27). Another example quoted by the paper is a study by sociologist Shiv Visvanathan who says: 'They [gurus] will not tell you to renounce everything and lead frugal lives: instead they offer "market-friendly" techniques to deal with life's stresses and problems' (Rajshekhar, 2003: para 28).

A senior communications scholar at the University of Hyderabad sees a direct link between the upsurge of Christian televangelism and the growth of Hindu televangelism. Professor Pavarala, firstly, sees the Hindu channels as a 'social oddity' as Hinduism historically does not have a tradition of discourse like the Judeo-Christian faiths. Secondly, Pavarala describes Hindu channels as 'imitative and reactive' in that they are 'aping Christian television and reacting to the hyper-Hindu sentiment of the previous Government' (Pavarala, 2006: interview).

The two Hindu epics, the *Ramayana* and the *Mahabharata* are making a comeback on television, this time with 'snazzy visual effects' and 'high-tech techniques such as those used in "The Lord of the Rings" films', according to a news article from Reuters (Jamkhandikar, 2008).

As pointed out earlier in the chapter, there is a link between Christian movies and the great Hindu mythologies on film. Davis (1946) argues that starting in the nineteenth century, Hinduism underwent a gradual transformation, largely through the influence of Christian missionaries. Many of the changes were in the areas of religious concepts, techniques and strategies like the introduction of public worship and united prayer in Hindu temples (Davis, 1946).

Even the name of the largest world-wide Hindu magazine *Hinduism Today* founded in 1979, bears a striking resemblance to its Christian counterpart *Christianity Today*, founded in 1955, by evangelical luminaries such as Billy Graham and Nelson Bell of the USA.

Is Hindu televangelism showing signs of being influenced by Christian Charismatic televangelism in keeping with the historical parallels of influence in Hindu cinema, temple worship and publications? Both Hindu leaders and senior Christian leaders were asked to comment whether they felt Hindu televangelism has borrowed aspects of Charismatic televangelism. A total of 55 per cent of the Christian leaders answered that there were elements from Charismatic televangelism that Hindu televangelists have taken on board (see Table 5.4).

Some of the features of the crossover include the marketing strategies, the entertainment aspect of televangelism and the self-help and life-skill type of teaching. Congregational singing and healing miracles, as well as 24-hour prayer lines, are other examples of techniques that seem to have crossed over from Charismatic televangelism to the Hindu channels. One Christian leader said: 'Unfortunately some Charismatic televangelists have made religion into a fine art and turned evangelists into celebrities...this is the American way...the Hindus are now making Gurus famous through satellite-assisted technology' (SCL, 2006).[1]

This sentiment is reflected in a news article about Hindu television:

> The religious [TV] business in India is very lucrative' said an executive of a [Hindu] religious channel who asked not to be identified. So fierce is the competition for media-exposure,...that lesser-known gurus typically pay religious channels for airtime; some have been known to record their sermons in private, 'then insert shots of a crowd from elsewhere and send us the tapes... (Lancaster, 2003: para. 14)

The article also mentioned that TV Guru Sudhanshu's Universal Awakening Mission operates 20 *ashram*s, a network of hospitals and

Table 5.4:   Is Hindu televangelism imitating Charismatic televangelism?

	Senior Christian leaders and key informants N = 30	Hindu leaders N = 30
1. Yes ... a little	10%	25%
2. Yes ... in a big way	45%	10%
3. No	*	20%
4. No, Christians are aping Hindus!	*	5%
5. Not sure/can't say	35%	40%

Source: Author.
Note: * Not answered.

schools with offices in Chicago and Los Angeles. Its main *ashram* occupies 17 acres in Delhi. It is a:

> [K]ind of religious theme park...stocked with white swans, a fire temple, a seminary for Hindu missionaries and a 60-foot high artificial mountain complete with cascading waterfall...an executive of the ashram acknowledged that for the guru's (Sudhanshu's) divinely inspired wisdom, he also had help from another source in building his spiritual empire. 'Television has created this', the executive said. (Lancaster, 2003: paras 18–19)

Shah (2006) differentiates between yesterday's spiritualists and today's Hindu televangelists:

> [M]odern spiritualists are unregulated multinational corporations. The Buddha renounced his life as a prince to find meaning for himself. But the Chopras of this world use a Rolex to put together a group of lost people and tell them they are actually found. (Shah, 2006: para 14)

Thirty-five per cent of the Hindu leaders agreed that Hindu televangelism is being influenced by Charismatic televangelism. Some of the aspects of influence singled out are in the area of 'the commercialisation of the religious programmes'; 'the slick production and techniques used' and the music. Five per cent of the Hindu leaders said that the Christians are the ones who are imitating the Hindus. One of the Hindu leaders said: '...they [Christians] are copying us. The Hindu religion has spread to the West and even TV shows in the USA use our words like "dharma" and "mantra" etc...so they are following us ...not the other way round' (HL, 2006).

Businessworld's investigative article on Hindu televangelism reports:

> [R]eligious television is offering them [gurus] a faster way to maximise reach and gain a following...Rakesh Gupta who started Sadhna, the third religious [Hindu] channel [says]: 'by coming on TV, the gurus can build a following. That is how they can command greater fees when they hold a discourse. The organisers will willingly pay more as they too will make more money—greater turnout, more donations'. (Rajshekhar, 2003: para 13).

Journalist Gupta (2006), who is critical of Christian televangelists, comments: 'Yes, there will be contemptible attempts to tar Hindu televangelists…We will hear of allegations of "crass commercialisation" of "telemarketing spiritualism", of catering to the "lowest common denominator"…' (Gupta, 2006: para. 10).

The two pillars of religious globalised television, seen in the Charismatic (Christian) and Hindu contexts are technology and the market. While technology is the new medium for the teaching and discourse of the faith, the market encourages the recoding of the message legitimising it for this world, rather than the world to come. Ravi Shankar and the Hindu TV gurus advocate a prosperity and 'feel good' message while unashamedly marketing a wide-range of spiritual products and paraphernalia.

Christian and Hindu televangelism both seem to have married their respective faiths to commercialisation. However, without the strong element of orthodoxy in Hinduism, Hindu televangelism seems even more commercialised than Christian televangelism earning it the dubious description 'Om Economics' to typify the disjunction of Hindu mediated faith in contemporary India.

This chapter revealed that the consequence of global televangelism combined with the rise of satellite television was the introduction of specialised Hindu TV channels operating in a similar fashion as the Christian channels. The Hindu televangelists on these Hindu channels preach a form of 'new age' Hindu spirituality while borrowing many production, marketing and rhetorical techniques and methods from Charismatic televangelists. It appears that Hindu television, while not being influenced by the biblical message, is influenced by the methods, marketing techniques and even the rhetoric of Christian televangelists. This, coupled with the complex interrelationships between the political economy of India, global capitalism and the nationalistic movement calls for more research in the burgeoning religious enterprise of Hindu televangelism.

Note

1. Since this chapter draws on primary research, the ideas and opinions of the respondents (many of whom wish to remain anonymous) are identified in the text in the following ways: MLP—Middle-Level Pastor/s; SCL-Senior Christian Leader/s; KI—Key Informant/s; HL—Hindu Leader/s and ML—Muslim Leader/s.

Chapter 6

Interpreting Charismatic Televangelism: Pastors and the Divided Church

This chapter examines how Charismatic and non-Charismatic pastors in urban India are impacted by global and 'glocal' Charismatic televangelism primarily through the transnational satellite networks of *God TV* and *Miraclenet*.

In the first section the results of the findings on global televangelism are examined. This is followed by the second section where the results of the findings of 'glocal' televangelism, in particular, CBN's *Solutions* programme are examined.

To study the influence of Charismatic televangelism on the Protestant Church, I felt it was important to start with the church leaders. I decided to measure the reactions to and the influences of Charismatic television on selected Protestant pastors. I was also seeking their perceptions of televangelism's influence. In India, elders and leaders are generally regarded as the decision makers and gate keepers of society. Therefore, I deliberately did not interview church members for two reasons: first, it would threaten the pastors if their communicants were interviewed; second, studying the response of the church members really constitutes a separate study which is beyond the scope and resources of this project.

This chapter draws heavily from primary research. Sixty middle-level pastors (from Charismatic and non-Charismatic persuasions) were chosen from Mumbai and Hyderabad to respond to a questionnaire on the impact of televangelism on the church. The results of their responses were shared with 30 senior Christian pastors and key informants for cross-checking and discussion. In the second section on 'glocal' televangelism, only the views of the senior Christian leaders were sought in an ethnographic study. The ideas and opinions of the respondents (many of whom wish to remain anonymous) are identified in the text in the following ways: MLP—Middle-level Pastor/s; SCL—Senior Christian Leader/s; KI—Key Informant/s; HL—Hindu Leader/s and ML—Muslim Leader/s.

Results of Findings on Global Televangelism

The following results are based on responses to a questionnaire for 60 middle-level pastors in Mumbai and Hyderabad, India as well as qualitative interviews with senior Christian leaders and key informants. These findings are discussed below under the following headings: significant influences in the church, sources of Charismatic influences, access to Charismatic televangelism and attendance, degree of influences, positive influences, negative influences, culturally appropriate issues and culturally inappropriate issues.

Significant influences in the Church

In response to the question, 'What are some significant changes that have occurred in the church in the last ten years?' (see Table 6.1). 63 per cent of Charismatic pastors indicated that the style of preaching has transformed into what they term 'prophetic'. Further analysis of this term with senior Christian leaders revealed that it is a reference to the shift from expository preaching of the text of scripture to a more

Table 6.1: Significant Church influences (10 years)

	Charismatic pastors N = 30	Non-Charismatic pastors N = 30
Preaching style (Prophetic)	63%	*
Use of spiritual gifts	27%	*
Worship—contemporary	10%	70%

Source: Author.
Note: * Not answered.

'spirit-led' and 'spirit-revealed' message that gives people immediate understanding of what God is saying, to the congregation here and now, with reference to healings, prophetic utterances or a word of knowledge specific to a person's immediate need.

Twenty-seven per cent of Charismatic pastors indicated that another change in the last 10 years is increased use of 'spiritual gifts'. Further research indicated that this is a reference to the use of miraculous and 'sign' gifts like healing, prophecies and tongues.

Non-charismatic pastors did not see preaching or use of gifts as a significant change in their respective churches. Non-Charismatic pastors (70 per cent) revealed that for them the significant change occurred in the area of worship and especially the use of contemporary songs in the Church. Further research with these pastors indicated that the church service now has a contemporary worship segment of up to 15 minutes. This is usually led by young people and it is called the 'praise and worship' time. During this time the Church gives the youth and the more contemporary members of the Church a chance to sing praises with musical instruments in a 'Charismatic' worship style.

The common denominator in all these significant changes mentioned seems to be the Charismatic movement. In other words, it is interesting to note that both Charismatic and non-Charismatic pastors have linked the main change in the last 10 years to the Charismatic movement. This led me to the next question: 'How do you think these Charismatic influences have come about?'

The comment by senior leaders that Indian Christians may watch Charismatic television but not cross over into Charismatic churches lends itself to comment and questioning. While my anecdotal experience in certain Indian churches (like the Mar Thoma and Brethren Churches) certainly points towards the fact that it is generally difficult for Indian Christians to cross over into other denominations, the question that arises is: where is the growth in Charismatic churches coming from? This will, no doubt, be a topic for subsequent research.

Charismatic influences

According to the middle-level pastors, the Charismatic para-church groups like Full-Gospel Associations exert more influence than the local Charismatic churches. Senior Christian leaders commenting on this explained that India has its own Pentecostal Churches which are considered indigenous Churches. However, senior leaders asserted that Christians from mainline Churches would not cross over into these Churches. Para-church groups, according to these senior leaders, hold meetings in hotels, in the work place and factories and so they have a tendency to reach more people than the local Church (SCL, 2006).

Senior Christian leaders also drew attention to the fact that, even though television may be the source of 'informing' other Christians of an alternative style and theology of Christianity, most Indian Christians are traditional at heart. They explained that it is hard for members of established Indian Christian families such as, the Mar Thoma Church or the Brethren Assemblies, to go to a different church from the one the father attends. In a sense 'Indian Christians have taken the community-mindedness of their culture into the Church...so a man would be born, married and buried in the same Church as his father' (SCL, 2006). Therefore, even though some non-Charismatic Christian may be influenced by Charismatic television, it does not necessarily mean that these Christians will give up their existing memberships to join Charismatic churches.

Thirty-five per cent of both Charismatic and non-Charismatic pastors felt that in the last 10 years, the influence of Charismatic theology and worship has come via television, videos, DVDs and books. When asked what percentage of the influence was primarily from television, the pastors indicated it would be anywhere from 50–60 per cent. Hence, television is a key agent in impacting the Indian church. Twenty per cent of the pastors agreed that foreign Charismatic preachers have influenced Indian churches through their rallies and healing crusades.

Senior Christian leaders agreed with these findings and added that foreign Charismatic missionaries (short-term and long-term) would also need to be mentioned, as these missionaries start Charismatic churches and Bible colleges in India and the influence widens (SCL, 2006).

Senior Christian leaders interpreted this question as significant and drew attention to the fact that, within the causes influence categories, number one and number four should be seen together (Table 6.2). For example, some world-renowned foreign Charismatic leaders, like Benny Hinn, had their programmes on Indian TV long before they set foot into India.

The TV media built up their image and aura before they came and paved the way for a phenomenal gathering when Hinn arrived. Other foreign Charismatic leaders launched their TV ministries after coming to India and so their share of the TV audience gathered

Table 6.2: Sources of Charismatic influence

Charismatic pastors and non-Charismatic pastors N = 60	Percentage
1. Visiting Charismatic preachers from overseas	20
2. Local Charismatic churches within India	3
3. Para-church organisations within India (e.g., Full Gospel chapters)	6
4. TV and other related media like videos, books, DVDs	35
5. Indian Christians who travel abroad	1
6. Not known/unanswered	35

Source: Author.

momentum because of their large crusades in key Indian cities. The complimentary books and videos given out at many of the crusades and pastors' seminars also needed to be taken into account in the discussion on the sources of Charismatic influence on the Church in India (SCL, 2006).

Access to televangelism and attendance

Hundred per cent of the pastors (Charismatic and non-Charismatic) had access to Charismatic televangelism through cable TV. All respondents (100 per cent) named three televangelists as the most popular Charismatic TV televangelists: Joyce Meyer, Benny Hinn and Creflo Dollar (Table 6.3).

Ninety-three per cent of Charismatic pastors, compared to 46 per cent of non-Charismatic pastors, reported that they attended public rallies or seminars when Charismatic TV evangelists visited India (Table 6.4). Senior Christian leaders, commenting on this finding, said that, whereas it is understandable that such a high percentage of Charismatic pastors would attend meetings by Charismatic TV evangelists, they were rather surprised that such a high figure of non-Charismatic pastors also attended these meetings. A key informant Christian leader explained that many non-Charismatic pastors would go to these meetings perhaps on a one-off basis to check out the pastors. This is not necessarily

Table 6.3: Access to and knowledge of televangelistic programmes

Charismatic pastors and non-Charismatic pastors N = 60	Percentage
1. Access? (Yes)	100
2. What type? (Cable TV)	100
3. Most popular Charismatic evangelists?	Meyer, Hinn and Dollar

Source: Author.

Table 6.4:   Attendance at Charismatic TV evangelists' meetings

	Charismatic pastors N = 30	˙ Non-Charismatic pastors N = 30
Yes	93%	46%
No	7%	54%

Source: Author.

an indication of a shift in theological thinking and or practice (KI, 2006). He added that 'Charismatic TV evangelists are quite a novelty, and a person like Benny Hinn attracts all kinds of people even Hindus and Muslims...the key is this...what happens to them after attending these meetings...is there a mass conversion? That is really doubtful...' (KI, 2006).

The pastors, who answered 'yes' to the question of whether they attended public meetings of visiting Charismatic TV evangelists, identified Benny Hinn (combined pastors 96 per cent); Joyce Meyer (combined pastors 26 per cent) and Pat Robertson (combined pastors 14 per cent) as the evangelist whose meeting/s they attended (Table 6.5). Senior Christian leaders commented that it is significant that even though Pat Robertson has been on Indian television since 1977 (longer than anyone else), only a combined total of 14 per cent of pastors attended his public meetings. On the other hand, Benny Hinn's televised miracles; 'showmanship', 'aura' and general controversy were probably what bought the crowds to his meetings in India, according to the senior Christian leaders. Key informants also added that the Benny Hinn public meetings were a very costly and well advertised 'media' event involving local politicians, celebrities and local 'mega' churches, which in part explains the phenomenal crowds he attracted (KI, 2006).

Degree of influences

When it came to aspects of Charismatic influence, 7 per cent of Charismatic pastors are not at all influenced by Charismatic

Table 6.5: Identifying the meetings attended

	Charismatic pastors N = 30	Non-Charismatic pastors N = 30
Benny Hinn	56%	40%
Joyce Meyer	13%	13%
Pat Robertson (CBN)	7%	7%

Source: Author.

televangelism, whereas 7 per cent of non-Charismatic pastors are very much influenced by Charismatic televangelism.

In a similar vein, 33 per cent of Charismatic pastors are very much influenced by Charismatic television, whereas 33 per cent of non-Charismatic pastors are not at all influenced. Sixty per cent of both Charismatic and non-Charismatic pastors responded that Charismatic televangelism had a limited influence on them.

When we add categories number two and three together in Table 6.6, 93 per cent of Charismatic pastors are influenced by Charismatic television, whereas 67 per cent of non-Charismatic pastors are influenced by Charismatic television. Although Charismatic pastors are more influenced by Charismatic television, it is significant that the percentage of influence among non-Charismatic pastors is fairly high.

Senior Christian leaders expressed surprise over this finding, but added that in the Indian context, it is possible to be positively influenced by a phenomenon like the Charismatic movement without a total shift in perspective and practice. They added that Indian Christians may watch Charismatic TV 'in the comfort of their homes, seeing it as a novelty or even adapting certain worship styles into their Churches... but only a few would cross over to become full-fledged members of Charismatic Churches' (SCL, 2006).

Positive influences

Under the aspect of what influenced them positively, the pastors mentioned two issues: preaching and worship, as seen in Table 6.7.

Further analysis revealed that the 40 per cent of non-Charismatic pastors who were influenced by the 'preaching content' were impressed by the delivery techniques of the preachers and the clever ways in which the sermon was put together (the use of alliteration) rather than the content *per se*. In contrast to this, 70 per cent of Charismatic pastors expressed the fact that they were influenced both by the preaching content as well as the delivery.

Table 6.6: Influence of Charismatic televangelism

	Charismatic pastors $N = 30$	Non-Charismatic pastors $N = 30$
1. Not at all influenced	7%	33%
2. Limited influence	60%	60%
3. Very much influenced	33%	7%

Source: Author.

Table 6.7:   Aspects of the positive influences

	Charismatic pastors N = 30	Non-Charismatic pastors N = 30
Preaching content	70%	40%
Worship	30%	40%
Not answered	–	20%

Source: Author.

Thirty per cent of Charismatic pastors reported they were influenced by the worship (singing of choruses, prayer times); whereas 40 per cent non-Charismatic pastors reported they were influenced by the worship. Worship, according to further analysis from both persuasions, refers to the contemporary music, the free-flowing style (as opposed to the stiff liturgical style) and the overall ease and sway in which the prayers and music are interspersed during the worship time.

Negative influences

With regard to negative aspects of Charismatic televangelism, several areas were raised, as reflected in Table 6.8.

Fundraising was one of the most discussed issues by both Charismatics and non-Charismatics. It is mentioned here as well as in the section on 'culturally inappropriate issues'. In this section, 53 per cent of Charismatic pastors and 46 per cent of non-Charismatic pastors (combined 99 per cent) named the fundraising aspect of Charismatic televangelism as negative. According to one senior Christian leader, the average Indian Christian is not materialistic; in fact 'he or she is attracted by one's resignation to wealth and prosperity rather than the possession of a lavish lifestyle such as that seen on many Charismatic programmes' (SCL, 2006). The following example was used by one

Table 6.8:   Negative influences

	Charismatic pastors N = 30	Non-Charismatic pastors N = 30
Fundraising style	53%	46%
Local church affected (e.g., funds, attendance)	40%	10%
Superficial content	–	13%
Commercialisation of the gospel	–	30%
Not answered	7%	1%

Source: Author.

of the senior Christian leaders to illustrate how televangelists have embarrassed local Christians on the *Miraclenet* channel with funding appeals: '…during the times of prayer one of the leaders said "send us Rs 500 and we will pray for you…send us Rs 1000 and we will put your name on a 24-hour prayer chain"…' (SCL, 2006). Every night, Michael Hughes, the American director of *Miraclenet*, a Chennai-based Charismatic TV network, announces the names, prayer items and amount of donations sent in by viewers. He then invites the audience 'to say the "miracle prayer"' (a ritual prayer for prosperity, health and general well-being). Senior Christian leaders also expressed concern that Charismatic televangelists give the impression that 'if you want blessings or favours from God…give to our ministry'. This, according to the leaders, is tantamount to 'twisting the Scriptures' (SCL, 2006). Two of the senior Christian leaders asserted that Charismatic televangelists should add this disclaimer in their appeals: 'Do not neglect the work of your local churches when you give to us' because local church pastors have been affected by church members giving to other ministries rather than the local church (SCL, 2006).

Forty per cent of Charismatic pastors and 10 per cent of non-Charismatic pastors bemoaned the fact that local churches were affected negatively by Charismatic televangelists. Four aspects were mentioned: funds, church attendance (as well as denominational loyalties), doctrinal confusion (and church splits in some situations) and popular expectations in preaching, worship and church administration.

1. Funds

Although the middle-level pastors and senior Christian leaders could not give figures to substantiate their claims, their general feeling was that a proportion of their congregational members had given finances to TV evangelists because '…our Indian Christians are very spiritual and if a preacher appeals to them or has blessed them, they will give to them…' (SCL, 2006). The senior Christian leader gave the example of Black American televangelist, Bishop Jakes, who says on TV: 'Don't forget who blessed you'. The senior Christian leader continued,

> …[A]lso the Christian message is mediated in very relevant and appealing format so there is an element of novelty…how long they (Christians) will continue to give is a question I have, but I am not surprised that they give to TV evangelists. (SCL, 2006)

2. Church attendance

In terms of attendance, pastors and senior leaders commented that they have not lost a huge number of communicants, but there have been a few church members who, as a result of watching these programs, end up moving to Charismatic Churches. Two leaders commented that at least 5 to 10 per cent of their communicants would 'be in two camps, that is, attending my church as well as going to another midweek or Sunday afternoon service organised by Charismatic groups'.

Senior Christian leaders, especially those from mainline denominations, expressed fear that with so many 'independent charismatic' Churches springing up, denominational loyalties may be threatened in the coming generation or so.

3. Doctrinal confusion

Three of the senior Christian leaders also lamented the absence of balance in the teachings of Charismatic preachers, pointing out that there is an 'unhealthy emphasis on healing, prosperity, and miracles rather than the teaching of the main tenets of Scriptures and leading people to a personal relationship with Jesus Christ'. Senior Christian leaders referred to the Benny Hinn crusade in India as a good example of the current craze for healing and the spectacular manifestation of gifts mediated through the televised 'aura' of Hinn (SCL, 2006).

Other senior leaders commented that Charismatic leaders seem not to be presenting the simple message of Christ but 'more techniques sometimes with spiritistic tendencies'. 'Slaying in the spirit' and 'power evangelism' were mentioned as examples of new techniques in the church. One senior leader said that Charismatic televangelists combined showmanship with spiritual techniques and some evangelists are known for the symbolic way in which they represent themselves. For example, one televangelist need only raise his finger and the people are 'slain in the spirit'. All these can create doctrinal confusion, according to three of the senior leaders (SCL, 2006). Two instances were given, one in Mumbai and one in Chennai where churches have actually split up over the issue of the doctrines of the Charismatic movement (SCL, 2006).

Smith and Campos (2005) had similar findings in their study of televangelism in Guatemala and Brazil:

The technologisation of evangelism has had a profound impact on the content of the Christian message in Latin America. Religious faith and especially conversion are enormously complex phenomena. However television demands simple messages. Thus, the earliest producers of evangelistic messages for the electronic media came to conceive of religious conversion in simplified, individualistic terms as demanded by the principles of marketing...

The great innovation of the Neo-Pentecostal media preachers has been to simplify the message even further, eliminating doctrine and reducing the message to a commercial transaction of symbolic goods. They have deepened and more effectively individualized the emotive content of religious television. 'Do you want hope? Do you long for forgiveness...Do you need healing, wealth, power? Demonstrate your faith by entrusting your offering to me...I give you this symbol of the sacred...Use the sacred substance...God will liberate you...and resolve your problems'. (Smith and Campos, 2005: 60–61)

The practice of being 'slain in the Spirit' was identified as one of the over-emphasised techniques that has led to the superficiality of the preaching. An experience conveyed by one of the senior Christian leaders of a Charismatic gathering in Mumbai, which had attracted many young people, whereby a Muslim young man went forward at the end of the service and started falling backwards even before the Pastor's hands were laid on him. A Christian who brought the Muslim to the church reported that when asked why he fell back so easily, the Muslim youth replied: 'I saw on TV that when they place their hands you have to fall back.' The senior leader explained '...in other words, the Muslim youth's experience was a learned response picked up through his viewing of television...' (SCL, 2006).

Thirty per cent of non-Charismatic pastors said they were grieved by the way the gospel had been commercialised. The pastors referred to the marketing and 'worldly techniques' that are used as well as the 'overuse of advertising and the repeated sale of products very much like commercial TV programmes' (SCL, 2006).

4. Popular expectations

Popular expectations on the part of the congregation in preaching, worship and church administration was yet another way in which the local church had been affected. A senior leader mentioned that local pastors were constantly being compared 'to the superstars on TV and this puts considerable pressure not only in our preaching but in the entire way we administer the Church and even the philosophy of the Church' (SCL, 2006).

This problem is similar to what the American church faced when televangelism was introduced into the USA:

> ...televangelism's popular religiosity has seriously challenged the traditional, institutional and denominational church.... Televangelism has created popular expectations that have forced many pastors and denominational prelates to change the ways their churches are organised and the ways church life is practiced. Televangelism has helped introduce to congregations such things as entertainment-oriented worship, charismatic preaching individualistic thinking and anonymous attendance... (Schultze, 1989: 204–205)

Thirteen per cent of pastors of non-Charismatic background listed superficial content as a negative aspect of Charismatic televangelism. Further analysis revealed that this was a reference to the 'dumbing down of the truths of the gospel...by simplistic teachings that are an embarrassment to the historic teachings of evangelicalism...' (SCL, 2006). Instant healing, individualistic blessings, prosperity are all taught in a topical fashion, 'using a series of proof texts, sometimes without due consideration to the overall context of the biblical passages...' (SCL, 2006).

Culturally appropriate issues

Thirteen per cent of non-Charismatic pastors identified traditional songs used in Charismatic programmes as culturally appropriate. These songs comprised traditional hymns (English) as well as traditional songs played with Indian instruments. Only 7 per cent of Charismatic pastors identified traditional songs as culturally appropriate. Five of the senior Christian leaders explained this finding by pointing out that there was 'paradigm shift in the whole approach to preaching and worship' which the Charismatic movement has introduced (SCL, 2006). This has also 'somewhat influenced the rest of the evangelical Church'. The preaching has become more 'experience-based and the worship more contemporary and loud with choruses taking over traditional hymns' (SCL, 2006). Therefore, for the Charismatic pastors, traditional songs are a thing of the past and contemporary songs are the measure of a good worship service. This explains why only 7 per cent of Charismatic pastors saw traditional songs as culturally appropriate.

A senior Christian leader explained further that 'Charismatic culture takes precedence over the culture of the community...that is why there is a core group of similarities in the Charismatic movement and the worship whether in USA, India or Brazil...' (SCL, 2006).

'Identification with people' was registered by 13 per cent of Charismatic pastors and 7 per cent of non-Charismatic pastors (Table 6.9). This, according to the majority of middle level pastors and the senior Christian leaders, is the ability of the programmes to connect with the audiences. Some examples of the ability to connect are: contemporary music for the youth, prayers especially for healing, messages that speak to the fears and aspirations of people and uplifting testimonies shared by pastors and teachers (SCL, 2006).

Table 6.9: Culturally appropriate issues

	Charismatic pastors N = 30	Non-Charismatic pastors N = 30
Traditional songs	7%	13%
Identification with people	13%	7%
Not answered/not known	80%	80%

Source: Author.

It is noteworthy that 80 per cent of respondents from both Charismatic and non-Charismatic persuasions did not answer or could not name specific aspects of culturally appropriate issues in Charismatic televangelism. Three of the senior Christian leaders and two specialist Christian leaders attributed this to the fact that there are more examples pertaining to culturally inappropriate issues than culturally appropriate issues. However, the leaders were also quick to add that this does not necessarily mean that there are no further examples of culturally appropriate elements. They advised that the way to get around this silence is to get pastors to actually view footage of a specific programme and get them to respond to appropriate and inappropriate elements in the particular programme. This method of eliciting specific responses was used in the section on 'glocal televangelism' in this chapter and in Chapter 7 as well.

Culturally inappropriate issues

Under the aspect of 'what was culturally inappropriate' in Charismatic televangelism, strong views were expressed in the areas of dress code, liberal trends and the perceived overemphasis on fundraising.

Further research and analysis revealed that 'dress code' refers to females wearing short skirts and low-cut tops as well as males being 'overly casual' in their dress. A combined total of 54 per cent (of Charismatic and non-Charismatic pastors) felt that the dress code portrayed on Charismatic televangelism was inappropriate, whereas 27 per cent of Charismatic pastors described 'liberal trends' as inappropriate (Table 6.10). The editor of an evangelical magazine in Mumbai confirmed the conservative nature of Indian Christians even in a media-savvy city like Mumbai. He reported that he receives many negative letters to the editor over the issue of dress code on Christian television. Senior Christian leaders also felt that there should be more adherences to the Indian culture with regard to dress code: '... Televangelists should change from wearing suits and ties to Indian-style clothing so as to be more connected with our culture' (SCL, 2006).

Table 6.10:   Culturally inappropriate issues

	Charismatic pastors N = 30	Non-Charismatic pastors N = 30
Dress code	27%	27%
Liberal trends among youth	27%	–
Western, commercial style of presentation	–	10%
Overemphasis on fundraising	13%	35%
Western songs	–	7%
Use of Hindi cinema tunes	–	7%
Political messages	9%	9%
Anti Hindu and Muslim rhetoric	7%	8%
Not answered/not known	17%	–

Source: Author.

'Liberal trends' refer to dancing during worship, somewhat like a rock concert, lavish sets where the broadcasts are taped and depiction of Western-style churches. A well-known senior Christian leader commented that Indian Christians are not comfortable with the blending of the sacred and the secular entertainment aspects of televangelism as 'it seems to take away the reverence and awe of Christian worship' (SCL, 2006). The Manager of India's leading Christian Music outlet confirmed some of these findings when he revealed that Australia's Hillsong Music, although a hit in many Asian countries like Singapore, is not catching on in India. This could be due to the 'rock concert' flavour of Hillsong. In contrast to this, The Gaither Vocal Band, a conservative hymn-singing American group, is currently leading the sales figures for Christian music in India (KI, 2006).

Thirteen per cent of non-Charismatic pastors described the Western and commercial style of presentation as inappropriate. Further analysis revealed that these concerns were based on the fact that the gospel is presented in the English language (Western) through Westerners, in Western song and dance. These all portray to Hindus, especially in northern India (where people are more conservative), a foreign religion that is not really suitable for India.

The overemphasis on fundraising was deemed inappropriate by 35 per cent of non-Charismatic pastors and 13 per cent of Charismatic pastors. It is significant that a total of 48 per cent of pastors from both persuasions listed fundraising on Charismatic television as inappropriate. It is also significant that the issue of fundraising was raised again in connection with the negative aspects of Charismatic televangelism.

Western songs and Hindi cinema tunes (7 per cent) were identified as inappropriate by non-Charismatic pastors. Discussion on this topic ensued with senior Christian leaders, the majority of whom agreed that there is a large group of conservative Christian who associate Hindi movies and 'going to the cinema' as taboo and so for Charismatic televangelists incorporating Hindi cinema tunes (albeit sung with Christian lyrics) into their programmes is considered 'quite outrageous by many conservative Christian families' (SCL, 2006). *Miraclenet*'s Director, an American by the name of Michael Hughes is married to a south Indian woman. During one of the programmes, Hughes' Indian wife sits on an elephant and sings Christian songs according to the most contemporary Bollywood cinema tunes. One of the senior leaders commented on this, saying '...for the Americans this may be great fun but for us it is a form of mockery...' (SCL, 2006). Thomas and Mitchell (2005) confirm these attitudes about the cinema in their own study of television in Mar Thoma Christian homes:

> Once I entered college in a nearby town, it was an adventure to go to the cinema since it was done without the knowledge not only of parents, relatives or neighbours but also of anyone who might know me from my church. Watching film was not an acceptable practice for a good Marthomite. Even today it would be a scandal if a priest or bishop was seen to have gone to a cinema or theatre in Kerala...

> Despite the similarity of television and cinema as audiovisual media Marthomites have divergent dispositions towards them. Cinema continues to evoke shame, fear and apprehension whereas television evokes confidence, enjoyment and prestige. (Thomas and Mitchell, 2005: 30, 36)

Nine per cent of Charismatic pastors and 9 per cent of non-Charismatic pastors mentioned that the political messages in certain Charismatic programmes were culturally inappropriate. One of the middle-level pastors expressed his disdain when the founder of the *God TV*, an Englishman, together with an interview guest prayed for President Bush at the start of the Iraqi war. The pastor's comment was 'they are meant to be Christian pastors and instead of praying for peace...they were praying for war and taking sides with USA and the coalition of Western nations...'. Senior Christian leaders commenting on this finding said, that the association of politics and Charismatic Christianity is most unfortunate '...and really we cannot adequately explain this position to the Indian Christian population let alone the Hindu community' (SCL, 2006).

Four of the senior Christian leaders mentioned the case of Pat Robertson of CBN's *700 Club* who virtually did the same thing—praying for the success of the American-led wars. The leaders felt that such practices have really widened the rift between Christianity and the Hindu community in India.

Seven per cent of Charismatic pastors and 9 per cent of non-Charismatic pastors made strong references to the anti-Hindu and anti-Muslim rhetoric of certain Charismatic televangelists. The example was given of Pat Robertson's denigrating references to Hinduism on TV—so much so that fundamentalist Hindu groups have placed Robertson on the infamous 'Hindu hit-list' (SCL, 2006).

Leslie (2003) in a case study based on a framing analysis of the CBN programme *700 Club* found the following:

> On 5/27, a news story titled 'Saudi's Deport Christians' reported that two Philippine Christians were deported when a Bible and Christian music were found in their houses. The 'Christians Persecuted' story on 8/8 told of a Jihad terrorist striking in Indonesia. The 'Muslim warriors' attacked a Christian community. Indeed the 700 Club maintains an anti-Muslim stance almost consistently whenever Islam or Muslims are invoked. (Leslie, 2003: 11)

As one might expect, Charismatic televangelism is influencing the Charismatic pastors more positively than the non-Charismatic pastors in urban India. However, both Charismatics and non-Charismatic pastors have strong reservations about the following: fundraising and cultural issues such as dress code and Western practices and ideas. The way the Christian message is packaged in certain Western cultural ways seems to be a real hindrance to its overall effectiveness, creating tensions within the church community in India. These tensions in global Charismatic televangelism have led some groups to consider more localised and culture-specific television productions. The results of a study on CBN's glocal televangelism production, *Solutions* are now examined.

Glocal Charismatic Televangelism

In this section, I use a case study to examine CBN's *Solutions* programme. *Solutions* is a hybrid production, which combines the use of American funding and technology with local Indian production and acting talent.

Is *Solutions* a culturally appropriate localised Indian programme or is it creating a disjunction and being perceived more like what I term 'Masala McGospel' (a fusion of the American gospel with some aspects of Indian culture)?

Historical sketch of CBN India

Christian Broadcasting Network Inc (CBN), headquartered in Virginia Beach USA, is the televangelistic ministry started by Pat Robertson in 1970. According to the CBN website, its mission is:

> ...to present the world with the Gospel message. It partners with other ministries and organizations in strategic use of mass media for spreading the message in a culturally relevant manner throughout the world, training leaders in Biblical principles, and discipling the millions who come to Christ. In addition, through its strategic partnership with Operation Blessing International, human suffering is alleviated through relief efforts, water wells and cisterns, free medical care, micro-enterprise, and lifeskill programmes. Innovation, excellence, and integrity are the principal [sic] guiding values in these tasks. (CBN, n.d.: para 2)

In November 1997 the *700 Club*, a magazine-type TV programme produced by CBN, premiered in India. Today, CBN has its own local office and broadcast facility in India (CBN India) and its programmes are telecast on several Indian cable channels—*Zee Music*, *Zee English*, *Zee Cinema*, *God TV*, *Jaya* TV and *Maa* TV. CBN International India telecasts programmes in the following languages to cater for India's multi-linguistic population: English, Hindi, Tamil and Telegu. Initially only English programmes produced in USA were aired like the *700 Club*, but in the 1980s specific and localised programmes were introduced for the Indian audience. One of the most successful locally produced English programmes is *Solutions*, a half-hour programme aired weekly 'reaching one million people every month with a message of hope' (CBN India, n.d.: paras 2–3). It is shown on both secular and Christian stations, mostly during prime time (Periasamy, 2006: interview).

According to the promotional material on CBN's website, *Solutions* is a programme that:

> …consists of actual testimonies of how lives have been transformed by the Lord Jesus Christ… The programme also includes the humanitarian activities of CBN International India touching lives through medical camps, ministries to street children, and provision of drinking water. To support the vast response from viewers of *Solutions*, our call center provides professional counselling and prayer for those who call our toll free number. With fifteen call stations, we attend to more than five thousand calls per month. Our counsellors are spirit-filled and sensitive to the physical and spiritual needs of the callers… *Solutions* is also produced in Hindi, Tamil and Telegu. (CBN India, n.d.: para 4)

CBN India is registered as a business corporation in India and is contracted by CBN International to produce programmes for India. As such there are US directors on the board of CBN India, which has a staff of around 140 Indian employees. Hundred per cent of the funding cur-rently comes from the USA, although CBN India is also encouraged to raise local funds for its humanitarian arm *Operation Blessing* which is registered as a non-government organisation with a local board (Periasamy, 2006: interview).

Content analysis of solutions

Episode number three of *Solutions*, a novel televangelistic programme with a magazine format, was analysed (see Table 6.11). The entire programme was approximately 27 minutes long, with the bulk of the time allocated to the story of a Hindu lady named Nila, a widow who 'turned to Christ' after her husband passed away in a car crash. The story of Nila is narrated in a professional news documentary style. Soon after the story the compere, Shekar Kallianpur (a pastor

Table 6.11: Content analysis of Solutions—episode 3

Segment	Description	Key statements	Time (in minutes)
Introduction	Compere at studio set	'Welcome to *Solutions* …'	2
Mini documentary of *Operation Blessing* in Afghanistan and fundraising	Story of schoolgirl helped by CBN India	'Your gifts have helped a school girl in Afghanistan'	4½
Promo of *Solutions*	A dialogue between two people	'Call us, our counsellors are waiting'	2½
Compere introduces main story	Compere at studio set	'The Bible has a definition of true religion … visit widows …'	1½
Interview of young people in city centres	Roving reporter fields questions	'Would you marry a widow?'	3
Story of Nila the widow	Documentary style story	'I was so down I prayed to Jesus'	7½
Compere closes the story	Compere at studio set	'Jesus is the only one who could help Nila'	3½
Closing comments	Compere at studio set	'Call our Counsellors'	2½
TOTAL TIME			**27**

Source: Author.

of a Mumbai Charismatic Church), shares the gospel message and invites people to turn to Christ because Christ accepts the rejected of society. Nila's story is preceded by interviews of young people in large cities. They are asked: 'How does society treat widows?' The men are asked, 'Would you marry a widow?' Eight out of ten men say 'No'. This lead-up to the story is significant as it establishes the point that widows are stigmatised in Indian society.

The other major time slot is devoted to a segment of CBN's relief work in Afghanistan after the fall of the Taliban. It shows CBN's India director, Kumar Periasamy, in action in Afghanistan. It basically informs the audience of the social and relief arm of CBN *Operation Blessing*. In a dramatic way, it zeroes in on how CBN's development work in an Afghanistan village has helped one school girl who otherwise would not have had basic schooling.

Results of Findings on the Impact of *Solutions*

Eighty-five per cent of the Christian leaders felt that the production quality was good, with 10 per cent stating it was excellent. Only 5 per cent thought that it needed improvement, specifically in the areas of photography and lighting.

Approximately 65 per cent of the respondents felt the programme was 'culturally appropriate' to the Indian context, whereas 35 per cent felt there were features in the programme that were definitely inappropriate to India. When the pastors were asked what was culturally appropriate, nearly 60 per cent listed the following items: the compere, Indian music, content and the style of presentation (Table 6.12). The compere, an Indian man wearing Indian clothes, related well to the audience. Another feature of the programme that was deemed culturally appropriate was the choice of the story/testimony of the widow. Most of the pastors felt this was a culturally relevant issue in India and therefore the subject of widows in the programme would touch the hearts of the Indian community. In short, to quote one Christian leader, the programme involved 'Indian people involved in an Indian problem handled as much as possible in an Indian way' (SCL, 2005).

Even though only 40 per cent felt there were features in the programme that were culturally inappropriate, the sentiments they expressed were very strongly and convincingly worded. First, the issue of dress

Table 6.12: Culturally appropriate and inappropriate elements in
***Solutions*—Christian leaders**

Appropriate	Inappropriate
Indian compere dressed in Indian clothes	Style of production: programme divided into segments
Story of Indian widow	Western dress code
Some Indian music	Western music
Gentle style of presentation	Western ways of relating and communicating
	Compere in a luxurious studio setting
	Incomplete gospel presentation: 'Jesus is my husband'
	Taliban (Afghanistan) mini documentary

Source: Author.

code was addressed. Before the story of the widow was presented, reporters were fielding questions from the public about the plight of widows and posed the question: would a man marry a widow in India today? Several pastors felt some of the girls and women folk interviewed were 'scantily dressed with short pants and short skirts', which is offensive to Indian Christians (SCL, 2005). It was also pointed out that the compere, although dressed in Indian clothes, was in luxurious surroundings and this is contrary to how pastors live in India. In other words, the pastor in the TV programme was portrayed as an American or British pastor rather than a local pastor. The Western clothes, luxurious setting and some of the trendy Western idioms and words reflect a foreign Western identity. This sentiment concurs with Moorti's research findings on TV game shows in India:

> While in the West the clothes that the men wear may signify being very casual, within the Indian context these items serve as markers of distinction...Women appearing in many of the national programmes and especially on music-related shows are very fashionable and scantily clad. They signify a cultural and symbolic capital that is still available to only a limited slice of the population. (Moorti, 2004: 556)

Three of the leaders felt that there are two levels of communication: on the first level, the Christian message is explained; on the second level, a message of Western cultural superiority is implied. This may cause young people and the rising middle class to aspire more and more towards Western ways of living.

Production and music was the second issue. The whole programme was 'too slick' according to one of the pastors. 'The half hour show was divided into too many segments and it was hard to follow' was another response (SCL, 2005). The fast-paced cuts and quick transitions from one scenario to another can be quite confusing to many Indians who are not accustomed to the Western mode of television production. For nearly 40 years, American pre-schoolers have been raised on a television diet of *Sesame Street*, which trained a whole generation to learn 'through the jazzy techniques of...quick cuts, animation, humour' (Hymovitz, 1995: para 7). It is significant that the creator of *Sesame Street*, Joan Ganz Cooney, initially used the television advertisement or commercial as the model for *Sesame Street* and then went on to incorporate all of television's formats: 'Its shows are an encyclopaedia of TV forms; minute-long soap operas with soppy organ music to teach the importance of trees,...Imitation of MTV videos, sitcoms, talk shows, TV award ceremonies—you name it...' (Hymovitz, 1995: para 6).

Solutions uses many of these production techniques from the USA, as they are now part of the standard production procedures; however, Indian audiences may take a while to get used to them. Hence, this is a clear example of the medium not being properly formatted to the Indian mindset. One of the leaders likened this to Indian pastors who go overseas to undertake seminary training and then return to India and preach 'three point sermons', an approach which is different from the 'cyclical' approach to traditional Indian preaching (SCL, 2005). According to this leader, those who communicate the faith to audiences, whether in Church or on TV, need to use culturally-sensitive techniques of communication.

One pastor lamented over the fact that, although it was an Indian story, they used 'Western music too liberally' rather than 'sticking to Indian music' (SCL, 2005). Indian culture was mentioned next. The whole atmosphere and style of the interview was quite foreign to the Indian context. 'Men and women do not sit next to each other and talk so freely' commented one pastor. It was mentioned that even today in a majority of Indian churches the women sit in separate sections of the Church during services. Therefore, to place the Christian message 'sandwiched between these foreign cultural values seems to jar my sensibilities' the pastor continued (SCL, 2005). Two other pastors agreed with this comment and added that Indian Christians and the general public were still very conservative and these subtle points need to be taken very seriously by Christian broadcasters.

Another pastor commented that the way the *Solutions* programme asked young people for their opinions was also quite foreign to the Indian culture where the parents, elders and leaders were the decision makers in the community.

The last item that was not culturally appropriate was the story of the plight of the people in Afghanistan and CBN's relief work there. The situation in Afghanistan was too removed for people in India to respond to, especially in the area of giving their funds. If this was an Indian relief operation, it might have been more acceptable. As this was an evangelistic programme geared to non-believers, many of the pastors felt that the fundraising aspect should have been omitted as viewers would have misunderstood its motives.

The pastors also felt that theologically the programme fell short in certain basic ways. For example, around 50 per cent of the pastors pointed out that after the widow story, an attempt was made to encourage people to turn to Christ. The compere 'was too rushed', the pastors felt and did not lead the audience to understand the implications of this significant and decisive act (SCL, 2005). Furthermore, there was no 'sinner's prayer' (a prayer traditionally used by Churches where the non-believer 'asks Jesus into his/her heart'). Other pastors pointed out that a simplistic evangelistic approach was used. Yet other pastors criticised the way the widow expressed 'Jesus is now my husband', which 'reduced the Lord Jesus to a product on offer to lonely widows very similar to Charismatic televangelists who say "come to Jesus and you will be healed"' (SCL, 2005).

When asked how their church members would respond to *Solutions*, 60 per cent of the pastors said that their members would respond positively. To support this view, pastors said the presentation was non-confrontive, gentle and it stimulated fresh thinking amongst Christians with regard to evangelism. The remaining 40 per cent said that there was danger in this kind of simplistic gospel presentation and continual exposure to these programmes would make it difficult for Christians to discern the true gospel and the evangelical doctrines of Christianity.

When asked how Hindus in the community would respond, 30 per cent of the pastors said the Hindus would respond positively to this kind of presentation. This is a 'soft sell approach' and therefore quite positive and novel. The pastors estimated that perhaps around 20 per cent of the Hindu community would be open to such presentations and these would be mainly from the middle to lower class economic brackets. Strong sentiments were expressed that many Hindus may still see this as part of the 'conversion agenda' of Christianity:

At least the TV programme may open their eyes [the pastors said], but it is a long road. It is hard for Hindus to go against the strong tide of community influence. Rarely do people come to Christ on the basis of a TV programme like this. (SCL, 2005)

Pastors also added that the unfortunate association with Western ideals, technology and funding needed to produce such programmes would add to the negative response of many Hindus to *Solutions*.

Is this an indigenous or localised programme? Around 45 per cent of respondents said it is indigenous and 55 per cent said it was a hybrid—a fusion of Indian and Western cultures. 'It is two parts Indian and three parts American', said one pastor (SCL, 2005).

What is the best way to reach India with the gospel? The leaders responded that whereas television was a good tool to reinforce the thinking and ideals of people who are already believers, it was not a good evangelistic tool for non-believers. They felt that one-on-one evangelism with pastoral care and nurture was still the best method for evangelising Hindus in India. In many respects these responses tell us a great deal about the mindset of the pastors, which is clearly conservative in its orientation and allows for a number of inferences to be made about the nature of Christianity in contemporary India.

I began the book in Chapter 1 with Stanley Jones' analogy of the women friends of the bride quietly taking leave when they finish their task of accompanying the bride to the bridegroom's house. If *Solutions* is typical of localised televangelism in India, then we can liken this to some of the bride's friends still lingering in the house, at the risk of violating their mores. It would seem that until this situation changes, localised televangelism in India will continue to be described somewhat cynically as 'two parts Indian and three parts American' or 'Masala McGospel'. However, it must be pointed out that from a communicational and missiological point of view, CBN India has set the pace in indigenising its programmes and is poised to be the forerunner of a unique cultural adaptation of the Christian gospel on Indian television.

The foregoing chapter sought to examine the impact of Charismatic televangelism on the Protestant Church in urban India. In the main global Charismatic televangelism is more appealing to Charismatic Church leaders, although both Charismatic and non-Charismatic pastors have pointed out the serious tensions created by this phenomenon in the Protestant Church in India, especially in the areas of culture, dress code and fundraising.

The findings of the impact of 'glocal' televangelism, in the form of a case study of CBN's *Solutions* programme, were also reported. 'Glocal' televangelism, according to the majority of pastors was truly a 'breath of fresh air', compared to global televangelism. However, the pastors pointed out that, on the whole both the message and the underlying elements behind the message still contained culturally inappropriate issues. In essence it was found that the hybrid nature of *Solutions* is creating a disjunction of meaning and understanding in the minds of both Charismatic and non-Charismatic pastors.

This paves the way for the next chapter, where the views and opinions of Hindu community leaders are explored with respect to global and 'glocal' televangelism.

Chapter 7

Interpreting Charismatic Televangelism: Hindu Leaders and the Contested Nation

Amerian recording artist Ray Stevens (1987) sings a song about televangelists entitled *Would Jesus Wear a Rolex*:[1]

Woke up this mornin' turned on my TV set
There in livin' color was somethin' I can't forget
This man was preaching' at me..yeah..layin' on the charm
Asking me for 20 with 10,000 on his arm

He wore designer clothing and a big smile on his face
Selling me salvation while they sang Amazing Grace
Asking me for money when he had all the signs of wealth
Almost wrote a check out… yeah…then I asked myself

Would He wear a pinky ring, would he drive a fancy car
Would His wife wear furs and diamonds, would His dressing room
have a star
If he came back tomorrow there's something I'd like to know
Would Jesus wear a rolex on His television show

Would Jesus be political if he came back to earth
Have his second home in Palm Springs .. yeah .. but try to hide his
worth
Take money from those poor folks when He comes back again
And admit He's talked to all those preachers who said they beenatalking
to Him

Would He wear a pinky ring, would he drive a fancy car
Would His wife wear furs and diamonds, would His dressing room
have a star
If he came back tomorrow there's something I'd like to know
Could ya tell me Would Jesus wear a rolex

Would Jesus wear a rolex
Would Jesus wear a rolex on His television show

If Americans find their own televangelists disconcerting, how would the Hindu community in India respond to US televangelists on Indian TV?

Whereas the previous chapter examined the influence of Charismatic televangelism on the Protestant Church in urban India, this chapter will examine the influence of Charismatic televangelism on the Hindu community in urban India. Thirty respondents, Hindu community leaders, were drawn from various city temples, Hindu organisations and institutions in Mumbai and Hyderabad. Originally, I planned on including Muslim leaders as research participants. However, very few Muslim leaders showed interest and only two leaders attended the first research meeting. Therefore, I abandoned the plan and concentrated on Hindu and Christian pastors. I have recorded in the study, some of the responses of the Muslim leaders, wherever it was deemed appropriate.

The responses of these leaders were shared with senior Christian leaders and some key informants for cross-checking, dialogue and further comments. As stated in the previous chapter, respondents are identified in the text as: MLP—Middle-Level Pastor/s; SCL—Senior Christian Leader/s; KI—Key Informant/s; HL—Hindu Leader/s and ML—Muslim Leader/s.

The chapter is divided into three parts: the impact of global Charismatic televangelism, the impact of 'glocal' Charismatic televangelism and a summary of the significant findings.

Global Televangelism and the Hindu Community

Cox (1973) shares his experience while in the poverty-stricken city of Recife in Brazil. The children switched on the TV and the programme *The Flintstones* was featured:

In the United States, mired in...a consumer culture, insulated in a thousand ways from our own people's poverty, the Flintstones on TV seem like one tiny insult among others...In Recife, on the other hand, surrounded by sickness, hunger and hopelessness, the humour seemed obscene, a mortal trespass... (Cox, 1973: 302)

Australian academic Shoesmith (2004) recalls a similar situation when he was in India and saw several American televangelists on various Indian TV channels. He wondered what the social impact of this new trend would be on a conservative nation with a large Hindu population.

The following results are based on qualitative interviews that were conducted with 35 Hindu community leaders, 20 senior Christian leaders and key informants between the years 2005 to 2006. The results are recorded in this order: restraints to cable access, cultural resistance, gender and dress code, Hindu and Muslims perceptions, the politics of culture and conversion and cultural acceptance.

Restraints to cable access

A key informant disclosed that although global television programmes from the *God TV* and *Miraclenet* are available in India, Hindu nationalist groups (which follow the *Hindutva* agenda of a Hindu India) such as the Rashtriya Swayamsevak Sangh (RSS) have put pressure on cable operators not to carry Christian programmes in many states like Madhya Pradesh, Bihar and Uttar Pradesh, traditionally known as the 'Hindu belt'. However, people who had installed private satellite dishes in their homes were able to receive these programmes (KI, 2006).

Two of the Christian leaders in Mumbai reiterated that access is a problem in certain Hindu states, but added that even in the suburbs of Mumbai access to Christian channels and other secular channels may occasionally stop without notice as cable operators 'are, by and large notorious for changing the programme and price schedules randomly' (SCL, 2006).

In Madhya Pradesh (MP) the cable channels are owned by people with RSS leanings and so Christian Channels are not accessed (KI, 2006). Joyce Meyer is heard on other secular channels but the 'general attitude in MP and other parts of North India is anti-Christian and so very few people watch Christian programmes' (KI, 2006). The same informant disclosed that when *The Life of Christ* was shown some years ago on *Doordarshan* TV '...quite a few Hindus watched this...Hindus do not mind stories of the life of Christ...but they generally do not watch Christian sermons on TV' (KI, 2006). As already mentioned in Chapter 5, Phalke, the father of Indian cinematography was greatly influenced by the film *The Life of Christ*, not in the way of Christian devotion, but in the way of his prolific productions of Hindu movies about the life of Hindu gods. Thus, this strange interplay between Christianity and Hinduism is not without historical precedent.

Cultural restraints

In answer to the question, 'What is your response to Christian tele-vangelism?', one of the Hindu leaders mentioned that there are funda-mental differences between Hinduism and Christianity:

> Hinduism is not a 'closed' religion like Christianity or Islam in the sense that they require the adherents to constrain themselves to only one faith...there is no dogma in Hinduism that says 'my religion is truth and others are evil'. Because of this, evangelism does not make sense in our Hinduism faith. (HL, 2006)

So then, Xians that support this belief are things more Hindu than Xian?

Another Hindu leader agreed with this view and added '...that is why we (Hindus) do not stress about our own Hindu "evangelism" and why we find Christian evangelism and televangelism offensive' (HL, 2006). According to another Hindu leader, a further difference be-tween Hinduism and Christianity is the view of spiritual evolution:

> Hindus believe that everyone has an *athma* (inner true self). Thus, depending on our stage of evolution, we understand spiritual matters differently. Hinduism does not provide a fixed path for people to follow...rather we believe there are many *margs* (paths) to the same goal. For example, there are different ways of Yoga that one can practice: *Karma Yoga* (path of action and service); *Gnana Yoga* (path of knowledge); *Bakthi Yoga* (path of devotion) and others...

> Because of our view of spiritual evolution, Hindus leave other indi-viduals to choose their own *marg* (path) based on their spiritual stage...we do not propagate one single system. (HL, 2006)

Two of the Hindu leaders shared their concern that Christian televangelists 'are using television to condemn our culture and our religion' (HL, 2006). One of them reported that he read in a publication that Pat Robertson, the founder of the *700 Club*, had made derogatory remarks about Hinduism on his *700 Club* TV programme. The article he was referring to, from *Hinduism Today*, gave the following details of the programme in question:

> It's not that unusual for Pat Robertson's daily Christian TV show, the *700 Club*, to portray other religions in less than complimentary light. Jews, Muslims and occasionally Hindus are singled out for a scathing recounting of their spiritual errors. Still, I was shocked to see Robertson on his March 23rd show label Hinduism as 'demonic' and advocate keeping Hindus out of America. My concerns intensified when President Clinton later implicated hateful talk in the hateful Oklahoma City bombing.
>
> Robertson was already a well-known figure in the conservative Christian community when his 1988 bid for the US presidency shot him into national attention and effectively anointed him leader of the Christian right wing. Talented and industrious, he is head or founder of numerous organizations, including a 1,400 student university. (Rajan, 1995: paras 1–2)

In answer to the question: 'Who is watching Christian televangelism?', a Hindu leader said '…conservative Hindus do not watch Christian television. They are not interested in Christian sermons and Charismatic messages' (HL, 2006). It was estimated by Hindu leaders from two well-known Hindu organisations that approximately 20–25 per cent of India's Hindu population would be in the conservative category. These Hindus would resist the religious flows of Charismatic televangelism because of their strong devotion to Hindu Gods and beliefs, as well as the very strong supportive network of family and friends. They also reported that the sense of belonging is strong among conservative Hindus and associated with this are the emotions of honour and shame, which seem to keep the conservative Hindus rather intact as a community (HL, 2006). According to the two Hindu leaders, most of this 20–25 per cent of Hindus would also be members of the high caste (HL, 2006). As pointed out in Chapter 4 the 'high caste' refers to the Brahmins, the intellectual and priestly caste who are top in the hierarchy, followed by the Kshatriyas, the Vaishyas and the Shudras.

Other groups of resistant people among the Hindus, according to two Hindu leaders and verified by the majority of Christian leaders, are those belonging to the upper middle and high class. These are the Hindus who would have a monthly earning capacity of approximately Rs 15,000 (US$ 275) and above (HL, 2006; SCL, 2006). The writings of Indian ecumenical Christian leader, M. M. Thomas (1996: 44) and veteran American missionary, Jones (1925: 17–18), indicate that historically Christian conversions took place among the middle to lower classes of Hindus and especially the low castes who saw conversion as a 'liberation from caste oppression'.

Two of the senior Christian leaders, while agreeing with the 20–25 per cent resistant Hindu figure, gave evidence of a few individuals from this group who, because of crises such as illness, unemployment and financial loss might become more open to the Christian message through televangelists.

According to one senior Christian leader, a well-known Bollywood actor, Dev Anand was reported to have said: 'thank God that Benny Hinn came to Bombay'; this was said soon after Hinn's mega meeting in Mumbai. Another senior Christian leader added this disclaimer about the statement:

> I too heard Benny Hinn in Bombay and it is not hard to explain why Dev Anand gave such a commendation—Benny Hinn only preached Jesus the healer,...he did not mention Jesus the saviour and so both Hindus and Muslims found him acceptable. (SCL, 2006)

The leader continued 'quite a few in this category of so-called resistant people may watch televangelists but it does not mean they accept the Christian faith in toto' (SCL, 2006).

A female Hindu leader shared insights about the family and societal pressures in Hindu society: 'Conversion to Christianity is resisted primarily because of the strong family bonds' (HL, 2006). Recalling the experience of her sister, the Hindu leader talked about how, over a period of time 'she [sister] was lost to Christianity as she went to Porta (Catholic) Church for miracles' (HL, 2006). The leader mentioned that her sister who now 'does not go to the temple, put ash on her forehead or light lamps' is ostracised by her family and the community (HL, 2006).

When told that 85 per cent of the global Charismatic programmes were in the English language, three of the Hindu leaders who served previously in north India said this puts a lot of the Indians off especially in the northern part of India where English is not so widely used. One of the leaders added '...in a cosmopolitan city like Mumbai, even though many people speak English they would rather watch their own Hindi or vernacular programmes like movies, news or music video shows...than the English programmes...' (HL, 2006).

Eighty per cent of the Christian leaders agreed with this comment pointing out that it is quite typical of most mainline denominational churches to have up to seven–eight services in various languages every Sunday besides the English service. These vernacular services, they added, are very well attended (SCL, 2006).

One of the senior Christian leaders remarked that even though there are many English speakers in India, from his experience many Indians may not be able to follow the accents, the colloquial expressions and humorous anecdotes used by the global televangelists (SCL, 2006).

A conservative Hindu leader, the head of the Arya Samaj group, when asked how many people in his flock of 75,000 followers in Mumbai city would watch Christian televangelism, answered: 'According to my knowledge none' (HL, 2006). The Arya Samaj which came into being, primarily through the influence of colonial Christianity is a minority Hindu sect in India. It is important to point out that, as the principal researcher, I was almost denied an audience with this leader because of the fact that I was a foreigner from Australia. When told by the local research assistant that I had an Indian background, the leader then asked 'Can he speak Hindi?' The fact that I did not speak Hindi did not help and almost meant the loss of the interview, had it not been for the persuasiveness of my research assistant.

When I arrived at the huge headquarters of the reform movement, I was aware of the fact that both the research assistant and I were the only ones dressed in Western clothes. There was a half an hour wait for the leader and while waiting I saw something of what goes on in this sectarian community. Pre-schoolers were in one part of the building, young mothers were in a yoga session with a female yoga instructor and young men were in another room listening to a religious talk. It dawned on me that even though the research assistant and I were of Indian background, there was a huge cultural divide between us and the followers of the Arya Samaj movement because of the fact that we were dressed differently, we spoke English and we were not members of this sectarian Hindu group.

The leader of the Arya Samaj, Randher, asserted that the cultural differences in Christian television would not appeal to his flock of 75,000 families in Mumbai. In explaining this point he added '...in our culture we are vegetarians, our dress code is different, our way of thinking is different...so when we see Western culture portrayed [on TV] it is offensive and not acceptable' (HL, 2006). Furthermore, the leader claimed that 'the Arya Samaj is not a religious group but a group to protect the culture of India from deterioration as it is exposed to the influences of Jainism, Buddhism, and other religions' (HL, 2006).

When asked what his advice would be if a follower of the group talked to him about Christian television, the leader said it would be for the person to stop watching it because 'our people do not have idols ...they are vegetarian and they do not smoke or drink...they practice yoga...our people are not attracted to televangelism' (HL, 2006).

The leader added that most of the people in his group are aspiring to attain to the high caste status or are in the high caste already. Randher informed us that he himself was born into the Kshatriya caste but because of 'good works' he is now a Brahmin, the highest caste. Therefore, there is a strong motivation for the followers of this sect to live a strict, disciplined and almost austere lifestyle so they could move up in the caste hierarchy through good works (HL, 2006). Hence their repulsion to all forms of Westernisation including Christian or Charismatic televangelism as these things stand in the way of the followers' upward move towards the Brahmin caste. This is a classic case of what is referred to as '*sanskritisation*'—a term coined by Srinivas (1952) which refers to the process by which Hindu lower caste members seek upward mobility by emulating the rituals and practices of the upper castes.

Randher, the leader of the *Arya Samaj* reluctantly watched some footage of global Charismatic televangelism in English, and although his English was limited it was interesting that the first thing he pointed out was the lavishness of where the programme was taped—the large church and the 'rich clothing' worn by the televangelist. Randher reacted negatively to these and asserted that his followers would be repulsed by these: '...in our group there is a rule that people should not spend money lavishly for entertainment even for weddings...these are organised as simple ceremonies...We believe the treatment of souls is more important than any of the external things...' (HL, 2006).

⤷ oh, i. only the Church!

Gender and dress code

Gender was another ambivalent issue raised by the Hindu leaders. In contrast to the 85 per cent of televangelists who preach only in English, American female televangelist Joyce Meyer, who is also of the Charismatic persuasion, is heard in seven Indian languages several times a day on Indian television. Meyer's programmes are dubbed into the following languages: Hindi, Tamil, Punjabi, Malayalam,

Marathi, Telegu and Kannada. It is not surprising, therefore, that 100 per cent of the pastors rated Joyce Meyer as the one of the three most popular Charismatic televangelists and 90 per cent of all the women participants from both Christian and Hindu persuasions recognised Joyce Meyer's name (MLP, 2006; HL, 2006). Furthermore, a total of 60 per cent of these female respondents (Christian and Hindu) said they found her programmes helpful and uplifting, with 20 per cent expressing reservations about her lavish settings, expensive wardrobe and casual references to spiritual matters (MLP, 2006; HL, 2006).

A Hindu leader commented that he read in a newspaper article which revealed that when Meyer wore a dress on TV for a programme, chances are people would never see her wear that dress again (HL, 2006). The leader continued:

> [W]hether this is true or not I can't say, but every time I see her [on TV] she seems to be showing off her looks…this creates a bad taste in our Indian culture as the Western woman and Western dress sense are slowly becoming introduced into Indian culture… (HL, 2006)

This sentiment is reflected in Mitra's (1994) findings in a study of gender advertising in the USA and India, which predicts that Western women may soon become the standard of glamour in certain aspects of Indian society especially the youth culture (Mitra, 1994).

A Hindu *Sanyasi*, an itinerant guru, made these interesting comments on the Indian dress code compared to the Western dress code seen on television and even on Christian TV:

> Indian culture has religious significance…dress has religious as well as aesthetic significance. Indian dress demonstrates elegance and simplicity can be easily produced in village shops. The lady's *sari* and the man's *dhoti* are simply pieces of cloth which do not require expensive tailoring. (HL, 2006)

A female Hindu teacher pointed out that clothing for women in Indian society 'emphasises modesty not sexual allurement (like the Western people's dress code) and simple elegance rather than fashion…' (HL, 2006).

Two Hindu leaders pointed out that they felt uncomfortable about the 'Western ways that are added to the Christian gospel' (HL, 2006). One of the leaders referred to a TV show where the husband and wife enjoyed 'an intimate moment' for the first few minutes and then started preaching. The leader said such things are objectionable in the Hindu cultural context and he wondered why local (Indian) Christians do not object to their Western counterparts about these inappropriate actions seen on Indian TV 'under the name of the Christian gospel' (HL, 2006). Through further investigations, I discovered that the TV programme referred to was a global Charismatic programme called *Messenger International* hosted by American preachers John and Lisa Bevere. The same leader went on to say that the wife (Lisa) is the main preacher and her husband (John) is present 'more as a prop' (HL, 2006). Again the leader pointed out that the Christians should do more research on Hindu society before evangelising, as India's culture is primarily a male-dominated one (HL, 2006). Two of the Christian leaders agreed that these aspects of gender do not resonate well in Indian society (SCL, 2006). One of the senior Christian leaders pointed out that there is an increase in female preachers (especially Charismatic) on the three Charismatic TV networks. For example, the latest female televangelist is Pastor Scarlett Scanlon Gambil 'from the Charismatic Abundant Life Ministries from the United Kingdom. She is seen on God TV several times a week...' (SCL, 2006). The senior Christian leader added that there are inappropriate gender issues in Gambil's programme as 'she has female guests sitting closely on the same couch with male guests talking to each other in very intimate conversational fashion, which we would not do in the Indian Christian context' (SCL, 2006).

Another Christian leader added that there is an increase of programmes with 'husband and wife teams' on television like James Robison's programme which features his wife, Betty and 'the wife's name appears first in all the introductions and promotions' (SCL, 2006).

Hindu and Muslim perceptions

Hindu and Muslim perceptions of Christians and Christianity can act as roadblocks to Charismatic televangelism. One of the Hindu leaders asked a rhetorical question which revealed his dilemma about Christian TV:

> Why should I watch Christian TV?...the other day I was flicking through the channels...first there was Fashion TV from the USA which featured near-naked women, then another channel showed an American programme where Christians were dancing as though they were in a nightclub/disco and in another channel I saw an American drama where a couple were in a very intimate lovemaking scene...in another channel there was

an American televangelist wearing an expensive suit preaching about miracles and asking for donations... (HL, 2006)

This sentiment reveals the shape of Hindu perceptions: the West is invariably associated with Christianity. This leader had apparently put all American TV programmes in the same category because they all originated 'from a Christian country' (HL, 2006). In his mind, Fashion TV, MTV and Christian televangelism are one and the same.

When this perception was conveyed to the senior Christian leaders, 100 per cent of them agreed that this is a typical Hindu response. One of the Christian leaders gave the example of a Bollywood movie that depicted a Christian girl: 'The girl wears a mini skirt (something quite abhorrent in Indian society) and she drinks and goes out to parties' (SCL, 2006). This is the 'standard depiction of Christians in the Hindu context ...but not only in the Hindu context...even Muslims see Christians in such stereotypical ways...' (SCL, 2006).

A Muslim leader agreed that Muslim and Hindu perceptions of Christians could be a barrier to Christian televangelism. Many Muslims see Christians as 'wine drinkers, pig eaters and our parents say to us "do not mix with Christians"' (ML, 2006). Some Hindus also see Christians as 'beef eaters' or 'those who go for dances' (HL, 2006). The majority of senior Christian leaders commenting on these responses said that such perceptions are fairly ingrained in many non-Christians and one Christian leader added that when people see worship services on television conducted like rock concerts, with dancing and loud music, 'this simply reinforces the wrong perception that many Hindus and Muslims have of Christians and Christianity' (SCL, 2006). Another Christian leader commented '...the Hillsong TV programme has done harm...as it feeds the Hindu/ Muslim perception of Christians as dancers, drinkers and partygoers' (SCL, 2006).

Tennent (2005) discovered that distorted perceptions and wrong associations refer not only to big issues but even to what may be considered as minor and incidental aspects of culture and faith:

> Hindus, for example view Christians as disrespectful because they keep their shoes on during services of worship. They often look on Christians as culturally foreign because they sit on pews rather then on the floor,

or use Western musical forms rather than bhajans...they simply do not understand why women will no longer wear bangles or participate in popular cultural festivals... (Tennent, 2005: para 3)

Another aspect of perception is the affluence and technological superiority of the West, which means slick Christian programmes are 'being dumped into countries like India. The US have the funds, technology and personnel to invade our airwaves with the Christian teaching...they should spend their money more wisely on doing relief and social work...' (HL, 2006).

A senior Christian leader commenting on this perception said:

[T]he West is associated with wealth...when Westerners are seen with us [locals] in our slum churches or orphanages somehow, the constituency immediately comes to two conclusions—number one we [the local leaders] are getting tons of money from the West...we are paid to make converts for the West and number two—we are doing all this work not because of our genuine love for the people we are serving but because we are employed by the West to do a job... (SCL, 2006)

Another senior Christian leader agreed with the previous comment and added: 'That is why in our mission we are careful not to invite or bring Western visitors to our mission sites...sometimes it is very hard to explain to our prayer partners in Western countries about this sensitive situation...' (SCL, 2006).

A key informant, a Christian leader who works in the 'Hindu belt' maintained that in his 20 years of ministry to Hindu families he had not allowed a single Western visitor to come and see his work '...this is not easy to maintain but I have to stick to my convictions...the minute I allow one [Westerner] to come...my credibility will be lost forever' (KI, 2006).

These views on Hindu perception of Christians add to the growing tensions between Christianity and Hinduism. Christian theologians like Smith (2003) are aware of these challenges:

The tendency of churches to adopt Westernized patterns of behaviour, to worship in ways that suggest that reverence for God is not one of the fruits of the gospel, and to reduce the message of Christ to a religious product, all of this reinforces Muslim [and Hindu] perceptions of Christianity as the religious carrier of a Western secular modernity. (Smith, 2003: 112)

The politics of culture and conversion

One of the Hindu leaders expressed his opinion that televangelism is a 'clever kind of warfare' as it is based on the battle for the minds of people: '...the site of the battlefield is the mind through the airwaves...' (HL, 2006).

When asked to explain this observation, the Hindu leader, a committee member of the RSS said he sees 'televangelism' as a new strategy for Christian propaganda, different from the strategy used by the British in the colonial days, when military technology and commercial know-how was twinned to 'Christianise' India. The leader added that 'the West these days is still making its presence felt in the "independent" countries like India through high-powered satellite technology' (HL, 2006).

The Hindu leader added that he himself is open to televangelism. He went on to say that in his thinking, how people's problems are solved (by Christians or Hindus) is not the issue '...so long as the problem is solved that is the issue' (HL, 2006). However, the leader added, others may not think this way. The Hindu clergy may not accept this and more importantly 'the politicians would find conversions to Christianity problematic and that is the crux of the issue...' (HL, 2006).

A key informant, who agreed with the Hindu leader, stated that it is quite paradoxical that Christians have been persecuted by extremist Hindu groups in the last 10 to 20 years, when India today is a secular, progressive nation, led by members of three minority groups: a Sikh Prime Minister, a Muslim President and an Italian-born Catholic woman as head of the ruling Congress party (KI, 2006). Yet the key informant is aware of the increase in persecution:

> Persecution against non-Hindu minorities has increased since the 1980's when Hindu nationalism was promoted as the agenda of the Bharatiya Janata Party (BJP). In 1998, the BJP won the elections and during their term of office persecution [against Christians] was at its highest level. (KI, 2006)

The BJP believes that previous indigenous movements like Gandhianism, pro-Western modernism and Marxist Communism have failed and will not profit India. Only '*Hindutva*'—the notion of a Hindu theocratic state, can help India: 'Veer Savarkar is considered to be the father ...of Hindutva. Savarkar wrote a book *Hindutva* in

1923... [it] gives [the] historical background to the word "Hindu", explains in detail the idea of Nationalism and establishes Hindutva as a secular form of Bhartiya nationalism' (Bal, 2007).

Even though *Hindutva*'s original perspective was nationalistic, the BJP's current understanding of *Hindutva* is seen more in religious terms. The BJP defines *Hindutva* in terms of 'Indian-ness and Hindu cultural nationalism but it does so in...religious terms' (Hawkins, 2006). The BJP website states that the BJP: 'has nothing against Muslim Indians...But it has no doubt that we were and are a Hindu nation; that change of faith cannot mean change of nationality' (BJP, n.d.). Therefore, Hinduism, a religion is defined as the principal attribute of Indian nationhood. Hiebert (2000) defines *Hindutva* as a:

[T]otalitarian ideology because it aspires to fill the whole space occupied by society and because it seeks to endow individuals with the selfless ideal of total submission (*ekchalak anurvartita*) to the ascetic leader (*pracharak*). It rejects a transcendent God and demands that Indians worship Mother India and make nationalism the source of all other values. (Hiebert, 2000: 54)

Kendal (2007) analyses and delineates the key elements of the *Hindutva* agenda:

1. Hinduise the animist tribal masses through religious conversions and 'reconversions' of Christian groups.
2. Create for political gain, a climate of fear and anger, enough to motivate Hindus to unite against a perceived threat to their security.
3. Promote the idea that Christianity is the greatest threat to national harmony, security and sovereignty.

I was in India in the early part of 2006 when a massive *Kumbh Mela* (a reconversion festival) was organised for some 160,000 people in Gujarat in an effort to bring thousands of Christians (who were allegedly deceived into becoming Christians) back into the fold of Hinduism.

A senior Christian leader commented that the event was openly organised by well-known sister groups of the Hindu BJP party and even the Chief Minister of Gujarat was in attendance because:

Hindus account for 80 per cent of India's population and Christians are less than three per cent of the total population. However 15 per cent of the Dangs [the tribal people of Gujarat] are Christians. The Hindus are concerned about this and they want to 'reconvert' the tribal Christians back to Hinduism. (SCL, 2006)

Virendra Solanki, the organiser of the event, said: 'Dangs have a history of Hindu tribal lords and we will not allow Christian missionaries to continue their programme of converting illiterate, unemployed tribals' (Solanki quoted in Green, 2006: 6).

A senior Christian leader commented on Solanki's statement and found it interesting that the Hindu organiser admitted that the Dangs were under Hindu tribal lords: The truth is that they [Dangs] were exploited by high caste Hindu people...Dang villages were kept in poor conditions...only the high caste Hindus were given important jobs and government positions (SCL, 2006).

Another senior Christian leader asserted that this anxiety about Dang conversion is all about the 'politics of caste':

When the Dangs become Christians they are told of their rights and privileges and the Hindu tribal lords do not like this...Christianity threatens the status quo of the high caste Hindus (SCL, 2006). A Hindu leader admitted that Hindu nationalist groups are concerned with the politics of conversion and he added: 'In one sense they [Hindu nationalist leaders] are less concerned about televangelism than they are about Christian missionaries working in the tribal areas. Televangelism does not touch the illiterate tribals...it speaks to the urban, educated Hindus' (HL, 2006).

Another Hindu leader disagreed with the above comment because Hindu nationalist groups are still concerned about televangelism '...the fact that they block cable reception in the Hindu belt shows that they are concerned about televangelism...' (HL, 2006). To substantiate his point, the Hindu leader talked about the controversial *Tehelka* report that exposed the conversion agenda of Christian groups in India with financial backing from the Bush administration (HL, 2006). The leader went on to say: 'Some 30–40 Christian groups were blacklisted in the report including the Christian Broadcasting Network (CBN) which has a base in India and produces the *700 Club* and other programmes in India' (HL, 2006).

The *Tehelka* report was a piece of investigative journalism by two Hindu journalists who assumed Christian identities to find out about the nature and scope of American-funded evangelistic activities in India. The report (which is deliberately quoted at length) found that:

As part of AD 2000, Christian organisations in most countries, including India, had embarked on an ambitious national AD 2000 initiative.

In India the Evangelical Fellowship of India was central to the fulfill-ment of the goals set by this initiative. According to the founders of AD 2000 (and that includes Bush's pal Billy Graham) north India is the 'kairos', the key. India is where the era of modern missionary effort began nearly 200 years ago with the arrival of William Carey, the father of modern evangelical missions. However, the nine north and central Indian states of Bihar, Rajasthan, Madhya Pradesh, Uttar Pradesh, Delhi, Jammu and Kashmir, Punjab, Himachal Pradesh and Haryana were considered areas of immense strategic importance for the follow-ing reasons: The Gangetic belt is one of the most heavily populated regions of the world. Forty per cent of the Indian population lives here; New Delhi is the capital and centre of political power in India; It is the most socially deprived area of India (the Hindi belt has a literacy rate of 30 per cent, infant mortality is double the national average and the government of India officially designates our of these states as BIMARU (sic); This area of India is known as the heartland of Hinduism, a re-ligion that boasts of some 33 million gods; and it has the smallest Christian presence in all of India. According to the 1991 census, the Christian population of north India is 0.5 per cent of the total population.

Clearly, north India was strategically important for the missionaries. What made things easier for them was the new buoyancy in India-US relations. Therefore, it was open to researchers and their research plans. Billy Graham and his ilk openly admit that they dispatched spying missions to India. 'Just as Joshua sent out the spies to survey the land and report on its condition before the children of Israel moved out in obedience to God's command, many more missionaries and Christian workers are finding research information invaluable in laying their plans,' say the AD 2000 and Beyond Movement documents. Over the past eight years, tremendous energies and resources have been spent on spying out the land and its inhabitants.

The India Missions Association (IMA) in partnership with Gospel for Asia, another big American missionary outfit, researched and published very informative and accurate books that unraveled the intricate mosaic that is India. Some of those books are in Tehelka's possession. One of the big achievements of the Chennai-based IMA was conducting a detailed India-wide PIN code survey. India's postal service is one of the world's largest and it is important to understand why American mission agencies picked on India's postal system to devise their covert conversion strategy. The Indian postal system has a network of 152, 786 post offices—89 per cent of them in villages, which means one post office for 23.12 sq. km of rural land and one for every 3.16 sq. km of urban stretch, or one for a village with 4612 people or one for 12 294 people in a town or city. (Shashikumar, 2004)

Periasamy (2006), the CBN India director, dismissed the *Tehelka* report as 'a sensational piece of journalism with factual inaccuracies' (Periasamy, 2006: interview). Only 8 per cent of the senior Christian leaders took the *Tehelka* report seriously, whereas 34 per cent of the Hindu leaders felt that it was an accurate representation of the status of Christian work (see Table 7.1).

One senior Christian leader said that one of the weaknesses of the report was the fact that it linked the Christian agencies in India to the US Bush administration, which he described as 'too far-fetched' (SCL, 2006). Another senior Christian leader voiced his view that even if there are such far-fetched notions in the report 'we have to take these views seriously as this is a reflection of the perception of the Hindus towards Christianity...' (SCL, 2006). The Christian leader continued: '... [C]an we blame the Hindus for linking Christianity in India with the Bush administration? When I watched the *700 Club* during the Iraq war, Pat Robertson [the host] was praying for the President [Bush] and the US troops...' (SCL, 2006).

A Hindu leader also observed that one morning as he was watching TV he came across an American televangelist:

>...his name was John something...he was standing in front of the US Capitol building preaching about saving America...his topic was 'Covenant'...he was asking for funds from viewers...to me this was a clear case of mixing politics with [the] Christian religion...Therefore the Tehelka report is quite right about Christian mission in India and the Bush Government's involvement. (HL, 2006)

Further investigations revealed that the programme in question is hosted by John Hagee, a Charismatic evangelist whose global programme uses discourse which blends the biblical text with personal views of

Table 7.1:   The *Tehelka* report: Accurate?

	Senior Christian leaders and key informants N = 30	Hindu leaders N = 30
1. Yes	8%	34%
2. No	60%	5%
3. Not sure	10%	15%
4. Have not heard of it/have not read it	22%	46%

Source: Author.

politicians (such as the Israeli Prime Minister) in what is referred to as 'the politics of representation' (Reddy, 2006: interview).

There is another angle to the issue of politics and Christianity. One of the local newspapers alleged that the Benny Hinn meetings in India were supported by the ruling Congress party and in particular by Sonia Gandhi (Star of Mysore, 2005). This is because (as mentioned in Chapter 4), several Congress party Chief Ministers were in attendance at Hinn's meetings.

Two senior Christian leaders admitted that the fact that there were local politicians and even Hindu leaders on stage at Hinn's crusades lent itself to various rumours that large sums of money were given by the Hinn organisation to politicians and Hindu leaders to attend these meetings (SCL, 2006).

Cultural acceptance

The evidence as argued above, points to the fact that the Hindu groups that would be most open to Christian television are those from the middle class and below. The content of Charismatic televangelism, with messages on 'prosperity' and 'success', would strike a chord with these groups. Many Hindus in these groups would view televangelism programmes and pick and choose whatever is helpful to them (HL, 2006). Hindu leaders who are familiar with Charismatic programmes commented that many of them would have no problems with the ideas put forth by certain televangelists, pointing out that some of the teachings would make them and the Hindus who watch these programmes 'better Hindus' (HL, 2006).

Another Hindu leader pointed out that there is more similarity between Christian teaching and Hinduism than he realised before: 'As I watched many Christian preachers...they talk about getting success, healing and prosperity through a spiritualistic framework...this is what our gurus are also saying...so in the end both are saying "get what you want through spiritual techniques"' (HL, 2006).

This is a clear reference to the message of Charismatic televangelists which incorporates Western materialism with Christian theology.

One of the Hindu leaders commented: 'We have millions of Gods... to add one more would not be a major problem for Hinduism...we can choose Christ or Allah or both...' (HL, 2006).

Another Hindu leader added that to understand this issue of Christianity in India, a fundamental truth about Hinduism is necessary:

'Hinduism is an accepting religion...one that accepts all spiritual positions...Hindus do not see Jesus as a Christian ...Jesus is a holy "avatar" who is for all people...including Hindus' (HL, 2006).

This comment resonates with the experience of Shavnaka Rishi Das, a Hindu teacher, who sees Jesus through Hindu eyes:

> I've an Indian friend who, when he was seven moved with his family...to England...he was asked to speak to the class about a saint from his Hindu tradition...he began to tell the story of the saint called 'Ishu'... born in a cowshed...visited by three holy men...walked on water...Of course he was telling the story of Christ...he was bewildered to hear that the teacher laid claim to 'Ishu' for herself.. this was her Lord...not his... (Das, n.d. : para 1)

Das posits the belief that Hinduism is a syncretistic religion with a high premium on practice as opposed to belief:

> ...in a sense Hindus don't see Jesus as a Christian at all...In Hindu thought church or temple membership, or belief is not as significant as spiritual practice (which is called sadhana in Sanskrit). As there is no Church of Hinduism everyone holds their own spiritual and philosophical opinions...It is more common to hear someone ask, 'What is your practice (or sadhana)?' than, 'What do you believe?' (Das, n.d. : para 2)

A senior Christian leader, commenting on the Hindu perceptions argued that Charismatic televangelism, because of its doctrinal shallowness would attract certain Hindus because of the syncretistic nature of the Hindu religion (SCL, 2006).

A majority of the senior Christian leaders commenting on this finding from Hindu leaders warned that a new form of 'Christo-Hinduism', a fusion of Hinduism and Christianity, may eventually come into being, as a result of this one-sided preaching of the gospel. Boyd (1977) discusses this concept under the theme of indigenous Indian theology; however, his treatment basically focuses on Sanskritic Hinduism ignoring Dalit traditions. Hoefer's (1991) research and discovery of 'churchless Christianity' (which is alluded to in Chapter 4) that there are many followers of Christ in India, flourishing outside the established churches, was mentioned by one of the senior Christian leaders (Hoefer, 1991; SCL, 2006). The leader pointed out the difference in television converts and converts referred to in Hoefer's research. Hoefer's research was based on:

...unbaptised Indians who still had strong links with some members of the established church...hence they are not 'secret Christians' but open and public in their links with Christians...

in the case of TV viewers...it is hard for the local churches to locate the so-called believers and harder still to give them any training and discipleship in the faith...TV Christians end up as anonymous Christians... (SCL, 2006)

Another Christian leader observed that the onus is on the churches that produced the TV programmes, to 'disciple and nurture the TV believers...whether this is happening or not is left to be seen' (SCL, 2006).

The concern of syncretistic Christianity is reinforced by Peter van der Veer's research findings that in India religious identities can be shaped over periods of time by various social and cultural forces, which include the media (van der Veer, 1998: ix–x). A similar form of this syncretistic Christianity, which the Indian Christian leaders are concerned about, has developed in the Korean context where according to Mullins (1994), Charismatic Christianity has effectively blended Shamanism with the gospel. The Indian Christian leaders also warned that this new form of syncretistic Christianity, which they loosely label 'popular Christianity', does not call for any commitment in the areas of church membership, accountability or Christian maturity and discipleship (SCL, 2006). Lyon (2000) alludes to this reality when he says that in today's 'post-denominational world...believing without belonging is an increasingly popular religious position' (Lyon, 2000: 72).

A key informant shared his views that more and more Hindus would be drawn to aspects of Christianity while retaining their Hindu beliefs in a syncretistic way (KI, 2006). The leader added: '[T]his is already happening and will happen more now with the airwaves filled with various Charismatic teachings...The comments of some of the Hindu leaders point toward an uncritical acceptance of the blending of Christianity and Hinduism...' (KI, 2006).

'Glocal' Televangelism and the Hindu Community: A Case Study of Solutions[2]

The 'glocal' televangelism programme *Solutions* (produced by CBN India) was the subject of a case study with pastors, the results of which were explored in Chapter 6. The same episode of *Solutions* was viewed by Hindu leaders with the following findings.

Seventy-five per cent of the Hindu community leaders felt the production quality of *Solutions* was good, with 25 per cent stating it was excellent (15 per cent more than the church leaders). Not one of the Hindu leaders felt the programme needed improvement in the technical or production aspects unlike the Church leaders.

Twenty-five per cent of the community leaders found elements in the programme that were culturally appropriate (see Table 7.2). When asked what was culturally appropriate, about 40 per cent of the respondents listed the story of Nila the widow, whereas only 10 per cent listed the Indian compere. In the Indian context, the concept of Karma (or the law of transmigration) is strong and there is an aversion for marrying a divorcee or a widow. Hence the widow story was 'highly emotional' and 'attention getting' according to one of the respondents (HL, 2006). With respect to the Indian compere, it was noted that Christians still take leadership from 'the Europeans' and so it is refreshing to see an Indian compere leading the programme 'not in conjunction with a white man' (HL, 2006).

Whereas 40 per cent of Church leaders saw elements of cultural inappropriateness in *Solutions*, a total of 75 per cent of the community leaders deemed aspects of the programme culturally inappropriate (see Table 7.3). Of these, 30 per cent felt the issue of widows was not fairly handled as not all Hindu widows are treated this way in India. It was pointed out that there are Hindu agencies in India, like the Ramakrisha Mission, which undertake social and rehabilitation work for the marginalised in society. Three of the leaders felt the broadcaster was negative about widows and this negative image would not help young people in this generation. A replay of the *Solutions* programme showed that the leaders had misunderstood the intent of the programme (it was to describe the negative views about widows prevalent in India,

Table 7.2: Culturally appropriate and inappropriate elements in *Solutions*—Hindu leaders

Appropriate	*Inappropriate*
Story of Indian widow (Nila)	Issue of widows reported unfairly
Indian compere	Presentation of Jesus as the 'only Saviour'
Helps one to be a 'better Hindu' in terms of improvement	Taliban (Afghanistan) mini documentary

Source: Author.

Table 7.3:   Summary and weighting of responses to *Solutions*

	Culturally appropriate	Culturally inappropriate	How Church members would respond?*		How Hindus would respond?*	
			Positive	Negative	Positive	Negative
Christian leaders N = 30	60%	40%	50%	40%	30%	40%
Hindu leaders N = 30	25%	75%	–	–	25%	50%

Source: Author.
Note: *These do not amount to 100% as all participants did not answer the question.

not to prescribe such views). However, the fact that such misunder-standings could easily take place was noted as significant. The same three leaders expressed doubt over the sincerity of Nila's conversion, alluding to the fact that if the Christians had so much funding to pro-duce such programmes; Nila might have been offered money to convert.

Two of the leaders found the Taliban story too out of place cul-turally for India pointing out that such fanaticism as experienced in Afghanistan is generally not seen in India and therefore should not be associated with India. The communal tensions between Hindus and Muslims in the north Indian pilgrimage centre of Ayodhya in 1984 and 1987 were noted by the leaders in their assessment of this viewpoint (van der Veer, 1998).

Two other leaders took exception to the closing comments by the compere, that we should accept Jesus as 'the only Saviour'. 'All gods are equally valid therefore to name Jesus as the only God doesn't go well in Hindu society', remarked one leader (HL, 2006).

An interesting discussion took place on the aspect of how the Hindu community would respond to *Solutions*. Fifty per cent of the com-munity leaders felt that the response among Hindus would not be positive based on the issue of the exclusive claim of Jesus Christ. Four of the community leaders felt the programme would be positively received by Hindus. Yet, two out of the four felt that, even though this programme would be accepted by Hindus, it may not necessarily lead to conversion to Christianity. The programme makes you 'a better Hindu' and 'improves your situation' (HL, 2006). 'What happened to the widow can happen to me', said one female respondent '... regardless of caste or religion, I know I am more in touch with God and his love' (HL, 2006). These Hindu leaders have obviously interpreted Christianity from a syncretistic point of view.

When this finding was presented to the Christian leaders, they responded that this is not surprising as basically Hinduism is a religion that accepts other faiths. Indian business and marketing companies today are using the Indian syncretistic propensity as a positive value. This is revealed in the writings of Shivakumar who says:

> Marketers who understand and address the Indian knack of uniting conflicting values in their lives are the ones who will succeed with the changing Indian consumer...The Indian way of managing change is to find the 'and' in every potential conflict. (Shivakumar, 2006: para 1)

Rapaille, author of *The Culture Code*, agrees with this view when he says 'India has a different cultural code to China. The collective unconscious of India has a way to integrate the outside world without losing its soul' (Rapaille, quoted in Shivakumar, 2006: para 11). India's foremost psychoanalyst and social commentator, Sudhir Kakar, also supports this view when he talks about the cultural ideal of Indian society as 'a receptive absorption rather than an active alteration and opposition' (Kakar, quoted in Shivakumar, 2006: para 18).

Ten per cent of the Hindu community leaders answered 'cannot say' to the question of Hindu responses to the programme, whereas the remaining 10 per cent said it may be positive for some and negative for others depending on the following factors: the strength of the individuals' faith; how strong their Hindu family network is; what economic class they belong to and the amount of Western influence they have experienced. These leaders highlighted the complex nature of Hindu society, pointing out that the cultural networks and social practices are part and parcel of life. Some of these practices were listed as oral tradition, folklore, symbols and rituals. Because the Hindu is imbedded in a culture, there are social practices and arrangements that constitute the ethos of a person. It was estimated that 20–25 per cent of Hindus would be resistant to Christian television including *Solutions*. These, according to the Hindu leaders, are Hindus from the high caste as well as the high class. The middle to lower level class Hindus would be the ones more open to Christian televangelism.[3]

Another significant finding raised by the Hindu leaders was the level of need of a person: 'when your level of pain exceeds your level of fear (fear of community reprisals, etc.) you will change' (HL, 2006). In other words, when people have needs and they are not getting answers or relief from their temples or priests, in desperation they turn to other faiths. Examples were given of Hindus and Muslims who go to Porta Church (Catholic) or to Novena Catholic Church at

Mahim (a suburb in Mumbai) for healing and miracles. When asked whether the 20–25 per cent resistant Hindus with deep needs would turn to Christ on the basis of Christian televangelism, 30 per cent of the Hindu leaders indicated that this might take place among a small minority depending on the level of their needs.

When Hindu leaders were asked who among the group of less resistant Hindus would be watching Christian televangelism, they indicated the middle to lower class and some Western educated Hindus. Out of these groupings it was thought that women would be more open to *Solutions*. 'Women are more open and honest about problems and also they are the "culture-carriers" who make plans for family celebrations, gatherings and rituals in the Indian context' (HL, 2006). This corresponds with Moorti's findings that women are the primary viewers of secular primetime TV programming in India even though the producers seem to target the male audiences (Moorti, 2004). Interestingly enough, the 2001 census report reveals that there are more female Christians than male Christians in India unlike the Hindu and Islamic communities where males are in the majority. The Christian population has the highest female to male ratio of 1009 females per thousand males at the 2001 census, compared to 936 females per thousand males for the Muslim population and 931 females per thousand males for the Hindu population (Amalraj, 2004).

Analysis and Implications of Solutions (Christian Pastors and Hindu Leaders)[4]

1. Source

It appears from the findings that the positive issues raised are in the first category—the source. Both the Christian and Hindu leaders commend the Indian compere who dresses in Indian clothes, introduces the various segments of the programme and shares the gospel message at the end. The winsome and gentle presentation of the compere is altogether positive.

2. Message

Seventy per cent of the negative input from both Christian and Hindu leaders, was centred on the message—its content as well as the underlying elements used in the treatment of the message. The widow story was 100 per cent positive for Christian leaders but mostly negative for the Hindu leaders. This was an emotionally charged issue and was perceived by some Hindus as an unfair portrayal of Indian society. Misunderstanding of the intention of the producers was also apparent in the widow story.

Another point of contention was the treatment of Jesus Christ. The Hindus disagreed with the presentation of the 'exclusive Christ', whereas several Christians criticised the portrayal of the 'syncretistic Christ' (HL, 2006). Some Hindus who were positive about the programme welcomed the message of 'improvement'—that praying to Christ would make one a 'better Hindu' (HL, 2006). Yet other Hindus saw this as part of a veiled conversion agenda. The motives of Nila the widow were questioned as some felt she may have converted to Christianity because of the new lifestyle promised her by missionaries.

Christians felt the gospel was compromised because Jesus was presented merely as a miracle worker rather than Saviour. Hence *Solutions* was seen to be transforming the message of Christianity.

Whereas Hindus focussed merely on the negative aspects of the content *per se*, Christians tended to focus on the underlying elements of the content as well, such as music, dress code and culture. Christians expressed concern over the Western influences that have seeped into the presentation, pointing out that these subtle things can influence one's perception of the message. The Western dress code was particularly offensive to Christians. Therefore, it appears that both the content as well as the underlying elements of the message need to be subjected to further analysis.

3. Channel

Ten per cent of the overall negative input was directed at the channel. Both Hindus and Christians were highly impressed by the production excellence of *Solutions*. Hindus were generally more impressed than Christians. This being the case, it is interesting that both Christians and Hindus expressed concern that the use of high-powered technology and Western TV production methods point to an unholy alliance between the Church and the West.

Both Hindus and Christians pointed out that the production techniques and shots were geared more for those raised in the Western tradition of television. Some of the fast-paced cuts and slick editing were rather confusing at times to some Indian viewers. Therefore, Christianity mediated through technology (especially Western TV production techniques) does not seem to be fully comprehensible to certain Hindus and Christians even though India is generally know for its media-savvy outlook.

4. Receiver

We can attempt to draw a profile of an average viewer based on input from the community leaders. Among Hindus, the average viewer who is open to the message of *Solutions*, would be from the 25–30 per cent of Hindus from the lower to middle class and caste brackets. The degree of openness would depend on each receiver's level of need and the existing commitment to the Hindu faith, practices and the networks associated with the religion. However, the quality of responses was called into question when it was obvious that the message of *Solutions* was misunderstood by certain Hindu leaders. The fact that 10–15 per cent concluded that they can take Christian elements from the programme while still maintaining the Hindu faith is significant as it shows disparity between the intention of the producers and the interpretation of the receiver.

In the Christian community it is apparent that Christians are more open to the message of *Solutions* than Hindus. However, the concerns from Christian leaders to modify the programme in both the content and the underlying elements indicate a lack of complete satisfaction on the part of the Christian audience.

As mentioned in Chapter 4, global televangelism follows the literacy approach (where space and time is fixed) whereas, Hindu televangelism follows the orality approach (where there is a constant shifting between the past, present and future time frames).

Even though *Solutions* has elements of 'Indianness' in it structure, it follows the literacy approach of global televangelism. In this sense, *Solutions* does not represent the deeper essence of what Bhaktin (1981: 358) refers to as 'organic hybridity'. *Solutions* also falls short of the 'Hindu in culture, Christian in faith Dharmic model' referred to in Chapters 1 and 3, as it veers more towards the global, US model of televangelism. Therefore, even though *Solutions* is a 'glocal' programme its hybridity is merely on the peripheral level.

Summary and Significant Findings

In this chapter, the impact of Charismatic televangelism on the Hindu, urban community was examined from two standpoints of Charismatic televangelism: global and 'glocal'.

Qualitative interviews and content analyses revealed that global televangelism was deemed a threat in some states necessitating restraints to be placed on cable operators in certain states, by various Hindu organisations, resistant to Christian televangelism. However, it was seen that the cultural restraints that act as barriers to the flows of Charismatic televangelism are just as powerful as the physical restraints placed by the RSS and other groups. Some of these cultural barriers are: caste, class, language, gender and perception. The politics surrounding conversion were also noted as a barrier to global televangelism.

Hindus from the middle to lower classes were thought to be more open to Charismatic televangelism, although a syncretistic understanding of the Christian faith by these followers seemed inevitable without the nurturing of the local church community and the fellowship of other Christians. Converts from televangelism, unlike other traditional forms of missionary activity, seem to end up as 'anonymous Christians'.

Solutions, an example of 'glocal' televangelism, the hybrid phenomenon of the global and the local, was examined in terms of its impact on the urban, Hindu community. The programme contains elements of dialogue, ideas and storylines that have obviously helped in the adaptation of the gospel along Indian ways. Whereas, some Hindus responded positively with their own understanding of the 'syncretistic Christ' others reacted negatively to the 'exclusive Christ'. The most likely audience for *Solutions* was deemed to be Hindus from the 20–25 per cent lower to middle classes. Of these, women were thought to be more receptive. Although *Solutions* was commended for its attempts to incorporate Indian elements, 70 per cent of Hindus found culturally inappropriate elements in the programme and agreed with the Christian pastors who cynically referred to the programme earlier in Chapter 6 as 'two parts Indian and three parts American' (SCL, 2006). Even then, Hindu leaders could not fault the production excellence of *Solutions*.

Notes

1. *Would Jesus Wear a Rolex* (Archer and Atkins, 1987. Sung by Ray Stevens). Used with permission.
2. Please see Chapter 6 for an overview of the content of the CBN programme, *Solutions*.
3. 'Class' is always defined in terms of economic scaling whereas 'caste' is defined in terms of social scaling in Indian society. 'High caste' need not necessarily be 'high class'.
4. I use Berlo's (1960) four-step model based on: source, message, channel and receiver as a framework for my analysis of the findings for the programme *Solutions*.

Chapter 8

The Mediation of Charismatic Televangelism[1]

The 1937 coronation ceremony of George VI at the Westminster Abbey in England, was broadcast on radio by the British Broadcasting Corporation (BBC). The coverage was done simply by a reporter who worked with his equipment behind the scenes in a tiny room 'without intruding into the service' (Hoover and Lundby, 1997: 302). Although television technology was available to telecast the coronation, no TV cameras were allowed for this sacred event.

In contrast to this, Queen Elizabeth's coronation in 1953 was, after 'considerable discussion and restriction' opened to television (Hoover and Lundby, 1997: 302). Thus within 16 years, former fears that television would desacralise such an event had given way to the belief that television would portray the event with 'full religious significance' (Wolfe, 1984: 497).

If we compare our present media-saturated society (where television and religion are enmeshed), to the time of these earlier historical events, a question may arise in the reader's mind: Were the fears of keeping TV out of the earlier coronation justified?

In this chapter, we consider the issue of the mediation of televangelism. Cathcart and Gumpert (1993), two of the early scholars to use the term 'mediation', analysed its role in interpersonal communication and warned that technological intermediaries would eventually transform both mass communication and interpersonal communication. The word 'mediation' comes from the word 'mediator', which refers to an intermediary who negotiates or resolves issues between two parties. In academic usage and specifically in media and communication research, 'mediation' connotes understanding of the 'middleman' role played by the media, but with a greater degree of critical consideration. As the television medium (compared to the face-to-face medium and print medium) has become a highly organised industry with interlocking connections to the whole fabric of social life, its mediations present both positive as well as negative effects. Livingstone (2008) draws our attention to some of the concerns resulting from the ambiguous mediating role of the media:

> ...when we ask who controls these media institutions, whether global corporations or the state, and when we critically observe how mediated communication is subordinated to, shaped by, the inexorable logic of global capitalism—commodification, standardisation, privatisation, co-option, surveillance, and the rest—then we see this change for the worse. (Livingstone, 2008: para 15)

My perspective on mediation is informed by the writings of Stolow (2005); Hoover and Clark (2002) and Hoover and Lundby (1997) who place religion and media together, having observed how religious practitioners today are becoming more and more adept at extending their mediated reach.

Writing from his Latin American experience, media analyst Martin-Barbero (1993) takes a critical approach, in analysing how media enters the power struggles between dominant and weaker groups:

> Communication in Latin America has been profoundly affected by external transnationalisation but also by the emergence of new social actors and new cultural identities. Thus communication has become a strategic arena for the analysis of the obstacles and contradictions that move these societies, now at the crossroads between accelerated underdevelopment and compulsive modernisation. Because communication is the meeting point of so many conflicting and integrating forces, the centre of the debate has shifted from media to mediations. (Martin-Barbero, 1993: 185)

In exploring the topic of the mediation of Charismatic televangelism in India, I take the following approach: first, I explore the issue of the ownership of the main Christian networks; second, I focus on five aspects of the reinvention of Christianity by the Charismatic movement and finally, I conclude by considering how the interplay between technology and theology has implications for both the Church and the wider community in India.

Ownership and Related Issues

The four main 24-hour Christian networks in India (as mentioned in Chapter 4), are owned or have strong connections with overseas Charismatic organisations and media agencies. One of these networks is *God TV*, which was established by UK-based Rory and Wendy Alec. This 24-hour network sells space to the global fraternity of Charismatic televangelists like Hinn, Dollar, Robertson, Copeland, Duplantis and the like. In 2004, the Alecs, who take a pro-US political stance, decided to move their broadcast centre from the UK to Jerusalem, Israel thereby reinforcing their other agenda—the pro-Israel political/ spiritual standing, with the familiar slogan: 'broadcasting from the Holy Land to the ends of the earth'.

Another network is Christian Broadcasting Network (CBN), a Charismatic media giant in USA, which sold their Family Channel in 1997 to *Fox Kids Worldwide* (owned by media mogul Rupert Murdoch) and used the proceeds, to establish media branches in Indonesia, Philippines and India. CBN (India), which was born from this sale, is headquartered in Hyderabad and presently trying to establish its own local identity after a period of controversy arising from the derogatory remarks made about Hinduism by the CBN USA leader Pat Robertson. Robertson has strong political links in USA, with family members who have been in the US Senate and claims a bloodline that links him to two previous US Presidents (van Busen, 2005: interview). Whereas these political links may be well thought of in USA, they are rather offensive in some Indian Christian and Hindu circles (KI, 2006).

As we look at *God TV* and CBN from the perspective of their inter-connectedness to overseas funds, secular organisations, US politics, the global Charismatic body and the neo-conservative economic world order, we can appreciate the reason why this mix could be troubling to many Hindus, Muslims and even some conservative Christians. Charismatic televangelism today is not just about preaching the gospel, but about forging liaisons with the world of politics, economics and technology.

Charismatic churches and ministries operate on two levels—as local entities and as organisations that are linked through exchange and communication with transnational Charismatic churches and organisations. Coleman (2000) explains this phenomenon:

Charismatic Christianity has become a global culture or way of life based on perception of identities that are transmitted world-wide through high-tech media; international conferences; fellowships; prayer links and mega-churches ...Some mega-churches function like international corporations serving as advocates for smaller affiliates as well as exporting literature, tapes ... (Coleman, 2000: 66)

An example of a Charismatic megachurch is Hillsong Australia which is based in Sydney and has a regular televangelism programme on several Indian channels, *Hillsong TV*. The pastors and worship leaders on *Hillsong TV* present more as entertainers than typical pastors, using song and television in their overall approach. Hillsong's music and its unique style of using its stage for worship have been copied by churches all across the world, including churches in India (James and Shoesmith, 2006: 11). The annual Hillsong conference in Sydney attracts 25 000 people from all over the world, with speakers from the global fraternity of Charismatic TV evangelists, such as Joyce Meyer, T. D. Jakes and the like. At these conferences, the Hillsong albums (comprising the latest worship songs sung by world-renowned singer Darlene Zschech and others) are released and immediately purchased by the captive international audience, resulting in many of the albums released this way topping the coveted Australian Recording Industry Association (ARIA) music charts (James and Shoesmith, 2006).

Renowned historian of Indian Christianity, Frykenberg (2008: 467) confirms the world-wide affiliation that local Indian Pentecostals and Charismatics have established:

In historical terms, various forms of Pentecostalism have never been detached from extensive international contacts or partnerships such as Assemblies of God in America or congregations in Sweden, Australia ... Indian Pentecostals have become a rapidly emerging Worldwide Charismatic Christianity.

God TV, CBN and other networks like *Miraclenet*, together with the televangelists and programmes like Benny Hinn and *Hillsong TV* are expressions of the globalisation of a specific brand of Christianity— the Charismatic faith. This brand is both global and local, producing at times through diffusion and symbiosis, a 'glocal' version of the faith. In Chapter 1, I have referred to this global brand of Charismatic Christianity in India as McDonaldisation because it represents an expression of global Charismatic Christianity mediated in its generation and construction by the particular grammar, logic and identity of global Charismatic Christianity. Likewise, the 'glocal' brand of Charismatic Christianity has been termed Masala McGospel because global Charismatic Christianity is producing a form of cultural fusion—blending the global (American) logic, grammar and identity with Indian components.

The extensiveness of Charismatic Christianity, consumed globally through multi-modal means, including satellite television, is so great that it is perceived to be creating a transnational brotherhood, a form of 'Christian *umma*'—an Arabic term meaning 'mother nation', used in reference to the powerful, global Islamic population (Thomas, 2008).

The Reinvention of Christianity

It is my contention that Charismatic televangelism in India, which is part of the global project of the Charismatic movement with roots in the Azusa Street revival in the USA, is virtually 'reinventing' Christianity in several ways. It is creating:

1. A new hermeneutic;
2. A new theology of communication;
3. A new set of teachings and practices;
4. A new type of clergy;
5. A new liturgy.

The sociologist Bordieu (1984) argues that contemporary individuals choose their practices based on 'habitus'—a framework to evaluate and organise their lives. This framework is based on 'fields', that is, networks with which we have contact—business, religious, social and emotional. According to Bordieu, each field has its own 'capital'—goods or resources that benefit us. Jenkins (1992) elaborates on Bourdieu's concept of field and capital:

> A field is structured internally in terms of power relations ... by virtue of the access they afford to the goods and resources (capital) which are at stake in the field. These goods can be principally differentiated into four categories—economic capital, social capital ... cultural...symbolic. (Jenkins, 1992: 85)

Our decisions and our practices are informed by the concept of 'distinction'—the novelty, freshness, packaging and new image that is portrayed on television. In a similar way, Charismatic televangelism has succeeded in creating a 'distinction' between the new Church and the old church and the new Christianity as opposed to the old Christianity. Let us now consider the five aspects of this distinction.

1. A new hermeneutic

Using an historical approach, Hiebert (1989) analyses the philosophical and theological factors that gave birth to the Charismatic movement, mentioning the change in world view in Western thinking as a primary factor:

> The old foundations that provided the basis for Western thought for some two or more centuries are crumbling, and no one set of new foundations has replaced them. In such times of uncertainty and fear, prophets often emerge proclaiming a new worldview which, they promise, will guide people to a better life. (Hiebert, 1989: 20)

Hiebert (1989) goes on to explain that the current world view in the Western world is no longer the Biblical world view prior to the Reformation. This is not a society in which God is the Creator linked with all of creation, including spirits, humans and plants. The modern world view is 'neo-platonic and it postulates a separation between the supernatural world (of God, Satan, miracles) and the natural world (of science, natural laws etc)'. This change, according to Hiebert, has left Western Christians with a 'spiritual schizophrenia'—believing in God on the one hand and yet living in a very naturalistic and materialistic world where there is no room for God (Hiebert, 1989: 22).

One of the consequences of this world view change is to 'place humans at the top of nature' because God is now 'out of the picture'. Hence, the focus on self became the 'dominant theme in Western society during the last decade of the nineteenth century' (Hiebert, 1989: 48).

This collapse of the Biblical world view and its consequences has brought about the return to animism, magic and New Age practices in the world at large. The Church is not exempt from these dangerous trends as two major theologies have come about in the last half century or so: a theology of power—manifested in signs, wonders, deliverance ministries and a theology of wealth and healing (Hiebert, 1989: 48).

Barnhart (1990: 160) in his exposè of Charismatic televangelists has narrowed down the five main tenets of the prosperity gospel preached in churches and over the airwaves by Pat Robertson, Oral Roberts and other televangelists:

1. God has supreme power over everything including Satan;
2. God does not want any Christian to be sick;
3. Satan is the cause of disease and illness;
4. God can overcome the power of Satan;
5. The gift of healing is a two-edged sword–it allows the evangelists to make war with Satan and it brings people to 'a right relationship with God…opening the channels of healing'.

Charismatic theologians have a different approach to hermeneutics than the non-Charismatic theologians. Hermeneutics is a reference to the rules of interpreting literary texts that involve *exegesis* (searching for the original meaning of the text) (Arrington, 1988: 377). Whereas non-Charismatic theologians continue to use the historical-grammatical method of hermeneutics and the historical principles of the Protestant movement, Charismatic theologians use what they term the 'pneumatic' or charismatic method: 'the interpreter relies on the illumination of the Holy Spirit in order to come to the fullest comprehension' (Ruthven, 1994: 382).

Non-Charismatic theologians believe that the Scriptures are inspired by God through the Holy Spirit, but they feel this does not contradict their use of the historical-grammatical method for the Spirit which does not go against the rules of grammar, history and culture in their search for understanding the meaning of the text (Hiebert, 1989: 40).

Marshall (1970: 7), a non-Charismatic theologian, takes exception to the pneumatic hermeneutical method of the Charismatics:

Such people depended purely on what they conceived to be the Spirit's help and so landed themselves in a subjective approach. They failed to compare Scripture with Scripture and…they failed to listen to the voice of the Spirit as he spoke to other interpreters of Scripture within the fellowship of the Christian Church over the centuries. In scriptural interpretation, as in any other area, it is essential that we 'test the Spirits'. (1 John 4:1, quoted in Marshall 1970)

Some Charismatic and Pentecostal theologians themselves recognise the dangers of the 'pneumatic' hermeneutical approach. Arrington (1988), while supporting the Charismatic hermeneutic, also cautions the Church to its dangers:

> This danger lies in the potential that the interpreter confuses his or her own spirit (or some other spirit) with the Spirit of God. Because the interpreter has claimed divine guidance, the resulting interpretation is assumed to be above questioning and thus implicitly demands an authority on par with Scripture itself. (Arrington, 1988: 383)

This new hermeneutic is at the very heart of the distinctiveness of the Charismatic movement in that it deals with the fundamental issue of epistemology—how we know truth and doctrine, which then leads to how we practise the faith.

2. A new theology of communication

The Charismatic movement's espousal of mass media is based on its theology of communication. Charismatics believe the canonical text (the Bible) to be the word of God. At the same time they also put a high premium on an individual receiving sacred revelations, 'anointings', divine empowerments and visions. Coleman (2000) writing about the Word of Faith movement, a Charismatic ministry says:

> The stress on self as a vehicle for the divine results not only in search for physical well-being but also in a repertoire of bodily gestures that can convert any space into a context for the internalisation or externalisation of the Word. (Coleman, 2000: 142)

Therefore, according to this view, human bodies can become objects of God's presence and anointing. In the same way, an object like a worship hall can become a vehicle of God's presence:

> Internal features of a worship hall emphasise the power of the Word and the sense of words to be 'received from God' ... In the main hall ... the most significant objects are the lectern ... and the television cameras. (Coleman, 2000: 156)

In most Charismatic churches, all the services are video-taped and audio-taped for sale and some are recorded for television, for both local and overseas stations. The use of television and radio is based on the Charismatic belief that the eternal truths of God must be easily adapted to as many forms of media as possible because the word is 'literally diffused' by the use of modern mass media (Coleman, 2000: 167). Hence 'ideology and experience contained in electronic media become objectified and commodified...framed and recycled within mass-media formats' (Coleman, 2000: 167). Since all media is a gift of God, Charismatics believe media should be used for the furtherance of the kingdom.

Television, therefore, becomes the embodiment of the Holy Spirit's blessing and anointing, regardless of the fact that television is a shared space used for secular programmes and commercials as well which feature less than spiritual topics, images and stories. Many people who view Charismatic television claim to be healed by simply watching healing programmes and touching the TV screens.

Evangelist Benny Hinn, at the end of his programmes 'reaches out to the camera and implores viewers to come toward the screen. "I see cancer, Lord dissolve that cancer." Hinn proclaimed on a recent show ... "I see a leg losing feeling. Lord restore feeling to that leg"' (Romney, 1997). Furthermore, 'the capture of television [by Charismatics] is itself part of the struggle against Satan and his powers' (Thomas, 2008: 161). Hence the use of television itself represents a Charismatic victory against the forces of the world.

3. A new set of teachings and practices

The teachings of the Charismatic movement, as outlined in Chapter 2 are basically a juxtaposition of two essential elements—a belief in the text of the Bible based on a 'pneumatic' (or Spirit-led) hermeneutic (as opposed to the historical-grammatical hermeneutic) and a belief in the possibility of the believer speaking in tongues, receiving revelations, visions, healings and other divine powers.

My survey of middle-level pastors in Mumbai and Hyderabad (Chapters 6 and 7) revealed some interesting findings about the concept of the church worship service and the practices associated with worship in Charismatic churches. Seventy-five per cent of Charismatic pastors (as opposed to 25 per cent of non-Charismatic pastors) saw the Church and, in particular, the worship service, as the primary means for non-believers to come to a knowledge of faith in Christ. A senior Charismatic pastor commenting on this finding explained at the interview: 'We believe that the worship service is the meeting point between God and people. We invite people to come to our services to experience God's presence and power' (SCL, 2006).

A key informant gave his analysis of the above finding:

> The Charismatic strategy is not to go out to the community in the traditional sense, like what the non-Charismatic Churches are doing, but to ask people to come to them. They believe the services are anointed and miracles will take place; therefore, they [worship services] are recorded and taped and shown on TV to replicate the anointed blessings to the world. (KI, 2006)

In the survey research (mentioned in Chapter 6), 80 per cent of Charismatic pastors revealed that 'power evangelism' was the means by which people became followers of Christ during church services.[2] Non-Charismatic pastors in the research placed a high premium (60 per cent) on teaching and preaching as a method of evangelism with only 6 per cent who saw power evangelism, as a method of bringing people to Christ in their non-Charismatic churches. Miracles, signs and wonders were variously recorded as evidences of power evangelism by the middle level pastors. The two primary miracles specified were being 'slain in the Spirit' and healing. Frykenberg (2008) confirms that Pentecostal and neo-Pentecostal groups have a large following in India, primarily because of their interactions with people who are in need of healing and freedom (from the fear of 'demonic forces' and 'spirits'). Thomas (2008) observes that healing is a felt-need which is being addressed at crusades.

> Medical bills are impossibly high for the lower middle class—and it is not coincidental that a large number of those taking part in healing crusades hope to be healed for free ... I was told that many patients from hospitals around Bengaluru found their way to the Jakkur airfield to hear Pastor Benny, hoping for a miraculous recovery from their ailments. (Thomas, 2008: 158)

In short, the Charismatic gospel and televangelism have responded to a need, placing on the Christian market a new set of spiritual 'goods and services'—healing, deliverance, prosperity and success.

4. A new clergy

Charismatic televangelism has created a new type of pastor, one with slick personal grooming and smooth, electrifying rhetoric that fits well with the image-driven television industry. Lee and Sinitiere (2009), in their study of superstar evangelists, have this to say about Joel Osteen, a TV evangelist who attracts 40,000 people in Houston on Sundays and is seen on television by more than 7 million people around the world, including India: 'He understands the importance of TV and uses the language of contemporary American society—the language of psychotherapy, the language of Americans who watch Oprah and Dr Phil' (Lee and Sinitiere, 2009 quoted in Stern, 2009: para 4).

The new type of clergy, according to Bourdieu (1984), is not the 'priest'—who manages and administers the established faith but a 'prophet' who advances the cause of religion because of 'charisma' and special powers in healing and miracles. Engler (2003) amplifies Bourdieu's analysis: '...the priest plays a conservative role, attempting to maintain control over religious capital, and the prophet is an innovator producing a new variant of religious goods' (Engler, 2003: 447).

Benny Hinn's first crusade in Mumbai in 2004 was a highly debated phenomenon in several mainline churches. During one of the research sessions with the senior pastors, a non-Charismatic pastor commented: '[Benny Hinn] did not mention Jesus the Saviour even once, only Jesus the healer. So he preached a one-sided gospel' (SCL, 2006).

On the issue of miracles and healing, the value-added aspect of the new clergy, Caplan (1987) observes:

> The more miraculous their [Charismatic evangelists] achievements, the wider their notoriety. Some develop 'specialisations', that is, they become known for dealing effectively with particular kinds of problems ... Those who achieve supra-local fame do so because they are seen to stand above the innumerable local healers in terms of their charismatic powers. (Caplan, 1987: 374–375)

The new clergy are also strong advocates, not only of the media with its attendant technologies, but also of the market, as both media and market are critical for the worldwide spread of the gospel. As Hunt (2000: 344) has rightly observed, the market is a crucial link in the Charismatic chain: 'Pentecostalism serves to develop attributes, motivations and personalities adapted to the exigencies of the deregulated global market'.

5. A new liturgy: teleliturgy

Liturgy, from the Greek *leitourgia*, refers to the official public worship of the church service. Some churches have a more prescribed and sacramental form of worship, whereas others have a less formalised order of service. The basic understanding of liturgy comes historically from Jesus' last Passover supper where he instituted what is now practised as 'The Lord's Supper' or 'Holy Communion'. The challenge posed by televangelism is that while the liturgy of the pre-television era was one dominated by the written word and print communication, today's televised church is increasingly following a liturgy that is electronically mediated. The cameras, production techniques, images and symbols of television, together with the teachings and practices of the Charismatic faith, are generating a new liturgy.

The most obvious difference between yesterday's liturgy and what I term 'teleliturgy'—the liturgy mediated by Charismatic television—is that whereas the former presupposes community—a shared response of the body to what God has done through Christ—teleliturgy is produced for and focussed on individuals. Televangelists routinely look to the camera and say on television: 'What is your need today?' or 'God wants to heal your cancer'.

Liturgy in Church, especially during the communion services celebrates the sacrificial life of Christ. Teleliturgy celebrates the life of the individual and objectifies the body that is to be healed of diseases or empowered and slain by the Holy Spirit. The content analysis of Benny Hinn's *This is Your Day* programme revealed that more air time was spent on miracles and fundraising combined, than on the preaching of the message (Chapter 4).

Liturgy in Church focuses on the transcendent—that which is beyond this life. The typical communion service ends with the words 'until he comes'. Teleliturgy focuses on the immanent, the here and now, as well as the transcendent. The songs, the sermons and especially the miracles, point to the celebration of life here and now, rather than the call to spiritual preparation for the coming kingdom.

In short, the Charismatic movement and Charismatic televangelism have opened the eyes of people in Indian churches to a new church—one that dispenses new goods and services mediated by a new clergy in the market place of spirituality. This represents a paradigm shift in the hermeneutical framework with a new set of teachings and practices.

The Implications of Mediation

While televangelism, a product of Christianised America, is enjoying relative success in its country of origin as well as in some African and

South American countries, its success in India is somewhat muted. India's socio-religious context is fundamentally Hindu in nature; Christianity is in the minority (at best around 3 per cent). Furthermore when, we take into account India's relatively large Muslim population (15 per cent) and the ongoing inter-religious tensions and conflicts since independence, televangelism seems to be positioning itself in the arena of public contestation. This is made more problematic in the light of the McDonaldised version of televangelism that presents a standardised consumer gospel, bereft of cultural linkage to India and adds fuel to the fire with its insensitive treatment of Hinduism and the local belief systems, calling them 'heathen' and 'demonic'. This, when added to televangelism's pro-US stance and the open agenda of 'winning souls', has greatly intensified the contestation on a community level. Furthermore, the political economy of Charismatic televangelism in India is such that televangelism is primarily funded, driven and inspired by the American fraternity of global Charismatic television and this fact adds to the ongoing tensions in India's socio-religious context.

On the level of the Christian community, it appears that the Indian Church has also been affected by the large-scale and intense contestation of Charismatic televangelism over the resources, people, television space and local churches within India. Very few mainline churches have entered into the realm of television, but the newer Charismatic congregations, some aided by overseas funds, have been quick to establish TV ministries (Chapter 4). Senior pastors and middle-level pastors, mostly from non-Charismatic churches, have expressed their fears of a 'Charismatic takeover' (Chapters 6 and 7). The pastors, in particular, have expressed their concerns that mediated Charismatic televangelism is unsettling the 'habitus'—the views, perceptions and tastes of Indian Christians—and pressure is now being placed on traditional pastors to orchestrate their church services and adjust the rhetoric of their sermons to bring it more in line with the televisual church model. Although these are real fears, other leaders have expressed the opinion that the many mainline churches (which I refer to as 'post-colonial' in Chapter 1), some of whom have been perceived to be 'elitist', are struggling with various internal issues such as: property and litigation matters; materialistic concerns; theological liberalism and the like (SCL; KI, 2006). Therefore, the new church created by the Charismatic movement (and aided by televangelism) with its distinctives in hermeneutics, theology, practice and clergy, as disturbing as they are, may actually serve as a 'wake up call' to the established churches 'to get their spiritual act together' (SCL, 2006).

Religion has always been considered as a form of communication between human beings and God or Gods based on faith, both on the 'mentifact' level (belief as mental construction) and 'artifact' level (belief manifested in rites or physical constructs). Faith with the supernatural being is administered either directly or through mediators such as priests, pastors, shamans and various religious clergy. In the process, human beings divided their operational spaces/places as 'fane' (sacred) and 'profane' (secular). In the Indian context, a natural object like a stone or tree can be transformed from profane to fane by marking it with saffron and tumeric colours through a ritualistic process.

The 'sacred space' is backed by a religious system with rules prescribing how a person ought to comport himself or herself in the presence of sacred objects. Hence the spaces are clearly segmented in the Indian religious ethos. With the onset of televangelism (Christian and Hindu) the spaces between the two are blurred as the medium (television) itself is becoming the 'message'. That is why during the *Ramayana*, Hindu broadcast (Chapters 1 and 5), television itself was seen as sacred space and objectified into a fetish. However, this was only for a brief time, during the Hindu broadcast. After the broadcast television reverted to secular space. Thus, mediated religion is transforming both men and material significantly in this age of globalisation.

I believe the mediation of Charismatic televangelism has affected the individual worshipper in several ways. First, the sacred act of worship has now been reduced to a series of choices in the supermarket of Christianity, with the worshipper in the role of consumer. In a sense, life in the global society is all about the consumption of symbols and lifestyles. Image and space are replacing narrative and history. Cultural globalisation, which is part of the current post-industrial economy is organised around culture, cultural consumption, the media and technology. Therefore, Lash's (1990: 4–5) prediction that global society is a 'regime of signification', in which 'only cultural objects are produced' is becoming true. Second, Christian televangelism is, in essence, Charismatic televangelism, which is the consequence of the reinvention of Christianity by the global Charismatic movement. Hence, Christians and non-Christians have to negotiate the new hermeneutics, teachings and practices of this new paradigm of Christianity which is administered by a new clergy. Third, the worshipper's experience of worship is mingled with Western ideas, values and concepts even in 'glocal' televangelism programmes like *Solutions*. Hence, subtle aspects of Western culture such as dress code, lifestyle and humour are being conveyed in televangelism. Therefore, mediated Christianity inevitably entails a certain degree of Westernisation. Fourth, the worshipper has become more adept with new technologies. I met a retired couple from the Mar Thoma Church in Hyderabad, who watch an average of five hours of televangelism every day. Previously they were not able to use the internet, but since they started watching televangelism, their eagerness to download sermons and other resources from televangelists on their computer, has now forced them to learn to negotiate the technology of new media. Fifth, the worshipper's experience of worship is associated with entertainment, spectacle and even 'worldliness'. One of the senior Christian leaders remarked about global televangelism:

> The worldly rock music, the dancing, and the casualness about worship is taking away the guilt from our young people about living in two worlds—the Christian world and the secular world ... they [televangelists] are making it OK for our youth. (SCL, 2006)

Sixth, Christian worship, which traditionally was a communal experience, is shifting to a more privatised mode, where the worshipper may pray for 'individual blessings', call the toll free telephone number on the screen for prayer and donate online to various televangelism ministries. Furthermore, the worshipper does not have to feel bad about not attending a physical church, for he or she can now believe without belonging.

To sum up: The Charismatic movement and Charismatic televangelism are impacting India in a profound way. In this chapter, I have examined the mediation of Charismatic televangelism in India—that is, the intermediary role that the media is playing in broadcasting the faith. I have attempted to do this by: examining the ownership, relationships and global links of the televangelism industries in India; outlining the new variant of products and services offered by Charismatic teachings through televangelists and describing the implications of these in the church and the broader community in India.

Notes

1. Since I use references in this chapter from various pastors and leaders drawn from the field research, I indicate these sources as follows: SCL = Senior Christian Leader and KI = Key Informant.
2. 'Power evangelism', a term used by Charismatic preachers (especially from the Vineyard Movement) refers to various signs and wonders that accompany evangelism, such as deliverance from demonic possession and healing of all kinds of ailments.

Chapter 9

Faith's Flows, Fragments and Futures

McDonaldisation, Masala McGospel and Om Economics are three metaphors I have used throughout this book to describe the status of televisual faith in contemporary India. The first word picture, 'McDonaldisation', comes from America, with its origins traced to the global consumerist world of franchised food restaurants made famous by the fast-food chain, McDonalds.

The second, 'Masala McGospel', is a fusion of McDonalds and the traditional culture of India drawn from the formulaic 'masala mix' of the Bollywood film industry. The third, 'Om Economics', refers to the merging of Hinduism's sacred sound and syllable '*Om*' with contemporary commerce and the capitalism of the West.

Although these metaphors refer to three different types of televised faith—global Charismatic, glocal Charismatic and Hindu—they share two common characteristics.

First, they remind us that in the world of globalisation, the time and space co-ordinates that defined life in past generations, no longer underpin contemporary life. 'Flows' and 'fragments' (elaborated in Chapters 1 and 2) define the world of globalisation. Flows, which are the building blocks of 'imagined worlds' (B. Anderson, 1993: 20), can spread as complete communication, or as 'fragments'—bits and pieces of information that may become grafted with aspects of the receiving culture. In Charismatic televangelism, the global teaching of the movement is what 'flows' via the various media and may then take on local distinctives. In Hindu television, since Hinduism is orthopractic (based on a different set of duties, practices and rituals), what flows is 'fragments' of the various practices, rituals and traditions, which are then recombined into individual experiences. For example, when a Hindu watches televangelism, even though the featured guru may not be his or her favourite, 'fragments' of what is said and practised or sung in the form of *bhajans* may resonate with the viewer's faith, thereby reinforcing the worship experience. The diversity and what might seem to be 'cultural fragmentation', does not generally worry Hindu viewers, because unlike Christianity, which is based on a body of truths, Hinduism is based on a set of practices.

The second characteristic that unites these three forms of televised faith is that in the world of globalisation, culture, society and commerce are brought closer to each other than ever before, resulting in the commodification of culture and religion. Faith becomes a commodity in the supermarket of spirituality and both Gods and religion are actively marketed using the tools, rhetoric and technologies of the capitalist market economy. The research showed that whereas Charismatic televangelism relies on aggressive fundraising (with repeated pleas for donations for programmes on air) and sales of products, Hindu televangelism relies almost solely on sales of products, paraphernalia and spiritual objects. As illustrated in Chapter 5, some Hindu programmes are devoted entirely to the sales and marketing of spiritual products.

Therefore, it would seem that religion in the global world is forced to find new avenues and methods for establishing its reach. These two characteristics—the flows (and fragments) and the commercialisation—give rise to the phenomenon of McDonaldisation, Masala McGospel and Om Economics.

In this concluding chapter of the book: first, I give a synopsis of the study and analysis of the findings; second, I assess the impact of televangelism in India and, finally, I make some broad predictions about mediated faith in a globalised world.

Synopsis and Analysis

The aim of the study was to examine the influence of Charismatic televangelism in urban India in two different settings: the Protestant Church and the Hindu community. The study took place in two cities: Mumbai and Hyderabad.

The main methodology I used in this study was ethnography, a research method from the social sciences designed to gain an in-depth understanding of the views, perceptions, fears and aspirations of Christian pastors and Hindu leaders in the divergent cultural context of India. Through participant observation, I was able to get close to my respondents in their everyday settings. During the one and a half years of fieldwork, I managed to collect sufficient data to draw a profile of Christian pastors and Hindu leaders in India (Harris and Johnson, 2000).

I supplemented the ethnographic methodology with survey research, conceptual analysis and the relational-comparative analysis (for which I used an historical-comparative framework). I felt it was necessary to use the latter because the contemporary missionary outreach of televangelism is part of a long and sustained Christian activity and, therefore, it cannot be viewed in an historical vacuum. In fact, the missionary enterprise has a history dating to the apostolic times. In my historical-comparative framework, Christianity in India was divided into three eras—pre-colonial, colonial and post-colonial—to which I applied three fields of study: post-colonial studies, sociology of religion and missiology (study of Christian missions).

One of the overriding realities emerging from the study is that India is a huge nation-continent, with an unusual socio-cultural complexity. The people are so diverse, the patterns of church growth differ from north to south and the social and economic caste system almost makes it impossible for scholars to engage in generalisations, diagnoses and recommendations. Therefore, what is presented here is done so in a tentative and provisional manner.

In recent years, Christianity has faced perhaps its greatest challenge historically: a campaign of opposition led by Hindu extremists who have blended nationalism with the Hindu religion. According to those behind this campaign, conversions to any other religion are anti-Indian and Christianity is a foreign virus polluting and endangering India's noble civilisation. This effort to keep India 'pure' has resulted in a multiplicity of activities: reconversion ceremonies for the tribal and low-caste Hindus (who have converted), hate campaigns, burning of churches, murder, rewriting of history text books, promoting Hinduism in the community and the media, anti-conversion laws, restriction on missionary visas and foreign funding regulations. While I certainly do not condone the proponents of *Hindutva*, it is valid to say that the Christian Church, by and large, has not realised that cultural identity is at the heart of Hindu–Christian tensions. Therefore, the Church needs to come to terms with its own philosophy of mission, methods and strategies.

In the midst of this troubled state of affairs, Indian Pentecostal and neo-Pentecostal churches (many linked with Western counterparts) are leading the way with what might be termed bold and aggressive evangelism activities. Post-denominational, independent churches (mostly Charismatic) are changing the spatial presence of major cities, as well as the rural areas of India, with their emphases on healing, miracles, 'driving out the spirits' and prosperity. Many of these groups have espoused Western and American-based techniques and practices that are alien to India's social and cultural essence.

India has witnessed considerable expansion of Charismatic televangelism ministries in the past decade that is the consequence of the introduction of satellite and cable television and the changing Indian mediascape. The numbers these ministries draw and the methods they incorporate into their activities have attracted church, community and media attention. The inspiration for this religious activity is clearly American. Both the Charismatic movement and the hybrid phenomenon of televangelism have their origins in the United States of America. What we are seeing in India is a powerful example of the worldwide spread of Charismatic televangelism emanating from the USA. Having said this, it is equally true to say that what we are witnessing today is the backing of televangelism by a small but growing force of new churches in India that are linked with Western missions and organisations. The fact that media penetration in India is not uniform means that certain states (mainly in the South) and some key megacities are being more influenced by televangelism than states such as Uttar Pradesh and Madhya Pradesh.

Charismatic televangelism, with more than four 24-hour networks propagating an American blend of Christianity, with alien practices and perspectives, has indeed changed India's cultural and religious mediascape. The plethora of American televangelistic programmes and the marketing techniques that accompany them have influenced local Charismatic televangelists and even Hindu televangelists to adopt some of the new assortment of communication technologies in sophisticated ways. Worship has become another form of entertainment. The medium indeed has become the message. However, as the research shows, the local figures are shaping the message and the medium to local conditions rather than unthinkingly mimicking mid-Western demagogues. Therefore, it is the sensitivity to local matters that would enhance the power of these global and local Charismatic televangelists alike. Clearly Charismatic televangelists need to give attention to issues of class, caste, language, culture and perception as they act as barriers to televangelism.

In the Christian church, the Charismatic pastors are more in favour of Charismatic televangelism than non-Charismatic pastors. Non-Charismatic pastors are concerned primarily about Charismatic televangelism's cultural disjunction and to some extent its doctrinal confusion, calling for more indigenous varieties of Christianity. *Solutions*, a 'glocal' televangelism programme, was generally well accepted by pastors and Hindu leaders, but was thought to be not truly Indian. In the Hindu community, the members of both the high caste and the high class are resistant to Charismatic televangelism, whereas the middle to lower level economic classes are more open to Charismatic televangelism. Women generally are more responsive to televangelism than men. There are fears expressed by Christian church leaders from both Charismatic and non-Charismatic persuasions that the Charismatic message, with its emphasis on prosperity, blessings and spiritual experiences, may introduce a new form of syncretistic and 'popular Christianity' without allegiance to Christ and membership in the community life of the local church. For instance, the phenomenal Benny Hinn campaign in Mumbai has been perceived by some Christian leaders there as a symptom of today's society—where the masses seek spectacle rather than meaning, entertainment rather than exposition of the text.

Indian pastors (especially those from a non-Charismatic background) are threatened by the potential loss of church members, funding and personal influence. Hindu leaders feel threatened by the scale and intrusiveness of satellite-mediated Christianity because it is potentially accessible to every Hindu home. Furthermore, the uncritical use of Western technology and the methodology of Charismatic televangelism reinforce the sentiment promulgated by *Hindutva* activists that Christian evangelism is part of an international conspiracy to divide India.

The most obvious general outcome of this study is that Charismatic televangelism has generated a series of nuanced responses from both the Protestant pastors and the Hindu community leaders. These sometimes contradictory responses and effects on cultural-religious practices and beliefs call for greater observation and study. Whereas it is too early to predict the overall growth and significance of

Charismatic televangelism, it does appear from the research findings that the religious contours of India are being challenged, contested and reconfigured by this new phenomenon that is pervading the airwaves.

When I started work on this research it became apparent to me that I was treading on new ground as there was a dearth of literature and current research in the field of study. And when I initiated the field-work in India, the feedback from various pastors and Christian leaders echoed this sentiment. Many pastors thanked me for my interest in what they regard as an important issue.

Eight of the main assertions that stem from my ethnographic research of pastors and Hindu leaders are:

First, the Protestant pastors are more concerned about the cultural disjunctive forms of Charismatic televangelism than the underpinning theological and doctrinal differences posed by the Charismatic move-ment. What emerge in the ethnography are issues related to dress code, music, dancing, fundraising, gender issues and the like. It appears that Christianity in India has been influenced by Hinduism's orthopractic nature. This is evident in the primary criticism of Charismatic televan-gelism in India, which is not based on its doctrinal teachings, or even its political overtones, but rather its nonconformity with the Indian way of life. For Westerners, these matters seem quite peripheral, '...but in the Indian context it's the way you live and act that matters, not what you believe' (Bharati, 2004: 1).

Hinduism is known as *Sanatan Dharma* or the 'eternal duty of life', which implies devotees may believe in a multiplicity of truths, but they must participate in the common duty and activities of *Dharma* (the duty of life). Therefore, to sum up the response of Protestant pastors to Charismatic televangelism: they regard the practice and way of life of Christians as more important than the theological and doctrinal basis of their faith.

Second, on the whole, global televangelism is not as well received by both Christian and Hindu leaders as local and 'glocal' televangelism. Global televangelism is likened to 'McDonaldisation' because of its refusal to indigenise and adapt the gospel to India, assuming that 'one size fits all'. The McDonalds gospel is basically an American consumer-driven gospel that does not go down well with Indian audiences.

Third, 'glocal' televangelism pioneered by CBN India, in spite of its cultural deficiencies, is a bold attempt in the hybrid expression of Christianity in the Indian context. *Solutions* demonstrates that efforts have been made through research and study to indigenise the gospel to the Indian context. I envisage that more of such media expressions will follow based on this model, some of which hopefully will aspire to be more in line with 'organic hybridity' mentioned in Chapter 7.

Fourth, Charismatic televangelism, with its theology and practices borrowed from a variety of religions and spiritistic experiences (including Hinduism), will resonate well with Hindus who practise 'popular Hinduism' and those from the middle class and below. Therefore, Charismatic televangelism is helping to promote the 'Christo-Hinduism' practices amongst those open to Charismatic teachings.

Fifth, for the growing Hindu middle-class population (approximately 10–20 per cent), Charismatic televangelism, with its messages on prosperity, self-help and healing, may be an attractive way to move upward in the middle-class culture and lifestyle. This new form of *sanskritisation* is appealing to a segment of the Indian population who are young, ambitious, materialistic and part of the global business culture.

Sixth, just as colonial Christianity's greatest influence on Hinduism was the emergence of reformed Hinduism, Charismatic televangelism's greatest influence in India is the spawning of Hindu televangelism, patterned after the American model of consumer-marketing techniques and media-savvy production methods.

Seventh, Charismatic televangelism, which has borrowed elements of Hinduism, has moved away from 'religion' into the realm of 'spirituality', like its Hindu counterpart—Hindu televangelism. This new landscape of 'spirituality' has been referred to as 'inner forms of the sacred' in which the value of self and wellbeing (in terms of health and prosperity) are given a new spiritual foundation and value (Heelas, 2008: 1). Therefore, it is my assertion that both Charismatic televangelism and Hindu televangelism are on a common platform as Charismatic televangelism shifts its focus more and more from 'religion' to 'spirituality'.

Eighth, the juxtaposition of secular and Christian television programmes from the West has reinforced the already strongly-held perception in the minds of many Hindu leaders that global televangelism represents a foreign religion, with all the values, culture, materialism and technology of the West. Therefore, the perception is that televangelism is, at best, another carrier of Western, secular modernity, and at worst, part of an international conspiracy to divide India.

The theoretical framework, arising out of the historical-comparative analysis (Tables 1.1a and 1.1b) I have devised from: post-colonial studies, sociology of religion and missiology, was examined in conjunction with the pre-colonial, colonial and post-colonial era. This framework has added another dimension to my study and enabled me to sharpen my ideas with more strategic insights. I believe that this framework can be used as a basis for further study in this field, as well as serve to open up studies in related fields. The historical-comparative framework has led to the creation of two new assertions and a model as follows:

The full-circle accommodation assertion (Chapter 2, Figure 2.2) looks at Charismatic televangelism in India from an historical and global perspective. I have argued that the Charismatic movement has been influenced by many belief systems, including Hinduism, and now the Charismatic movement is influencing India via transnational television. A full-circle has been reached in terms of Wallace's (1956) theory of accommodation.

The historical roots missiology assertion (Chapter 3, Figure 3.1) links the current scholarship in India on indigenous missions (with the clarion call for a more indigenous and Dharmic Christianity) to the pre-colonial roots of Indian Christianity. It is my contention that to indigenise Christianity successfully today, the Indian Church needs to remember what happened with Indian Christianity in pre-colonial times when Christianity maintained the fabric of Hindu culture while being Christian in faith and Syrian in liturgy.

The indigenisation measurement scale (Chapter 3, Figure 3.2) is a useful tool to measure the various aspects of indigenisation. Nine levels are suggested in this scale. Any ministry that claims to be indigenous can now look at the various aspects and measure its level of indigenisation on a scale of one to nine (one being the ground level). As Western forms of Christianity continue to be looked upon with disdain by *Hindutva* forces, it is prudent for the Indian Church (as well as televangelism ministries) to become as fully indigenous as possible. Currently, Charismatic televangelism ministries such as CBN India get 100 per cent of their support from the USA, although efforts are being made to raise funds locally as well.

The phenomenon of televangelism in India highlights the fact that globalisation and transnationalism are intersecting with culture and religion as much as with economics and politics. This research points to the availability and production of new local, transnational, 'glocal' and Hindu sacred spaces in the context of multiple 'secular' spaces.

Global Charismatic televangelism represents a marriage between the sacred and the secular. It was noted in the content analysis that 'anointing' is one of the key words used by global televangelists. 'Anointing' sets the preacher, as a power and spiritual base, apart from the rest of the audience. However, through technology and the airwaves, Charismatic teachers believe that the preacher's anointing is transferred to the masses. Global televangelism in India seems to be a cultural anachronism; it may have been tolerated in colonial India but it certainly is out of place in contemporary India. Global televangelism, compared to other institutional forms that are more culturally embedded, is the least indigenised form of Christianity. Therefore, it is a form of 'McDonaldisation' of the American gospel. Hindus and Christians are being offered a menu of services for easy consumption. The gospel has been reduced to a commodity for the calculating buyer. The McDonaldised gospel is a marketplace spirituality of least resistance, which produces 'consumer worshippers' rather than worshippers who are 'consumed with God'.

'Glocal' televangelism, on the other hand, has a more promising future. Even though there are cultural elements that jar the sensibilities of both Hindus and Christians in *Solutions*, the 'glocal' programme pioneered by CBN, is far from being merely a form of 'Masala McGospel'. As I observed the facial expressions and responses by both Christian and Hindu leaders during various times of the screening of *Solutions*, I sensed an overall openness because there were enough elements of 'Indianness' in the programme. The water of life is being presented in an Indian cup, albeit mediated through technology. 'Glocal' televangelism, as evidenced in *Solutions*, is the start of a vital adaptation of Christianity, one that is catering to urban, televisual, Bollywood culture and changing the approach of Christianity in India in the process. Even though more indigenous Christian channels with Indianised programmes are springing up, especially in the South, *Solutions*, while falling short of the standards of 'organic hybridity' is unique in its overall philosophy and approach.

Historically, Christian mission to Hindus was successful because of three factors: indigenisation, meeting of felt-needs, and respect for the Indian social and kinship patterns. Therefore, if televangelism is to succeed in India, more efforts need to be undertaken in these three areas. 'Glocal' televangelism has made a start in its cultural adaptation of the gospel and the meeting of felt needs. To be truly successful, 'glocal' televangelism needs to be more 'organic' and perhaps work with groups such as the *Jesu Bhakta* movement (devotee of Jesus), the Churchless Christian movement and other like-minded groups which respect the Hindu social system (unlike the established and 'organised' churches).

Perhaps, just as *Solutions* caters to Bollywood India, other more indigenous productions may be launched to cater in the future for different segments of the Indian population, such as 'Churchless Christians', *Jesu Bhaktas* and *Ashram* believers. Televangelism can, therefore, play a unique and far-reaching role in India as the electronic church to the Churchless Christian community or to the Hindus who revere Christ but not the organised Church.

Impact of Televangelism in India

As has been noted in Chapter 3, India is a nation consisting of various sub-groups of people; one of the ways we can categorise India is to see it in three ways: urban Western-oriented, urban traditional—oriented and village traditional-oriented. It appears from the research that the urban Western-oriented Indian is the one most likely to respond to Charismatic televangelism. For some of these Indians the Charismatic gospel of health, wealth and success may induce a form of 'Sanskritisation', a term coined by Srinivas (1952) to refer to lower caste Indians who wish to move upwards in the social scale by adopting certain practices or acquiring certain qualifications (like learning to speak English as a means to get into the civil service in colonial times). Televangelism, both in its global and glocal forms, will continue to interest and inspire the Western-educated urban Indian who may not take on board the exclusive claims of Christ but fragments of Christianity that fit into the familiar trajectory of his or her Hindu lifestyle. In this way, a new form of syncretised Christianity or 'Christo-Hinduism' may eventuate.

The research also indicates that both the church and the wider segments of the Hindu community are generally resistant to forms of religions and cultural importation. Therefore, I can expect that more 'glocal' programmes like *Solutions* may be produced. In this way televangelism in India will follow the precedent established in Brazil, where what began as import substitution (from America) now enjoys more local productions and local independent networks as well.

Within the Indian Church, as televangelism extends its influence in both the global and glocal formats, the Christian Church will be impacted and challenged in new ways. Charismatic televangelism, I believe, is shifting in its role as the reinforcer and handmaiden of mission to that of the 'face' of mission in India. I envisage that we will see a blurring of denominational distinctives as the 'new' Christianity mediated by Charismatic televangelism finds its way into mainline churches primarily through the large numbers of young people, the leaders of tomorrow.

Charismatic worship—with its repertoire of upbeat songs, worship bands and worship singers—makes sense to the youth of today's churches and for them the long-held denominational distinctives observed by their forefathers are nothing more than traditional baggage. Therefore, mainline churches may become more Charismatic (at least in their mode of worship and liturgy) and more Charismatic churches will spring up—some as extensions of Western churches and others as independent churches.

Historically, it was the invention of print technology that led to breaking the stranglehold of the Catholic Church, giving birth to the Protestant movement. Could the introduction of satellite and digital technology bring about something as significant in the Indian church context?

While I believe that the traditions of historic Christianity are strong in India and, therefore, something as cataclysmic as what happened during the Protestant Reformation may not come to pass; yet it is equally true to say that Christianity in India is at the crossroads and time will reveal the future shape of Christianity.

In response to the 'Charismatisation' of the Church, we may also see the rise of certain conservative and fundamental groups within Indian Christianity who take on a more anti-Charismatic and traditional stance in an effort to resist the blurring of distinctives and keep the faith 'pure'.

The matrix of 'self' (Hindu) and 'other' (non-Hindu) in India has now come into operation because the 'other' is visible. Hindus have every reason to protect their self-identity as the 'other' increases in visibility and domination. With the onslaught of Charismatic televangelism, Hindus and Indian Christians now have access to view the worship patterns and styles of Christians from all parts of the globe. The 'other' is immediately perceived as 'foreign' and hence, there is a concerted move towards 'Hinduisation' or Christian indigenisation and the preservation of the cultural identity of 'self'.

Charismatic television in India's sensitive communal and religious context will indeed add to the contestation of faiths. For the average

Hindu, or Muslim for that matter, Charismatic televangelism is regarded as Christian televangelism. Hindus and Muslims are generally not aware of the theological and denominational differences and subsets within the Christian Church. As a result of the increase of Charismatic televangelism, I can expect tremendous growth and expansion in Hindu televangelism and more global links (financial, artistic and spiritual) established with Indians in the diaspora in USA, Europe and elsewhere. Hence, the media could inadvertently become the venue for 'culture wars' and the 'clash of civilisations'. At other times, the media will simply be a venue for the fragmentation of faiths, where multiple faiths are 'narrowcasted' to specific interest groups, with the various religions in a state of co-existence.

Predictions about Mediated Faith in a Globalised World

Both Charismatic televangelism and Hindu televangelism have created a new genre in the expanding television media market in India. The prime time for spiritual and religious television is 6.30 am to 8 am and 5.30 pm to 7.30 pm because Hindus consider these periods as holy times for devotion and worship. What used to be a quiet and uneventful period for television in general (the 6.30 am to 8 am slot) is now becoming a much sought after time for all kinds of religious programmes. So this is yet another way that religious television is making its mark in India.

Other religions, like Islam and Buddhism and even new religious movements and sectarian groups are likely to jump on the bandwagon to establish religious channels. Hence, religious TV in India may consist of a potpourri of religious discourses, ayurvedic cures, yoga, slaying in the spirit, miracles and teachings from the Vedas, the Koran and the Bible, with a new 'Babel' in the airwaves. As each religious group gets a foothold into the airwaves, financial, marketing and faith links will be established locally and overseas, thereby creating political economies that support and sustain their religious media enterprises.

Whereas the epicentre of Charismatic televangelism is in the West, primarily the USA, the epicentre of Hindu televangelism is in India. Islamic televangelism currently originates from Pakistan and the Middle East. Therefore, we are witnessing the makings of a new geopolitical and religious map. However, as I have indicated in earlier chapters, in the age of globalisation fixed spaces and locations are not as important as flows of information, capital and power. Even then, the overall picture that emerges of links, hubs and flows in connection with religious televangelism is interesting and significant. It calls for greater study, as well as a new paradigm, for understanding the changing patterns of mediated religion in the global world.

I predict that religious televangelism will become more strategic in the use of the various media, resulting in a greater convergence of the old and new media of television, internet, mobile phone and DVD. This is already happening to some extent as certain Hindu channels are offering to text a daily verse from the *Vedas* to interested mobile phone subscribers.

How will the growth of multiple religious television stations affect the 'secular' media? I believe the mainstream media will be constrained to have a growing appreciation of the significance of religion and religious television and may even cash in on its need to provide ritualistic and spiritual support to the community—especially during times of national or international crises, catastrophes and tragedies.

This is happening in the West where the funerals of religious leaders (like the Pope) or celebrities (like Michael Jackson) are presented by the secular media as live transmissions, giving the religious institution (the Church) for that moment the full benefit of conducting its ceremony with some sense of solemnity and dignity and therefore bringing a sense of closure to the collective grief of the people. It will be interesting to see whether the secular media in India turns to Christian, Hindu and Islamic faiths and television stations in days to come to give coverage to stories and events pertaining to the three world religions in India.

McDonaldisation, Masala McGospel and Om Economics is an attempt to trace the shape of televisual faith in India. Faith is indeed alive and actively searching for new modes of expression and new nodes for delivering spirituality. In the process, faith has found strange bedfellows in politics and the capitalist market. Through these means, televangelism is changing the church and the broader community in India, but at a more fundamental level, it is also changing the whole concept of religion in the modern world. How these changes will impact the generations to come is something that, hopefully, is deemed worthy of research.

References

Abelman, R. 1990. 'Who's Watching for What Reasons', in R. Abelman and S. Hoover (eds), *Religious Television: Controversies and Conclusions*. Norwood, New Jersey: Ablex Publishing Co.

Abraham, V. 1992. 'The Call of Indian Cities', *Aim*, 23(16).

Alexander, K. 1992. 'Roots of the New Age', in J. R. Lewis and J. G. Melton (eds), *Perspectives of the New Age*. Albany, New York: State University of New York Press.

Amalraj, J. 2004. 'The Highlights of the 2001 Census Report and its Implications for Indian Missions', in *Indian Missions* (October–December), pp. 38–47. Hyderabad, India: India Missions Association.

Ananthakrishnan, G. (26 April 2008).'Kerala Church Divided Over Invite to Advani'. *Times of India*, Hyderabad.

Anderson, A. 1999. 'The Gospel and Culture in Pentecostal Mission in the Third World', paper presented at the Conference of European Pentecostal, Charismatic Research Association, Hamburg, 13–17 July.

Anderson, B. 1993. *Imagined Communities: Reflections of the Origins and Spread of Nationalism*. London: Verso.

Appadurai, A. 2000. 'Disjuncture and Difference in the Global Cultural Economy', in D. Brydon (ed.), *PostColonialism: Critical Concepts*. London: Routledge.

Archer, M. and C. Atkins. 1987. 'Would Jesus wear a Rolex watch?' in *On Collection* [Music CD]. Nashville, TN: MCA Records.

Armstrong, B. 1979. *The Electric Church*. Nashville: Nelson.

Arrington, F. L. 1988. 'Historical Perspectives on Pentecostal and Charismatic Hermeneutics', in S. M. Burgess and G. B. McGee (eds), *Dictionary of Pentecostal and Charismatic Movements*, pp. 376–389. Grand Rapids, MI: Regency (Zondervan).

Arulappa, R. 1974. *Tirakurral a Christian Book?* Madras: Meipporul.

Asamoah-Gyadu, J. K. 2005. 'Anointing through the Screen: Neo Pentecostalism and Televised Christianity in Ghana', *Studies in World Christianity*, 11(1).

Asante, M. K. 1987. *The Afrocentric Idea*. Philadelphia: Temple University Press.

Ayrookuzhiel, A. M. A. (n.d.). 'The Ideological Nature of the Emerging Dalit Consciousness', in A. P. Nirmal (ed.), *Towards a Common Dalit Ideology*. Madras: Garukul Press.

Aythal, J. M. and J. J. Thatamanil. 2002. *Metropolitan Chrysostom on Mission in the Market Place*. Tiruvalla: CSS.

Bal, A. 2007. 'Hindutva Not a Way of Life'. Retrieved from http://hindurenaissance. com/index.php/yugabda-5109/20080126102/6-varshapratipada-april-2007/ articles/dharma/hindutv on 1 September 2009.

Barber, B. 1992. 'Civilization and Ideology: Jihad vs. McWorld', *The Atlantic Monthly*, 269(3).

Barber, B. 1995. *Jihad vs McWorld*. New York: Times Books.

Barnett, H. G. 1953. *Innovation: The Basis of Cultural Change*. New York: McGraw-Hill.

Barnhart, J. E. 1990. 'Prosperity Gospel: A New Folk Theology', in R. Abelman and S. Hoover (eds), *Religious Television: Controversies and Conclusions*, pp. 159–162. Norwood, New Jersey: Ablex Publishing.

Barron, B. 1987. *The Health and Wealth Gospel*. Illinois: IVP.

Bebbington, D. 1989. *Evangelicalism in Modern Britain: A History from the 1730's to the 1980's*. London: Unwin Hyman.

Benny Hinn Ministries. 2006. 'Television Reaches Around the World'. Retrieved from http://www.bennyhinn.org/Televison/televisiondefault.cfm on 10 March 2006.

Berelson, B. 1952. *Content Analysis in Communication Research*. Glencoe, Illinois: Free Press.

Berkowitz, B. 2006. 'Pastor John Hagee spearheads Christians United for Israel'. Media Transparency Website. Retrieved from http://www.mediatransparency.org/story.php?storyID=116 on 7 March 2008.

Berlo, D. 1960. *The Process of Communication: An Introduction to Theory and Practice*. San Francisco: Rinehart.

Berreman, G. D. 1979. *Caste and Other Inequities*. New Delhi: Ved Prakash Vatuk Folklore Institute.

Bhabha, H. K. 1990. *Nation and Narration*. New York: Routledge.

Bhaktin, M. 1981. 'Discourse in the Novel', in M. Holquist (ed.), *The Dialogical Imagination*. Austin: Texas University Press.

Bharati, S. 2004. *Living Water and Indian Bowl*. Pasadena, California: William Carey Library.

Bharatiya Janata Party (BJP). (n.d.). Website [Electronic Version]. Retrieved from http://www.bjp.org/ on July 2006.

Bhuskute, P. 2005. 'Merchants of Nirvana', *Deccan Chronicle*, Hyderabad, 31 July.

Birch, D., T. Schirato and S. Srivastava. 2000. *Asia: Cultural Politics in the Global Age*. Crows Nest, NSW: Allen and Unwin.

Bisset, T. 1980. 'Religious Broadcasting: Assessing the State of the Art', *Christianity Today*, 12 December, 24 (21).

Borgard, M. 1997. 'Indian Religion'. Retrieved from http://www.snu.edu/syllabi/history/s97projects/india/religion.htm on 10 November 2007.

Bourdieu, P. 1984. *Distinction: A Social Critique of the Judgement of Taste*. London: Routledge and Kegan Paul.

———. 1991. 'Genesis and structures of the Religious Field', *Comparative Social Research*, 13(1): 1–44.

Bowman, R. M. and P. Carden. 1991. 'Book Review: Good Morning Holy Spirit', *Christian Research Institute* (Spring), 36.

Boyd, R. 1977. *Khristadvaita: A Theology for India*. Madras: CLS Press.

Bruce, S. 1990. *Pray TV: Televangelism in America*. New York: Routledge.

Burgess, S. 2001. 'Pentecostalism in India: An Overview', *Asian Journal of Pentecostal Studies*, 4(1).

Caincross, F. 2001. 'Changing the World', in *The Death of Distance: How the Communication Revolution is Changing Our Lives*, pp. 1–18. Boston: Harvard Business School Press.

Caplan, L. 1987. 'Christian Fundamentalism as Counter Culture', in W. F. Fore (ed.), *Television and Religion: The Shaping of Faith, Values and Culture*, pp. 366–381. Minneapolis, USA: Augsburg Publishing House.

Cathcart, R. and G. Gumpert. 1993. 'Mediated Interpersonal Communication: Toward a New Typology', *Quarterly Journal of Speech*, 69(3): 267–277.

CBN. 2008. 'Hindu Nation: India's Religious Cleansing'. Retrieved from http://www.cbn.com/CBNnews/305889.aspx?option=print on 23 January 2008.

CBN India. (n.d.). 'Christian Broadcasting Network India'. Retrieved from http://cbnindia.org on 4 October 2004.

Cherian, Raju. 2006. Interviewed by the author on 10 March, Mumbai.

Cho, P. Y. 1979. *The Fourth Dimension* (Volume 2). New Jersey: Logos.

Chowgule, A. V. (n.d.). 'Christianity in India: The Hindutva Perspective'. Retrieved from http://www.hvK.org/Publications/Cihp/index.html on 26 December 2007.

Church of North India website. (n.d.). Retrieved from http://www.cnisynod.org/begning.htm on 10 July 2007.

Church of South India website. (n.d.). 'That All May Be One'. Retrieved from http://www.csichurch.com/main.htm on 10 July 2007.

Clark, L. S. 2003. *From Angels to Aliens: Teenagers, the Media, and the Supernatural.* New York: Oxford University Press.

Coleman, S. 2000. *The Globalisation of Charismatic Christianity: Spreading the Gospel of Prosperity.* Cambridge, England: Cambridge University Press.

Compaine, B. 2002. 'Global Media', *Foreign Policy*, 133 (November–December).

Contractor, D. 2009. Interviewed by author through email, 23 July, Mumbai.

Copley, A. 1997. *Religions in Conflict: Ideology, Cultural Contact And Conversion in Late-Colonial India.* New Delhi: Oxford University Press.

Cox, H. 1973. *The Seduction of the Spirit: The Use and Misuse of People's Religion.* New York: Simon and Shuster.

Cross, F. L. 2005. 'India', in F. L. Cross (ed.), *The Oxford Dictionary of the Christian Church.* Oxford: Oxford University Press.

Daniel, P. 1984. 'Theology of Conversion in the Indian Context'. Doctoral dissertation. Pasadena: California: Fuller Theological Seminary.

Das, G. 2004. 'The Respect They Deserve', *Time Asia.* Retrieved from http://www.time.com/time/asia/covers/501041206/two_indias_vpt_das.html on 5 March 2008.

Das, S. (n.d.). 'Jesus through Hindu Eyes'. Retrieved from http://www.bbc.co.uk/religion/religions/hinduism/features/hindu_eys/index.shtml on 4 April 2006.

Davis, G. 1946. 'Some Hidden Effects of Christianity upon Hinduism and Hindus', *The Journal of Religion*, 26(3): 119.

Dempster, M. W., B. D. Klaus and P. Douglas. 1999. *The Globalization of Pentecostalism: A Religion Made to Travel.* Carlisle: Paternoster Press.

Dennis, J. 1962. 'An Analysis of the Audience of Religious Radio and Television Programmes in the Detroit Metropolitan Area'. University of Michigan.

Dhanabalan, S. 2003. 'The Church in Singapore: Time to Distance from the West?', paper presented at the Graduates Christian Fellowship, Singapore, 5 September 2003. Retrieved from http://www.gcf.org.sg/resources/the-church-in-singapore—time-to-distance-from-the-west? on 3 May 2010.

Dharmaraj, J. 1993. *Colonialism and Christian Missions: Post-colonial Reflections.* New Delhi: Indian Society for Promoting Christian Knowledge.

Diem, A. G. and J. R. Lewis. 1992. 'Imagining India: The Influence of Hinduism on the New Age Movement', in J. R. Lewis and J. G. Melton (eds), *Perspectives of the New Age.* Albany, New York: State University of New York Press.

Dirks, N. 2001. *Castes of Mind: Colonialism and the Making of Modern India*. New Jersey: Princeton University Press.

Drane, J. 2001. *The McDonaldizaion of the Church: Consumer Culture and the Church's Future*. Macon, GA: Smyth and Helwys Publishing.

D'souza, J. 2004. *Dalit Freedom Now and Forever: The Epic Struggle for Dalit Emancipation*. Centennial, Colorado: Dalit Freedom Network.

Dumont, L. 1980. *Homo Hieracticus: The Caste System and It's Implications*. Chicago: University of Chicago.

Durkheim, E. 1961. *The Elementary Forms of the Religious Life*. New York: Collier Books.

Eapen, J. T. 2006. 'New Life Fellowship: Celebrating 25 Years', *Transformation by Word*, 1(1).

Eaton, R. 2000. *Essays on Islam and Indian History*. New Delhi: Oxford University Press.

Edwards, K. 2003. 'Televangelism and Political Ideology: A Study of Content and Ideology in the 700 Club', *Journal of Undergraduate Research*, 4(10).

Ellul, J. 1985. *The Humiliation of the Word*. Grand Rapids: Eerdmans.

Engler, S. 2003. 'Modern Times: Religion, Consecration and the State in Bourdieu', *Cultural Studies*, 17(3–4): 445–467.

Escobar, S. 1994. 'Mission in the New World Order', *Prism* 4 (December).

Evans-Pritchard, E. E. 1976. *Witchcraft, Oracles, and Magic among the Azande*. Oxford: Oxford University Press.

———. 1990. *Theories of Primitive Religion*. Oxford: Clarendon Press.

Farquhar, J. N. 1913. *The Crown of Hinduism*. London: Oxford University Press.

FCRA website. (n.d.). 'FCRA for NGO's'. Retrieved from http://www.fcraforngos. org/intro.htm on 1 January 2008.

Fore, W. 1987. *Television and Religion: The Shaping of Faith, Values and Culture*. Minneapolis: Ashburg.

Forrester, D. B. 1979. *Caste and Christianity: Attitudes and Policies on Caste of Anglo-Saxon Protestant Missions in India*. London: Curzon Press.

Frankl, R. 1987. *Televangelism: The Marketing of Popular Religion*. Illinois: Southern Illinois University.

———. 1998. 'Transformation of Televangelism: Repackaging Christian Family Values', in L. Kintz and J. Lesage (eds), *Media, Culture and the Religious Right*, pp. 163–189. Minnesota: University of Minnesota Press.

Freston, P. 1997. 'Evangelization and Globalization: General Observations and Some Latin American Dimensions', in M. Hutchinson and O. Kalu (eds), *A Global Faith: Essays on Evangelicalism and Globalization*. Sydney: Centre for the Study of Australian Christianity.

Frontline. 2001, 8–21 December. 'Hindutva Ire', *Frontline*, 18(25).

Frost, R. 2005. 'Local Success on a Global Scale'. Retrieved from http://www. brandchannel.com/features_effects.asp?pf_id+261 on 30 August 2006.

Frykenberg, R. E. 1996. *History and Belief: Foundations of Historical Understanding*. Grand Rapids, MI: Eerdmans, William B. Publishing.

———. 2004. 'Gospel, Globalization and Hindutva: The Politics of "Conversion" in India', in D. M. Lewis (ed.), *Christianity Reborn: The Global Expansion of Evangelicalism in the 20th Century*. Grand Rapids: William Eerdmans Publishers.

Frykenberg, R. E. 2008. *Christianity in India: From Beginnings to the Present*. Oxford: Oxford University Press.

Fukuyama, F. 1992. *The End of History and the Last Man*. New York: Avon Books Inc.

Gawain, S. 1985. *Creative Visualization*. New York: Bantam Books.

Gellner, E. 1992. *Plough, Sword, and Book: The Structure of Human History*. Chicago: The University of Chicago Press.

George, F. J. 1989. *Mother India Speaks*. Singapore: Scholastica Silva.

Giddens, A. 2000. *Runaway World*. London: Routledge.

Gifford, P. 2004. *Ghana's New Christianity: Pentecostalism in a Globalizing African Economy*. Bloomington and Indianapolis: Indiana University Press.

Gilliland, D. S. 1989. 'Contextual Theology as Incarnational Mission', in D. S. Gilliland (ed.), *The Word among Us*. Dallas: Word Publishing.

Gnanasigamani, V. 1981. *Agathiar Gnanam*. Madras: Gnanodhayam Publishers.

God TV. 2006. 'You Can be a Millionaire', Television Programme, March 9, 9.30 pm, Mumbai.

Gokran, S. 2006. 'Economic Origins of India's Middle Class', rediffnews.com. Retrieved from http://202.54.124.133/money/2006/nov/20guest.htm on 5 March 2008.

Gopal, S. 1993. 'Secularism: Historical Perspective', paper presented at the Third Bashir Memorial Lecture Trivandrum, India on 22 May 1993.

Government of India. 2003. 'Indian Cable Industry', White Paper, Government of India, New Delhi.

Graham, B. 1983. 'The Future of TV Evangelism', *TV Guide*, 31(10): 4–11.

Gramsci, A. 1978. *Selections from Political Writings 1912–1926* (Q. Hoare, Trans.). New York: International Publishers.

Green, S. 2006. 'Hindu Rally Sparks Fears'. *The Advocate*, p. 6.

Griswold, H. P. 1912. 'Some Characteristics of Hinduism as a Religion', *The Biblical World*, 40(3).

Gupta, K. 2006. 'Hindu Tele-evangelists'. Retrieved from http://thepioneer.english.indianpress.info/ on 19 March 2006.

Hadden, J. K. 1990. 'The Globalization of American Televangelism', *International Journal of Frontier Missions*, 7(1).

Hadden, J. K. and A. Shupe. 1988. *Televangelism: Power and Politics on God's Frontier*. New York: Henry Holt.

Hadden, J. K. and C. E. Swann. 1981. *Prime Time Preachers: The Rising Power of Televangelism*. Reading, MA: Addison-Wesley Publishing.

Hambye, E. R. 1952. 'The Syrian Christians in India', *Clergy Monthly*, 16(10).

Hare, J. B. 2007. 'Hinduism'. Retrieved from www.sacred-texts.com on 6 April 2007.

Haribabu, E. 2006. Interviewed by author, 5 October, Hyderabad.

Harris, M. and O. Johnson. 2000. *Cultural Anthropology* (5th ed.). Needham Heights, Massachusetts: Allyn and Bacon.

Hawkins, M. 2006. *Global Structures, Local Cultures*. Melbourne: Oxford University Press.

Haynes, J. 2003. 'Religious Fundamentalism and Politics'. Retrieved from www.law.emory.edu/ihr/worddocs/haynes5.doc on 15 January 2005.

Hedlund, R. 1982. *Building the Church*. Madras: Evangelical Literature Service.

———. 1999. 'Indian Christians of Indigenous Origin and Their Solidarity with Original Groups', *Journal of Dharma*, 24(1).

Hedlund, R. 2001. 'Previews of Christian Indigeneity in India', *Journal of Asian Mission*, 3(2).

——. 2004. 'The Witness of New Christian Movements in India', paper presented at the IAMS Conference, Malaysia on 31 July–7 August.

Heelas, P. 2008. *Spiritualities of Life: New Age Romanticism and Consumptive Capitalism*. Malden, Massachusetts: Blackwell Publishing.

Heelas, P., L. Woodhead, B. Seel, B. Szerszynski and K. Trusting. 2005. *The Spiritual Revolution: Why Religion is Giving Way to Spirituality*. Malden Massachusets, USA: Blackwell Publishing.

Hemphill, P. 1981. 'Praise the Lord–and Cue the Cameraman', in B. Cole (ed.), *Television Today: Readings From TV Guide*. New York: Oxford University Press.

Hendershot, H. 2004. *Shaking the World for Jesus: Media and Conservative Evangelical Culture*. Chicago: University of Chicago Press.

Hexam, I. and K. Poewe. 1994. 'Charismatic Churches in South Africa: A Critique of Criticisms and Problems of Bias', in K. Poewe (ed.), *Charismatic Christianity as a Global Culture*. South Carolina: University of South Carolina Press.

——. 1997. *New Religions as Global Cultures*. Boulder, CO: Westview Press.

Hiebert, P. 1987. 'Critical Contextualization', *International Bulletin of Missionary Research*, 11 (3): 104–12.

——. 1989. 'Healing and the Kingdom', in J. R. Coggins and P. Hiebert (eds), *Wonders and the Word: An Examination of Issues Raised by John Wimber and the Vineyard Movement*. Winnipeg, MB: Kindred Press.

——. 2000. 'Missiological Issues in the Encounter with Emerging Hinduism', *Missiology: An International Review*, 28(1): 47–63.

Hinn, Benny. 1990. *Good Morning, Holy Spirit*. Nashville, Tennessee: Thomas Nelson.

——. 1992. *The Anointing*. Nashville, Tennessee: Thomas Nelson.

History of Church of God Missions. 1943. Cleveland, Tennessee: Church of God Publishing House.

Hocken, P. D. 1988. 'Charismatic Movement', in S. M. Burgess and G. B. McGee (eds), *Dictionary of Pentecostal and Charismatic Movements* (3rd ed., pp. 130–160). Grand Rapids, Michigan: Regency.

Hoefer, H. 1991. *Churchless Christianity* (2001 ed.). Pasadena, California: William Carey Library.

Hong, Y. G. 2006. 'Encounter with Modernity: The "McDonaldization" and "Charismatization" of Korean Mega-Churches', *Cyberjournal for Pentecostal Charismatic Research*, 15. Retrieved from http://www.pctii.org/cyberj/cyberj15/Hong.html on 21 April 2010.

Hoover, S. 1987. 'The Religious Television Audience: A Matter of Significance, or Size?', *Review of Religous Research*, 29(2): 135–51.

——. 2005. 'Islands in the Global Stream: Television, Religion, and Geographic Integration', *Studies in World Christianity*, 11(1).

Hoover, S. and K. Lundby. 1997. *Rethinking Media, Religon And Culture*. Thousand Oaks, California: Sage Publications.

Hoover, S. and L. S. Clark. 2002. *Practising Religion in the Age of the Media: Explorations in Media, Religion and Culture*. New York: Columbia University Press.

Horsfield, P. 1984. *Religious Television. The American Experience*. New York: Longman.

Horsfield, P. 1985. 'The Mediated Ministry: Evangelism by Mail', *Journal of Communication*, 36(1).

———. 1990. 'American Religious Programmes in Australia', in R. Abelman and S. Hoover (eds), *Religious Television: Controversies and Conclusions*. New Jersey: Ablex Publishing.

Horsfield, P., M. Hess and A. Medrano. 2004. *Belief in Media: Cultural Perspectives on Media and Christianity*. Hampshire: Ashgate.

Human Rights Watch. 2007. 'India: Stop Hindu-Christian Violence in Orissa'. Retrieved from http://hrw.org/english/docs/2007/12/28/india17668.htm on 12 February 2008.

Hunt, S. 2000. 'Winning Ways: Globalisation and the Impact of the Health and Wealth Gospel'. *Contemporary Religion*, 15(3): 331–147.

Huntington, S. P. 1998. *The Clash of Civilizations and the Remaking of World Order*. London: Touchstone Books.

Hymovitz, K. S. 1995. 'On Sesame Street, It's All Show'. Retrieved from http://www.city-journal.org/html/5_4_on_sesame_street_html on 19 November 2006.

IEM website. (n.d.). 'Indian Evangelical Mission'. Retrieved from http://www.iemoutreach.org on 21 April 2010.

IPC website. (n.d.). 'Indian Pentecostal Church of God'. Retrieved from http://www.ipcgeneralcouncil.org/regions/asp on 25 December 2007.

Irwin, R. 2006. *For Lust of Knowing: The Orientalists and their Enemies*. London: Allen Lane.

James, J. and B. Shoesmith. 2006. *Hillsong, Benny Hinn and the Message of Health and Wealth: Looking at Technology and Religion*. Murdoch University, WA, Australia.

———. 2007. 'Masala McGospel: A Case Study of CBN's Solutions Programme in India', *Studies in World Christianity*, 13(2): 174–175.

James, L. 1994. *The Rise and Fall of the British Empire*. London: Little, Brown and Company.

Jamkhandikar, S. 2008. 'Hi-tech Remake of Hindu Epics Flood Indian TV,' Reuters Latest News [Electronic Version]. Retrieved from http://in.reuters.com/article/entertainmentNews/idINIndia-34475920080711 on 26 December 2008.

Jenkins, D. 2000. 'Overcoming Consumer Christianity'. Retrieved from http://members.aol.com/lcsharpe/000227.html on 6 April 2008.

Jenkins, P. 2002. *The Next Christendom: The Coming of Global Christianity*. New York: Oxford University Press.

Jenkins, R. 1992. *Pierre Bourdieu*. London and New York: Routledge.

John, P. K. (n.d.). 'Christians of Kerala [Electronic Version].' Kerala History Series. Retrieved from http://ananthapuri.com/Kerala-history.asp?page=christian on 3 December 2007.

Johnstone, P. and J. Mandryk. 2001. 'India', in *Operation World*. Cumbria, UK: WEC International.

Jones, E. S. 1925. *The Christ of the Indian Road*. New York: Abingdon.

Kane, J. H. 1971. *A Global View of Christian Missions*. Grand Rapids, Michigan: Baker Book House.

Keay, F. E. 1931. *A History of the Syrian Church in India*. Delhi: ISPCK.

Kendal, E. 2007. 'Recipe for Catastrophe In Working Together', *Australian Evangelical Alliance*, 2007(2): 11.

Kintz, L. and J. Lesage (eds). 1998. *Media, Culture and the Religious Right*. Menneapolis: University of Minnesota.

Kitchen, M. 1996. *The British Empire and Commonwealth: A Short History*. London: Macmillan Press.

Kooliman, D. 1983. *Conversion and Social Equality in India*. New Delhi: South Asia Publications.

Kopf, D. 1987. *The Indian World*. Arlington Heights, Ill: Forum Press.

Kreeft, P. 1987. 'Comparing Christianity and Hinduism', *National Catholic Register*, 5 (May).

Krippendorff, K. 1980. *Content Analysis: An Introduction to Its Methodology*. Newbury Park, CA: Sage Publications.

Kurth, J. 1999. 'Religion and Globalization', *The Templeton Lecture on Religion and World Affairs*, 7(7).

Lancaster, J. 2003. 'India: Peddling Religion on TV'. Retrieved from http://communalism. blogspot.com/2003/12/india-peddling-religion-on-tv.html on 9 November 2007.

Lash, S. 1990. *Sociology of Postmodernism*. London: Routledge.

Lee, S. and P. L. Sinitiere. 2009. *Holy Mavericks: Evangelical Innovators and the Spiritual Marketplace*. New York: New York University Press.

Lehmann, D. 1998. 'Fundamentalism and Globalism', *Third World Quarterly*, 19(4).

Leslie, M. 2003. 'International Televangelism/American Ideology: The Case of The 700 Club', paper presented at the International Conference on Television in Transition, Massachusetts Institute of Technology, Boston on 2–4 May.

Levinson, D. 1998. *Religion: A Cross-cultural Dictionary*. London: Oxford University Press.

Levitt, P. 2001. *The Transnational Villagers*. Los Angeles: University of California Press.

Lewis-Beck, M. S. 1990. 'Basic Content Analysis', in R. P. Weber (ed.), *Quantitative Applications in the Social Sciences*, Series Number 07–049. Thousand Oaks: Sage Publications.

Littell, J. F. 1976. *Coping with the Mass Media*. Evanston, Illinois: McDougal, Littell.

Livingstone, S. 2008. 'On the Mediation of Everything'. Retrieved from http://www. icahdq.org/conferences/presaddress.asp on 25 July 2009.

Luzbetak, L. 1970. *The Church and Cultures: An Applied Anthropology for the Religious Worker*. Techny, IL: Divine Word Publications.

———. 1985. 'If Junipero Serra Were Alive', *The American*, 41(4).

Lyon, D. 2000. *Jesus in Disneyland: Religion in Postmodern Times*. Cambridge: Polity/ Blackwell.

Macdonald, J. I. 1910. *The Redeemer's Reign: Foreign Missions and the Second Advent*. London: Marshall and Scott.

Malik, Rajiv. 2003. ' India's Bold New Religious TV', *Hinduism Today*, January–March. Retrieved from http://www.hinduismtoday.com/modules/smartsection/item. php?itemid=3768 on 26 October 2007.

Mallampalli, C. 2004. *Christians and Public Life in Colonial South India, 1863–1937: Contending with Marginality*. London: Routledge Curzon.

Mana's website. n.d.. 'Indian Religions: Ramayana Text'. Retrieved from www.sscnet. ucla.edu/ on 2 November 2006.

Mangalwadi, V., V. Martis, M. B. Desai, B. K. Verghese and R. Samuel. 2000. *Burnt Alive: The Staines and the God They Loved*. Mumbai: GLS.

Mankekar, P. 1999. *Screening Culture, Viewing Politics: An Ethnography of Television, Womanhood and Nation in Postcolonial India*. Durham, NC: Duke University Press.

Marshall, I. H. 1970. *Luke: Historian and Theologian*. Exeter: Paternoster.

Martin, B. 2001. 'The Pentecostal Gender Paradox: A Cautionary Tale for the Sociology of Religion', in R. K. Fenn (ed.), *The Blackwell Companion to the Sociology of Religion*. Oxford: Blackwell.

Martin, D. 1978. *A General Theory of Secularization*. Oxford: Blackwell.

———. 1990. *Tongues of Fire: The Explosion of Protestantism in Latin America*. Oxford, UK: Blackwell Publishers.

Martin, P. 1998. 'A Brief History of the Ceylon Pentecostal Mission', paper presented at the Indigenous Christian Movements Conference, Hyderabad on 27–31 October.

Martin, W. 1989. *The New Age Cult*. Minneapolis: Bethany House Publishers.

Martin-Barbero, J. 1993. *Communication, Culture and Hegemony: From the Media to Mediations*. London: Sage Publications.

Martinez, R. D. 2006. 'Strange Fires: Pentecostals and Charismatics', Spirit Watch Website. Retrieved from http://www.spiritwatch.org.firepcdif.htm on 24 March 2006.

Massey, J. (n.d.). 'Need of a Dalit Theology'. *CTC Bulletin*. Retrieved from http://www.cca.org.hk/resources/ctc/ctc01-04/ctc0101i.htm on 4 January 2008.

Mathew, C. V. (n.d.). 'Indian Theology'. *Elwell Evangelical Dictionary*. Retrieved from http://mb-soft.com/believe/txo/indian.htm on 7 April 2008.

Maxwell, D. 1988. 'Editorial', *Journal of Religion in Africa*, 28(3).

McConnell, D. R. 1988. *A Different Gospel*. Peabody: Hendrickson Publishers.

McGavran, D. 1955. *The Bridges of God: A Study in the Strategy of Missions*. New York: Friendship Press.

———. 1970. *Understanding Church Growth*. Grand Rapids: William Eerdmans.

McGee, G. 1999. '"Latter Rain" Falling in the East: Early Twentieth-Century Pentecostalism in India and the Debate over Speaking in Tongues', *Church History Studies in Christianity and Culture*, 68(3).

McGee, G. and S. Burgess. 2003. 'India', in S. M. Burgess and E. van der Maas (eds), *The New International Dictionary of Pentecostal and Charismatic Movements*. Grand Rapids, Michigan: Zondervan.

McGrath, A. E. 2001. *Christian Theology: An Introduction* (3rd ed.). Malden, Massachusetts: Blackwell Publishing.

———. 2002. *The Future of Christianity*. Oxford, UK: Blackwell Publishers.

McMahon, R. 1974. 'India', in J. D. Douglas (ed.), *The New International Dictionary of the Christian Church*. Exeter: The Paternoster Press.

Melton, J. G. 1992. 'New Thought and the New Age', in J. R. Lewis and J. G. Melton (eds), *Perspectives on the New Age*. Albany, New York: State University of New York Press.

Michael, S. M. 2003. 'Reaffirming Indian Pluralism', *Pluralism and Cultural Identity*, 6(3).

Middleton, V. J. 1977. 'An Andhra Pradesh Story', in R. Hedlund (ed.), *Church Growth in The Third World*. Bombay: Gospel Literature Service.

Mishra, N. 2006. 'Yogi in a Tangle'. *India Today*, 23 January. Retrieved from http://www.indiatoday.com/itoday/20060123/controvr.html on 19 July 2009.

Mitchell, J. 2005. 'Christianity and Television', Editorial in *Studies in World Christianity*, 11(1).

Mitra, A. 1994. 'Gender Advertising in US and India', *Media Culture and Society*, 16(3): 487.

Moffett, S. H. 1992. *A History of Christianity in Asia*. San Francisco, CA: Harper.

Moorti, S. 2004. 'Fashioning a Cosmopolitan Tamil Identity: Game Shows, Commodities and Cultural Identity', *Media, Culture and Society*, 26(4): 549–567.

Morente, C. 2006. 'Hindu Guru Shares Yoga, Meditation Practices in San Mateo', *Oakland Tribune*, San Mateo, 10 July.

Morgan, D. 2005. *Sacred Gaze: Religious Visual Culture in Theory and Practice*. Berkeley: University of California Press.

Muggeridge, M. 1977. *Christ and the Media*. London: Hodder and Stoughton.

Mullins, M. R. 1994. 'The Empire Strikes Back: Korean Pentecostal Mission to Japan', in K. O. Poewe (ed.), *Charismatic Christianity as a Global Culture*, pp. 87–102. South Carolina: University of South Carolina.

Mundadan, A. M. 1984. *History of Christianity in India* (Volume 1). Bangalore: Theological Publications.

Muthiah, S. 2006. 'The Legacy That Ziegenbalg Left', *The Hindu*, 2 July, Mumbai.

Nehru, J. 1964. *The Discovery of India*. Calcutta: Meridian Books.

Neill, S. 1970. *The Story of the Christian Church in India and Pakistan*. Grand Rapids, Michigan: William Eerdmans.

Newcomb, H. 1855. 'Syrian Christians', in *A Cyclopedia of Missions*. London: Charles Scribner and Sons.

Nicholls, B. 1995. 'A Living Theology for Asian Churches: Some Reflections on the Contextualization-Syncretism Debate', in K. Gnanakan (ed.), *Biblical Theology in Asia*. Bangalore: Asia Theological Association.

O'Connor, A. 2007. 'Lord Ram Row Dredges Up Religious Fury', *The Weekend Australian*, Sydney, 15–16 September.

O'Malley, L. S. S. 1935. *Popular Hinduism: The Religion of the Masses*. New York: Macmillan.

Oommen, G. 2000. 'The Emerging Dalit Theology: A Historical Appraisal', *Indian Christian History Review*, 35(1): 19–37.

Palmquist, M., K. Carley and T. Dale. 1997. 'Applications of Computer-Aided Text Analysis: Analyzing Literary and Nonliterary Texts', in C. W. Roberts (ed.), *Text and Analysis for the Social Sciences*. Mahwah, New Jersey: Lawrence Erlbaum.

Park, S. 2000. 'Christianity in India'. Retrieved from http:www.emory.edu/ENGLISH/Bahri/Chris.html on 9 January 2004.

Pavarala, V. 2006. Interviewed by author, 5 October, Hyderabad.

Peck, J. 1993. *The Gods of Televangelism*. Lexington, Massachusetts: Greenwood Press.

Periasamy, K. 2006. Interviewed by author, 10 March, Hyderabad.

Pope, G. U. 1886. *The Tirukurral*. London: W. H. Allen and Co.

Postman, N. 1985. *Amusing Ourselves to Death*. New York: Viking.

Pratt, M. L. 1991. 'Arts of the contact zone', *Profession*, 91(9).

Pullum, S. J. 1999. *'Foul Demons Come Out!' The Rhetoric of Twentieth-Century American Faith Healing*. Westport, CT: Praeger Publications.

Raj, E. S. 2001. *National Debate on Conversion*. Chennai: Bharat Joyti.

Rajagopal, A. 2001. *Politics after Television: Religious Nationalism and the Reshaping of the Indian Public*. London: Cambridge University Press.

Rajan, V. J. 1995. 'Using TV, Christian Pat Robertson Denounces Hinduism as "Demonic".' Retreived from http://www.geocities.com/CapitolHill/7027/htoday.html?20088 on 8 April 2008.

Rajendran, K. 2000. 'Evangelical Missiology from India', in W. D. Taylor (ed.), *Global Missiology from the 21st century: The Iquassu Dialogue*. Grand Rapids, Michigan: Baker Academic.

Rajshekhar, M. 2003. 'Om Economics: A Walk Through the Business Universe of Gurus and Religious TeleVision', *Businessworld*, 13 October. Retrieved from http://www.businessworldindia.com/oct1303/invogue01.asp on 3 May 2006.

Ram-Prasad, C. 2007. 'India's Middle Class Failure', *Prospect*, 138 (September).

Reddy, S. 2006. Interviewed by author, October 5, Hyderabad.

Richard, H. L. 2001. 'Evangelical Approaches to Hindus', *Missiology*, 29(2).

Richardson, J. (n.d.). 'What is a Charismatic?', John Richardson's Charismatic Movement Page. Retrieved from http://www.btinternet.com/~j.p.richardson/definitn.html on 24 March 2006.

Ritzer, G. 1993. *The McDonaldization of Society*. California: Forge.

———. 1994. *Sociological Beginnings: On the Origins of Key Ideas in Sociology*. New York: McGraw-Hill.

Robertson, R. 1995. 'Glocalization: Time-Space and Homogeneity-Heterogeneity', in M. Featherston, Scott Lash and Roland Robertson (eds), *Global Modernities*. London: Sage Publications.

Romney, L. 1997. 'Televangelist Hinn Building TV Studio, Ministry in O.C.', *Los Angeles Times*, Los Angeles, 24 August.

Roy, S. and R. G. Katoti. (eds). 2004. *Statistical Outline of India: 2004–2005*. Mumbai: Tata Department of Statistics.

Rubin, A. 1983. 'Television Uses and Gratifications: The Interactions of Viewing Patterns and Motivation', *Journal of Broadcasting*, 27: 37–51.

———. 1984. 'Ritualized and Instrumental Viewing', *Journal of Communication*, 34(3): 67–77.

Ruthven, J. 1994. 'Can a Charismatic Theology be Biblical? Traditional Theology and Biblical Emphases'. Retrieved from http://home.regent.edu/ruthven/ruthhome.html on 6 July 2004.

Samuel, G. 1977. 'Urban Growth Strategy: A Bombay Case-Study', in R. Hedlund (ed.), *Church Growth in the Third World*. Bombay: Gospel Literature Service.

Sanne, S. 2003. 'British Colonialism in India and its Influence on Indian Society'. Revised Internet. Retrieved from blog.designs-for-automotion.de/zeug/British%20Colonialism%20in%20India%20and%20its%20Influence%20on%20Indian%20Society.pdf on 11 December 2007.

Sanneh, L. 1991. *Translating the Message*. Maryknoll: Orbis.

Sanskar TV. (n.d.). Website. Retrieved from http://www.sanskartv.info/fcp_main.htm on 9 November 2007.

Satellite and Cable TV Industry. 2007. 'The Indian Market'. Retrieved from http://www.scatindia.com/indianmarket.html on 6 June 2007.

Schultze, Q. 1989. *Televangelism and American Culture*. Michigan: Baker.

Shah, S. 2006. 'The Globalization of Spirituality', CHOWK website. Retrieved from http://www.chowk.com/articles/11445 on 8 March 2008.

Shashidar, A. 2006. 'TV Viewers Tuned in to Piety Too', *Business Line*, 21 January.

Shashikumar, V. K. 2004. 'Preparing for the Harvest: Tehelka's Expose of Christian Work in India', *Tehelka: The People's Paper*, 1 (1), New Delhi.

Shaw, R. 1995. 'Contextualizing the Power and the Glory', *International Journal of Frontier Missions*, 12(3).

Shivakumar, H. (2006). 'And-ness the Key'. Retrieved from http://thehindubusiness line,com/catalyst/2006/10/10/26/stories/2006102600020100 on 26 October, 2006.

Shoesmith, B. 2004. Interviewed by author, 29 March, Perth.

Shourie, A. 1987. *Missionaries in India: Continuities, Changes, Dilemmas*. New Delhi: HarperCollins.

———. 2000. *Harvesting Our Souls: Missionaries Their Designs, Their Claims*. New Delhi: ASA Publications.

Singh, K. 1992. *India: An Introduction*. New Delhi: Vision Books.

Sinha, B. M. 1993. 'Satellite TV Invades India', *Hinduism Today*, Sydney. Retrieved from http://www.hinduismtoday.com/modules/smartsection/item.php? itemid=991 on 26 October 2007.

Smith, B. 1987. 'Exorcising the Transcendent: Strategies for Defining Hinduism and Religion', *History of Religions*, 27(1).

Smith, D. 1988. 'The Impact of Religious Programming in the Electronic Media on the Active Christian Population in Central America', *Latin American Pastoral Issues*, 15(1).

———. 2003. *Against the Stream: Christianity and Mission in an Age of Globalization*. Leicester: IVP.

Smith, D. and L. Campos. 2005. 'Christianity and Television in Guatemala and Brazil: The Pentecostal Experience', *Studies in World Christianity*, 11(1).

Soja, E. 2000. *Postmetropolis: Critical Studies of Cities and Regions*. Oxford: Blackwell.

Soper, E. D. (n.d.). *The Inevitable Choice: Vedanta Philosophy or Christian Gospel*. Nashville: Abingdon Press.

Srinivas, M. N. 1952. *Religion and Society among the Coorgs of South India*. Oxford: Oxford University Press.

Star of Mysore. 2005. 'Dr Bhyrappa Sees Sonia's Role behind Benny Hinn Concert'. Retrieved from http://www.christianaggression.org/item_display.php?type=NE WS&id=1106377228 on 19 March 2006.

Stern, G. 2009. 'Televangelist Promises Hope, Positivity'. Retrieved from http://www. lohud.com/article/2009904220354 on 18 June 2009.

Stewart, J. 1961. *Nestorian Missionary Enterprise*. Trichur: Mar Narsai.

Stock, F. and M. Stock. 1975. *People Movements in the Punjab*. Bombay: Gospel Literature Service.

Stolow, J. 2005. 'Religion and/as Media', *Theory, Culture and Society*, 22(4): 119–45.

Sundar, N. 2005. 'Adivasi vs. Vanvasi: The Politics of Conversion in Central India', paper presented at the Religious and Social Fragmentation and Economic Development in South Asia, Cornell University on 15–16 October.

Synan, V. 1984. ' Pentecostalism', in W. A. Elwell (ed.), *Evangelical Dictionary of Theology*, pp. 835–839. Grand Rapids, Michigan: Baker Book House.

Taylor, R. W. 1992. *Acknowledging the Lordship of Christ: Selected Writings of Richard W. Taylor*. Delhi: Indian Society for Promoting Christian Knowledge (ISPCK).

Tennent, T. C. 2005. 'The Challenge of Churchless Christianity: an Evangelical Assessment', *International Bulletin of Missionary Research*, 29(4): 171–176.

Tharamangalam, J. 2004. 'Whose Swadeshi? Contending Nationalisms among Indian Christians', *Asian Journal of Social Science*, 32(2).

The Catholic Encyclopedia. 1912. *St Thomas Christians* (Volume XIV). New York: Robert Appleton Company.

Theyvanayagam, P. (n.d.). *Aindhavithan Yaar?* Madras: Meipporul Publications.

Thomas, M. M. 1996. *The Church's Mission and Post-Modern Humanism*. New Delhi: OSS and ISPOK.

Thomas, P. 2007. 'Christian Fundamentalism and the Media in South India', *Media Development*, LIV 1/2007(1): 23–31.

———. 2008. *Strong Religion/Zealous Media: Christian Fundamentalism and Communication in India*. New Delhi: Sage Publications.

Thomas, S. and J. Mitchell 2005. 'Understanding Television and Christianity in Marthoma Homes, South India', *Studies in World Christianity*, 11(1).

Trinity Broadcasting Network (TBN). 2009. Website. About Us. Retrieved from http://www.tbn.org/index.php/3.html on 5 July 2009.

Turner, B. 1983. *Religion and Social Theory: A Materialist Perspective*. London: Heinemann.

———. 2004. *Postmodern Social Theory*. London: Sage Publications.

Tyrrell, H. 2003. 'Bollywood versus Hollywood: Battle of the Dream Factories', in F. Lechner and J. Boli (eds), *The Globalization Reader*. Malden, MA: Wiley-Blackwell Publishers.

van der Veer, P. 1998. *Religious Nationalism: Hindus and Muslims in India*. New Delhi: Oxford University Press.

Vasquez, M. A. and M. F. Marquardt. 2003. *Globalizing the Sacred: Religion across the Americas*. Brunswick, New Jersey: Rutgers University Press.

Viswanathan, G. 1998. *Outside the Fold: Conversion, Modernity and Belief*. New Jersey: Princeton University Press.

Vohra, R. 2001. *The Making of India: A Historical Survey*. New York: M.E.Sharpe Inc.

von Busek, C. 2005. Interviewed by the author, 14 February, California.

Wacker, G. 2001. *Heaven Below: Early Pentecostals and American Culture*. Cambridge: Harvard University Press.

Wagner, C. P. 1988. *The Third Wave of the Holy Spirit: Encountering the Power of Signs and Wonders Today*. Ann Arbor, Michigan: Servant Publications.

Wallace, A. F. C. 1956. 'Revitalization Movements', *American Anthropologist*, 58(2): 264–281.

Walls, A. 1996. *The Missionary Movement in Christian History: Studies in the Transmission of Faith*. New York: Orbis.

Warraq, I. 2007. *Defending the West: A Critique of Edward Said's Orientalism*. Amherst, New York: Prometheus.

Weber, M. 1990. *The Protestant Ethic and the Spirit of Capitalism* (T. Parsons and A. Giddens, Trans.). London: Unwin Hyman.

Webster, J. C. B. 1992. *A History of the Dalit Christians in India*. San Francisco: Mellen Research University Press.

Wilson, B. 1966. *Religion in Secular Society*. London: C.A. Watts.

Windahl, S. 1981. 'Uses and gratifications at the crossroads', *Mass Communications Review Yearbook*, 2: 174–185.

Wolfe, K. M. 1984. *The Churches and the British Broadcasting Corporation: The Politics of Broadcast Religion*. London: SCM Press.

Zayani, M. 1997. 'The McDonaldization of Society', Book reviews. Retrieved from http://findarticles.com/p/articles/mi_m2220/is_v39/ai_20183783 on 2 November 2006.

Zee Jagran website. (n.d.). About Us section. Retrieved from http://www.jagranchannel.com/aboutus.html on 20 July 2009.

Zito, G. V. 1975. *Methodology and Meanings: Varieties of Sociological Inquiry*. New York: Praeger.

Index

About the Author

Jonathan D. James is a researcher and writer on Media, Religion and Culture. His research interests include: cultural globalisation, the social effects of new media, new religious movements, indigenisation, diaspora Asians in the West and the image industry in Asia. With an early education in Singapore and later training in professional television production and media in the USA, he is currently an adjunct Lecturer at Edith Cowan University, Perth and well-known in the Asia-Pacific region as a consultant, lecturer and guest speaker. His articles have appeared in refereed journals in Australia, UK and North America including *The Journal of Religion and Popular Culture; Studies in World Christianity and Continuum: Journal of Media and Culture*. He is widely-travelled in Asia, North America and the Pacific in his role as director of a church-based international development and educational agency.

He is a research member of the culture and media group of CREATEC, the Centre for Research in Entertainment, Art, Technology, Education and Communications, at Edith Cowan University, and a member of the Cultural Studies Association of Australasia (CSAA). He is also President of Destiny Communications, an entity that provides newspaper and radio for community and educational purposes.